C-3777   CAREER EXAMINATION SERIES

This is your
PASSBOOK for...

Electrical Apprentice Aptitude Test

Test Preparation Study Guide
Questions & Answers

NATIONAL LEARNING CORPORATION®

COPYRIGHT NOTICE

This book is SOLELY intended for, is sold ONLY to, and its use is RESTRICTED to individual, bona fide applicants or candidates who qualify by virtue of having seriously filed applications for appropriate license, certificate, professional and/or promotional advancement, higher school matriculation, scholarship, or other legitimate requirements of education and/or governmental authorities.

This book is NOT intended for use, class instruction, tutoring, training, duplication, copying, reprinting, excerption, or adaptation, etc., by:

1) Other publishers
2) Proprietors and/or Instructors of "Coaching" and/or Preparatory Courses
3) Personnel and/or Training Divisions of commercial, industrial, and governmental organizations
4) Schools, colleges, or universities and/or their departments and staffs, including teachers and other personnel
5) Testing Agencies or Bureaus
6) Study groups which seek by the purchase of a single volume to copy and/or duplicate and/or adapt this material for use by the group as a whole without having purchased individual volumes for each of the members of the group
7) Et al.

Such persons would be in violation of appropriate Federal and State statutes.

PROVISION OF LICENSING AGREEMENTS – Recognized educational, commercial, industrial, and governmental institutions and organizations, and others legitimately engaged in educational pursuits, including training, testing, and measurement activities, may address request for a licensing agreement to the copyright owners, who will determine whether, and under what conditions, including fees and charges, the materials in this book may be used them. In other words, a licensing facility exists for the legitimate use of the material in this book on other than an individual basis. However, it is asseverated and affirmed here that the material in this book CANNOT be used without the receipt of the express permission of such a licensing agreement from the Publishers. Inquiries re licensing should be addressed to the company, attention rights and permissions department.

All rights reserved, including the right of reproduction in whole or in part, in any form or by any means, electronic or mechanical, including photocopying, recording, or by any information storage and retrieval system, without permission in writing from the Publisher.

Copyright © 2024 by
National Learning Corporation

212 Michael Drive, Syosset, NY 11791
(516) 921-8888 • www.passbooks.com
E-mail: info@passbooks.com

PUBLISHED IN THE UNITED STATES OF AMERICA

PASSBOOK® SERIES

THE *PASSBOOK® SERIES* has been created to prepare applicants and candidates for the ultimate academic battlefield – the examination room.

At some time in our lives, each and every one of us may be required to take an examination – for validation, matriculation, admission, qualification, registration, certification, or licensure.

Based on the assumption that every applicant or candidate has met the basic formal educational standards, has taken the required number of courses, and read the necessary texts, the *PASSBOOK® SERIES* furnishes the one special preparation which may assure passing with confidence, instead of failing with insecurity. Examination questions – together with answers – are furnished as the basic vehicle for study so that the mysteries of the examination and its compounding difficulties may be eliminated or diminished by a sure method.

This book is meant to help you pass your examination provided that you qualify and are serious in your objective.

The entire field is reviewed through the huge store of content information which is succinctly presented through a provocative and challenging approach – the question-and-answer method.

A climate of success is established by furnishing the correct answers at the end of each test.

You soon learn to recognize types of questions, forms of questions, and patterns of questioning. You may even begin to anticipate expected outcomes.

You perceive that many questions are repeated or adapted so that you can gain acute insights, which may enable you to score many sure points.

You learn how to confront new questions, or types of questions, and to attack them confidently and work out the correct answers.

You note objectives and emphases, and recognize pitfalls and dangers, so that you may make positive educational adjustments.

Moreover, you are kept fully informed in relation to new concepts, methods, practices, and directions in the field.

You discover that you are actually taking the examination all the time: you are preparing for the examination by "taking" an examination, not by reading extraneous and/or supererogatory textbooks.

In short, this PASSBOOK®, used directedly, should be an important factor in helping you to pass your test.

ELECTRICAL APPRENTICE APTITUDE TEST

The Electrical Apprentice Aptitude Test is administered to applicants seeking apprenticeship positions in the electrical trade industry.

The test consists of:

1. Basic Electricity
2. Tools of the Trade
3. Mechanical Aptitude
4. Reading Comprehension
5. Mathematical Ability
6. Abstract Reasoning

HOW TO TAKE A TEST

I. YOU MUST PASS AN EXAMINATION

A. WHAT EVERY CANDIDATE SHOULD KNOW

Examination applicants often ask us for help in preparing for the written test. What can I study in advance? What kinds of questions will be asked? How will the test be given? How will the papers be graded?

As an applicant for a civil service examination, you may be wondering about some of these things. Our purpose here is to suggest effective methods of advance study and to describe civil service examinations.

Your chances for success on this examination can be increased if you know how to prepare. Those "pre-examination jitters" can be reduced if you know what to expect. You can even experience an adventure in good citizenship if you know why civil service exams are given.

B. WHY ARE CIVIL SERVICE EXAMINATIONS GIVEN?

Civil service examinations are important to you in two ways. As a citizen, you want public jobs filled by employees who know how to do their work. As a job seeker, you want a fair chance to compete for that job on an equal footing with other candidates. The best-known means of accomplishing this two-fold goal is the competitive examination.

Exams are widely publicized throughout the nation. They may be administered for jobs in federal, state, city, municipal, town or village governments or agencies.

Any citizen may apply, with some limitations, such as the age or residence of applicants. Your experience and education may be reviewed to see whether you meet the requirements for the particular examination. When these requirements exist, they are reasonable and applied consistently to all applicants. Thus, a competitive examination may cause you some uneasiness now, but it is your privilege and safeguard.

C. HOW ARE CIVIL SERVICE EXAMS DEVELOPED?

Examinations are carefully written by trained technicians who are specialists in the field known as "psychological measurement," in consultation with recognized authorities in the field of work that the test will cover. These experts recommend the subject matter areas or skills to be tested; only those knowledges or skills important to your success on the job are included. The most reliable books and source materials available are used as references. Together, the experts and technicians judge the difficulty level of the questions.

Test technicians know how to phrase questions so that the problem is clearly stated. Their ethics do not permit "trick" or "catch" questions. Questions may have been tried out on sample groups, or subjected to statistical analysis, to determine their usefulness.

Written tests are often used in combination with performance tests, ratings of training and experience, and oral interviews. All of these measures combine to form the best-known means of finding the right person for the right job.

II. HOW TO PASS THE WRITTEN TEST

A. NATURE OF THE EXAMINATION

To prepare intelligently for civil service examinations, you should know how they differ from school examinations you have taken. In school you were assigned certain definite pages to read or subjects to cover. The examination questions were quite detailed and usually emphasized memory. Civil service exams, on the other hand, try to discover your present ability to perform the duties of a position, plus your potentiality to learn these duties. In other words, a civil service exam attempts to predict how successful you will be. Questions cover such a broad area that they cannot be as minute and detailed as school exam questions.

In the public service similar kinds of work, or positions, are grouped together in one "class." This process is known as *position-classification*. All the positions in a class are paid according to the salary range for that class. One class title covers all of these positions, and they are all tested by the same examination.

B. FOUR BASIC STEPS

1) Study the announcement

How, then, can you know what subjects to study? Our best answer is: "Learn as much as possible about the class of positions for which you've applied." The exam will test the knowledge, skills and abilities needed to do the work.

Your most valuable source of information about the position you want is the official exam announcement. This announcement lists the training and experience qualifications. Check these standards and apply only if you come reasonably close to meeting them.

The brief description of the position in the examination announcement offers some clues to the subjects which will be tested. Think about the job itself. Review the duties in your mind. Can you perform them, or are there some in which you are rusty? Fill in the blank spots in your preparation.

Many jurisdictions preview the written test in the exam announcement by including a section called "Knowledge and Abilities Required," "Scope of the Examination," or some similar heading. Here you will find out specifically what fields will be tested.

2) Review your own background

Once you learn in general what the position is all about, and what you need to know to do the work, ask yourself which subjects you already know fairly well and which need improvement. You may wonder whether to concentrate on improving your strong areas or on building some background in your fields of weakness. When the announcement has specified "some knowledge" or "considerable knowledge," or has used adjectives like "beginning principles of…" or "advanced … methods," you can get a clue as to the number and difficulty of questions to be asked in any given field. More questions, and hence broader coverage, would be included for those subjects which are more important in the work. Now weigh your strengths and weaknesses against the job requirements and prepare accordingly.

3) Determine the level of the position

Another way to tell how intensively you should prepare is to understand the level of the job for which you are applying. Is it the entering level? In other words, is this the position in which beginners in a field of work are hired? Or is it an intermediate or advanced level? Sometimes this is indicated by such words as "Junior" or "Senior" in the class title. Other jurisdictions use Roman numerals to designate the level – Clerk I, Clerk II, for example. The word "Supervisor" sometimes appears in the title. If the level is not indicated by the title, check the description of duties. Will you be working under very close supervision, or will you have responsibility for independent decisions in this work?

4) Choose appropriate study materials

Now that you know the subjects to be examined and the relative amount of each subject to be covered, you can choose suitable study materials. For beginning level jobs, or even advanced ones, if you have a pronounced weakness in some aspect of your training, read a modern, standard textbook in that field. Be sure it is up to date and has general coverage. Such books are normally available at your library, and the librarian will be glad to help you locate one. For entry-level positions, questions of appropriate difficulty are chosen – neither highly advanced questions, nor those too simple. Such questions require careful thought but not advanced training.

If the position for which you are applying is technical or advanced, you will read more advanced, specialized material. If you are already familiar with the basic principles of your field, elementary textbooks would waste your time. Concentrate on advanced textbooks and technical periodicals. Think through the concepts and review difficult problems in your field.

These are all general sources. You can get more ideas on your own initiative, following these leads. For example, training manuals and publications of the government agency which employs workers in your field can be useful, particularly for technical and professional positions. A letter or visit to the government department involved may result in more specific study suggestions, and certainly will provide you with a more definite idea of the exact nature of the position you are seeking.

III. KINDS OF TESTS

Tests are used for purposes other than measuring knowledge and ability to perform specified duties. For some positions, it is equally important to test ability to make adjustments to new situations or to profit from training. In others, basic mental abilities not dependent on information are essential. Questions which test these things may not appear as pertinent to the duties of the position as those which test for knowledge and information. Yet they are often highly important parts of a fair examination. For very general questions, it is almost impossible to help you direct your study efforts. What we can do is to point out some of the more common of these general abilities needed in public service positions and describe some typical questions.

1) General information

Broad, general information has been found useful for predicting job success in some kinds of work. This is tested in a variety of ways, from vocabulary lists to questions about current events. Basic background in some field of work, such as sociology or economics, may be sampled in a group of questions. Often these are principles which have become familiar to most persons through exposure rather than through formal training. It is difficult to advise you how to study for these questions; being alert to the world around you is our best suggestion.

2) Verbal ability

An example of an ability needed in many positions is verbal or language ability. Verbal ability is, in brief, the ability to use and understand words. Vocabulary and grammar tests are typical measures of this ability. Reading comprehension or paragraph interpretation questions are common in many kinds of civil service tests. You are given a paragraph of written material and asked to find its central meaning.

3) Numerical ability

Number skills can be tested by the familiar arithmetic problem, by checking paired lists of numbers to see which are alike and which are different, or by interpreting charts and graphs. In the latter test, a graph may be printed in the test booklet which you are asked to use as the basis for answering questions.

4) Observation

A popular test for law-enforcement positions is the observation test. A picture is shown to you for several minutes, then taken away. Questions about the picture test your ability to observe both details and larger elements.

5) Following directions

In many positions in the public service, the employee must be able to carry out written instructions dependably and accurately. You may be given a chart with several columns, each column listing a variety of information. The questions require you to carry out directions involving the information given in the chart.

6) Skills and aptitudes

Performance tests effectively measure some manual skills and aptitudes. When the skill is one in which you are trained, such as typing or shorthand, you can practice. These tests are often very much like those given in business school or high school courses. For many of the other skills and aptitudes, however, no short-time preparation can be made. Skills and abilities natural to you or that you have developed throughout your lifetime are being tested.

Many of the general questions just described provide all the data needed to answer the questions and ask you to use your reasoning ability to find the answers. Your best preparation for these tests, as well as for tests of facts and ideas, is to be at your physical and mental best. You, no doubt, have your own methods of getting into an exam-taking mood and keeping "in shape." The next section lists some ideas on this subject.

IV. KINDS OF QUESTIONS

Only rarely is the "essay" question, which you answer in narrative form, used in civil service tests. Civil service tests are usually of the short-answer type. Full instructions for answering these questions will be given to you at the examination. But in case this is your first experience with short-answer questions and separate answer sheets, here is what you need to know:

1) Multiple-choice Questions

Most popular of the short-answer questions is the "multiple choice" or "best answer" question. It can be used, for example, to test for factual knowledge, ability to solve problems or judgment in meeting situations found at work.

A multiple-choice question is normally one of three types—
- It can begin with an incomplete statement followed by several possible endings. You are to find the one ending which *best* completes the statement, although some of the others may not be entirely wrong.
- It can also be a complete statement in the form of a question which is answered by choosing one of the statements listed.

- It can be in the form of a problem – again you select the best answer.

Here is an example of a multiple-choice question with a discussion which should give you some clues as to the method for choosing the right answer:

When an employee has a complaint about his assignment, the action which will *best* help him overcome his difficulty is to
- A. discuss his difficulty with his coworkers
- B. take the problem to the head of the organization
- C. take the problem to the person who gave him the assignment
- D. say nothing to anyone about his complaint

In answering this question, you should study each of the choices to find which is best. Consider choice "A" – Certainly an employee may discuss his complaint with fellow employees, but no change or improvement can result, and the complaint remains unresolved. Choice "B" is a poor choice since the head of the organization probably does not know what assignment you have been given, and taking your problem to him is known as "going over the head" of the supervisor. The supervisor, or person who made the assignment, is the person who can clarify it or correct any injustice. Choice "C" is, therefore, correct. To say nothing, as in choice "D," is unwise. Supervisors have and interest in knowing the problems employees are facing, and the employee is seeking a solution to his problem.

2) True/False Questions

The "true/false" or "right/wrong" form of question is sometimes used. Here a complete statement is given. Your job is to decide whether the statement is right or wrong.

SAMPLE: A roaming cell-phone call to a nearby city costs less than a non-roaming call to a distant city.

This statement is wrong, or false, since roaming calls are more expensive.

This is not a complete list of all possible question forms, although most of the others are variations of these common types. You will always get complete directions for answering questions. Be sure you understand *how* to mark your answers – ask questions until you do.

V. RECORDING YOUR ANSWERS

Computer terminals are used more and more today for many different kinds of exams.

For an examination with very few applicants, you may be told to record your answers in the test booklet itself. Separate answer sheets are much more common. If this separate answer sheet is to be scored by machine – and this is often the case – it is highly important that you mark your answers correctly in order to get credit.

An electronic scoring machine is often used in civil service offices because of the speed with which papers can be scored. Machine-scored answer sheets must be marked with a pencil, which will be given to you. This pencil has a high graphite content which responds to the electronic scoring machine. As a matter of fact, stray dots may register as answers, so do not let your pencil rest on the answer sheet while you are pondering the correct answer. Also, if your pencil lead breaks or is otherwise defective, ask for another.

Since the answer sheet will be dropped in a slot in the scoring machine, be careful not to bend the corners or get the paper crumpled.

The answer sheet normally has five vertical columns of numbers, with 30 numbers to a column. These numbers correspond to the question numbers in your test booklet. After each number, going across the page are four or five pairs of dotted lines. These short dotted lines have small letters or numbers above them. The first two pairs may also have a "T" or "F" above the letters. This indicates that the first two pairs only are to be used if the questions are of the true-false type. If the questions are multiple choice, disregard the "T" and "F" and pay attention only to the small letters or numbers.

Answer your questions in the manner of the sample that follows:

32. The largest city in the United States is
    A. Washington, D.C.
    B. New York City
    C. Chicago
    D. Detroit
    E. San Francisco

1) Choose the answer you think is best. (New York City is the largest, so "B" is correct.)
2) Find the row of dotted lines numbered the same as the question you are answering. (Find row number 32)
3) Find the pair of dotted lines corresponding to the answer. (Find the pair of lines under the mark "B.")
4) Make a solid black mark between the dotted lines.

VI. BEFORE THE TEST

Common sense will help you find procedures to follow to get ready for an examination. Too many of us, however, overlook these sensible measures. Indeed, nervousness and fatigue have been found to be the most serious reasons why applicants fail to do their best on civil service tests. Here is a list of reminders:

- Begin your preparation early – Don't wait until the last minute to go scurrying around for books and materials or to find out what the position is all about.
- Prepare continuously – An hour a night for a week is better than an all-night cram session. This has been definitely established. What is more, a night a week for a month will return better dividends than crowding your study into a shorter period of time.
- Locate the place of the exam – You have been sent a notice telling you when and where to report for the examination. If the location is in a different town or otherwise unfamiliar to you, it would be well to inquire the best route and learn something about the building.
- Relax the night before the test – Allow your mind to rest. Do not study at all that night. Plan some mild recreation or diversion; then go to bed early and get a good night's sleep.
- Get up early enough to make a leisurely trip to the place for the test – This way unforeseen events, traffic snarls, unfamiliar buildings, etc. will not upset you.
- Dress comfortably – A written test is not a fashion show. You will be known by number and not by name, so wear something comfortable.

- Leave excess paraphernalia at home – Shopping bags and odd bundles will get in your way. You need bring only the items mentioned in the official notice you received; usually everything you need is provided. Do not bring reference books to the exam. They will only confuse those last minutes and be taken away from you when in the test room.
- Arrive somewhat ahead of time – If because of transportation schedules you must get there very early, bring a newspaper or magazine to take your mind off yourself while waiting.
- Locate the examination room – When you have found the proper room, you will be directed to the seat or part of the room where you will sit. Sometimes you are given a sheet of instructions to read while you are waiting. Do not fill out any forms until you are told to do so; just read them and be prepared.
- Relax and prepare to listen to the instructions
- If you have any physical problem that may keep you from doing your best, be sure to tell the test administrator. If you are sick or in poor health, you really cannot do your best on the exam. You can come back and take the test some other time.

VII. AT THE TEST

The day of the test is here and you have the test booklet in your hand. The temptation to get going is very strong. Caution! There is more to success than knowing the right answers. You must know how to identify your papers and understand variations in the type of short-answer question used in this particular examination. Follow these suggestions for maximum results from your efforts:

1) Cooperate with the monitor

The test administrator has a duty to create a situation in which you can be as much at ease as possible. He will give instructions, tell you when to begin, check to see that you are marking your answer sheet correctly, and so on. He is not there to guard you, although he will see that your competitors do not take unfair advantage. He wants to help you do your best.

2) Listen to all instructions

Don't jump the gun! Wait until you understand all directions. In most civil service tests you get more time than you need to answer the questions. So don't be in a hurry. Read each word of instructions until you clearly understand the meaning. Study the examples, listen to all announcements and follow directions. Ask questions if you do not understand what to do.

3) Identify your papers

Civil service exams are usually identified by number only. You will be assigned a number; you must not put your name on your test papers. Be sure to copy your number correctly. Since more than one exam may be given, copy your exact examination title.

4) Plan your time

Unless you are told that a test is a "speed" or "rate of work" test, speed itself is usually not important. Time enough to answer all the questions will be provided, but this does not mean that you have all day. An overall time limit has been set. Divide the total time (in minutes) by the number of questions to determine the approximate time you have for each question.

5) Do not linger over difficult questions

If you come across a difficult question, mark it with a paper clip (useful to have along) and come back to it when you have been through the booklet. One caution if you do this – be sure to skip a number on your answer sheet as well. Check often to be sure that you have not lost your place and that you are marking in the row numbered the same as the question you are answering.

6) Read the questions

Be sure you know what the question asks! Many capable people are unsuccessful because they failed to *read* the questions correctly.

7) Answer all questions

Unless you have been instructed that a penalty will be deducted for incorrect answers, it is better to guess than to omit a question.

8) Speed tests

It is often better NOT to guess on speed tests. It has been found that on timed tests people are tempted to spend the last few seconds before time is called in marking answers at random – without even reading them – in the hope of picking up a few extra points. To discourage this practice, the instructions may warn you that your score will be "corrected" for guessing. That is, a penalty will be applied. The incorrect answers will be deducted from the correct ones, or some other penalty formula will be used.

9) Review your answers

If you finish before time is called, go back to the questions you guessed or omitted to give them further thought. Review other answers if you have time.

10) Return your test materials

If you are ready to leave before others have finished or time is called, take ALL your materials to the monitor and leave quietly. Never take any test material with you. The monitor can discover whose papers are not complete, and taking a test booklet may be grounds for disqualification.

VIII. EXAMINATION TECHNIQUES

1) Read the general instructions carefully. These are usually printed on the first page of the exam booklet. As a rule, these instructions refer to the timing of the examination; the fact that you should not start work until the signal and must stop work at a signal, etc. If there are any *special* instructions, such as a choice of questions to be answered, make sure that you note this instruction carefully.

2) When you are ready to start work on the examination, that is as soon as the signal has been given, read the instructions to each question booklet, underline any key words or phrases, such as *least, best, outline, describe* and the like. In this way you will tend to answer as requested rather than discover on reviewing your paper that you *listed without describing*, that you selected the *worst* choice rather than the *best* choice, etc.

3) If the examination is of the objective or multiple-choice type – that is, each question will also give a series of possible answers: A, B, C or D, and you are called upon to select the best answer and write the letter next to that answer on your answer paper – it is advisable to start answering each question in turn. There may be anywhere from 50 to 100 such questions in the three or four hours allotted and you can see how much time would be taken if you read through all the questions before beginning to answer any. Furthermore, if you come across a question or group of questions which you know would be difficult to answer, it would undoubtedly affect your handling of all the other questions.

4) If the examination is of the essay type and contains but a few questions, it is a moot point as to whether you should read all the questions before starting to answer any one. Of course, if you are given a choice – say five out of seven and the like – then it is essential to read all the questions so you can eliminate the two that are most difficult. If, however, you are asked to answer all the questions, there may be danger in trying to answer the easiest one first because you may find that you will spend too much time on it. The best technique is to answer the first question, then proceed to the second, etc.

5) Time your answers. Before the exam begins, write down the time it started, then add the time allowed for the examination and write down the time it must be completed, then divide the time available somewhat as follows:
   - If 3-1/2 hours are allowed, that would be 210 minutes. If you have 80 objective-type questions, that would be an average of 2-1/2 minutes per question. Allow yourself no more than 2 minutes per question, or a total of 160 minutes, which will permit about 50 minutes to review.
   - If for the time allotment of 210 minutes there are 7 essay questions to answer, that would average about 30 minutes a question. Give yourself only 25 minutes per question so that you have about 35 minutes to review.

6) The most important instruction is to *read each question* and make sure you know what is wanted. The second most important instruction is to *time yourself properly* so that you answer every question. The third most important instruction is to *answer every question*. Guess if you have to but include something for each question. Remember that you will receive no credit for a blank and will probably receive some credit if you write something in answer to an essay question. If you guess a letter – say "B" for a multiple-choice question – you may have guessed right. If you leave a blank as an answer to a multiple-choice question, the examiners may respect your feelings but it will not add a point to your score. Some exams may penalize you for wrong answers, so in such cases *only*, you may not want to guess unless you have some basis for your answer.

7) Suggestions
   a. Objective-type questions
      1. Examine the question booklet for proper sequence of pages and questions
      2. Read all instructions carefully
      3. Skip any question which seems too difficult; return to it after all other questions have been answered
      4. Apportion your time properly; do not spend too much time on any single question or group of questions

5. Note and underline key words – *all, most, fewest, least, best, worst, same, opposite,* etc.
6. Pay particular attention to negatives
7. Note unusual option, e.g., unduly long, short, complex, different or similar in content to the body of the question
8. Observe the use of "hedging" words – *probably, may, most likely,* etc.
9. Make sure that your answer is put next to the same number as the question
10. Do not second-guess unless you have good reason to believe the second answer is definitely more correct
11. Cross out original answer if you decide another answer is more accurate; do not erase until you are ready to hand your paper in
12. Answer all questions; guess unless instructed otherwise
13. Leave time for review

  b. Essay questions
1. Read each question carefully
2. Determine exactly what is wanted. Underline key words or phrases.
3. Decide on outline or paragraph answer
4. Include many different points and elements unless asked to develop any one or two points or elements
5. Show impartiality by giving pros and cons unless directed to select one side only
6. Make and write down any assumptions you find necessary to answer the questions
7. Watch your English, grammar, punctuation and choice of words
8. Time your answers; don't crowd material

8) Answering the essay question

Most essay questions can be answered by framing the specific response around several key words or ideas. Here are a few such key words or ideas:

M's: manpower, materials, methods, money, management
P's: purpose, program, policy, plan, procedure, practice, problems, pitfalls, personnel, public relations

  a. Six basic steps in handling problems:
1. Preliminary plan and background development
2. Collect information, data and facts
3. Analyze and interpret information, data and facts
4. Analyze and develop solutions as well as make recommendations
5. Prepare report and sell recommendations
6. Install recommendations and follow up effectiveness

  b. Pitfalls to avoid
1. *Taking things for granted* – A statement of the situation does not necessarily imply that each of the elements is necessarily true; for example, a complaint may be invalid and biased so that all that can be taken for granted is that a complaint has been registered

2. *Considering only one side of a situation* – Wherever possible, indicate several alternatives and then point out the reasons you selected the best one
3. *Failing to indicate follow up* – Whenever your answer indicates action on your part, make certain that you will take proper follow-up action to see how successful your recommendations, procedures or actions turn out to be
4. *Taking too long in answering any single question* – Remember to time your answers properly

IX. AFTER THE TEST

Scoring procedures differ in detail among civil service jurisdictions although the general principles are the same. Whether the papers are hand-scored or graded by machine we have described, they are nearly always graded by number. That is, the person who marks the paper knows only the number – never the name – of the applicant. Not until all the papers have been graded will they be matched with names. If other tests, such as training and experience or oral interview ratings have been given, scores will be combined. Different parts of the examination usually have different weights. For example, the written test might count 60 percent of the final grade, and a rating of training and experience 40 percent. In many jurisdictions, veterans will have a certain number of points added to their grades.

After the final grade has been determined, the names are placed in grade order and an eligible list is established. There are various methods for resolving ties between those who get the same final grade – probably the most common is to place first the name of the person whose application was received first. Job offers are made from the eligible list in the order the names appear on it. You will be notified of your grade and your rank as soon as all these computations have been made. This will be done as rapidly as possible.

People who are found to meet the requirements in the announcement are called "eligibles." Their names are put on a list of eligible candidates. An eligible's chances of getting a job depend on how high he stands on this list and how fast agencies are filling jobs from the list.

When a job is to be filled from a list of eligibles, the agency asks for the names of people on the list of eligibles for that job. When the civil service commission receives this request, it sends to the agency the names of the three people highest on this list. Or, if the job to be filled has specialized requirements, the office sends the agency the names of the top three persons who meet these requirements from the general list.

The appointing officer makes a choice from among the three people whose names were sent to him. If the selected person accepts the appointment, the names of the others are put back on the list to be considered for future openings.

That is the rule in hiring from all kinds of eligible lists, whether they are for typist, carpenter, chemist, or something else. For every vacancy, the appointing officer has his choice of any one of the top three eligibles on the list. This explains why the person whose name is on top of the list sometimes does not get an appointment when some of the persons lower on the list do. If the appointing officer chooses the second or third eligible, the No. 1 eligible does not get a job at once, but stays on the list until he is appointed or the list is terminated.

X. HOW TO PASS THE INTERVIEW TEST

The examination for which you applied requires an oral interview test. You have already taken the written test and you are now being called for the interview test – the final part of the formal examination.

You may think that it is not possible to prepare for an interview test and that there are no procedures to follow during an interview. Our purpose is to point out some things you can do in advance that will help you and some good rules to follow and pitfalls to avoid while you are being interviewed.

What is an interview supposed to test?

The written examination is designed to test the technical knowledge and competence of the candidate; the oral is designed to evaluate intangible qualities, not readily measured otherwise, and to establish a list showing the relative fitness of each candidate – as measured against his competitors – for the position sought. Scoring is not on the basis of "right" and "wrong," but on a sliding scale of values ranging from "not passable" to "outstanding." As a matter of fact, it is possible to achieve a relatively low score without a single "incorrect" answer because of evident weakness in the qualities being measured.

Occasionally, an examination may consist entirely of an oral test – either an individual or a group oral. In such cases, information is sought concerning the technical knowledges and abilities of the candidate, since there has been no written examination for this purpose. More commonly, however, an oral test is used to supplement a written examination.

Who conducts interviews?

The composition of oral boards varies among different jurisdictions. In nearly all, a representative of the personnel department serves as chairman. One of the members of the board may be a representative of the department in which the candidate would work. In some cases, "outside experts" are used, and, frequently, a businessman or some other representative of the general public is asked to serve. Labor and management or other special groups may be represented. The aim is to secure the services of experts in the appropriate field.

However the board is composed, it is a good idea (and not at all improper or unethical) to ascertain in advance of the interview who the members are and what groups they represent. When you are introduced to them, you will have some idea of their backgrounds and interests, and at least you will not stutter and stammer over their names.

What should be done before the interview?

While knowledge about the board members is useful and takes some of the surprise element out of the interview, there is other preparation which is more substantive. It *is* possible to prepare for an oral interview – in several ways:

1) Keep a copy of your application and review it carefully before the interview

This may be the only document before the oral board, and the starting point of the interview. Know what education and experience you have listed there, and the sequence and dates of all of it. Sometimes the board will ask you to review the highlights of your experience for them; you should not have to hem and haw doing it.

2) Study the class specification and the examination announcement

Usually, the oral board has one or both of these to guide them. The qualities, characteristics or knowledges required by the position sought are stated in these documents. They offer valuable clues as to the nature of the oral interview. For example, if the job involves supervisory responsibilities, the announcement will usually indicate that knowledge of modern supervisory methods and the qualifications of the candidate as a supervisor will be tested. If so, you can expect such questions, frequently in the form of a hypothetical situation which you are expected to solve. NEVER go into an oral without knowledge of the duties and responsibilities of the job you seek.

3) Think through each qualification required

Try to visualize the kind of questions you would ask if you were a board member. How well could you answer them? Try especially to appraise your own knowledge and background in each area, *measured against the job sought*, and identify any areas in which you are weak. Be critical and realistic – do not flatter yourself.

4) Do some general reading in areas in which you feel you may be weak

For example, if the job involves supervision and your past experience has NOT, some general reading in supervisory methods and practices, particularly in the field of human relations, might be useful. Do NOT study agency procedures or detailed manuals. The oral board will be testing your understanding and capacity, not your memory.

5) Get a good night's sleep and watch your general health and mental attitude

You will want a clear head at the interview. Take care of a cold or any other minor ailment, and of course, no hangovers.

What should be done on the day of the interview?

Now comes the day of the interview itself. Give yourself plenty of time to get there. Plan to arrive somewhat ahead of the scheduled time, particularly if your appointment is in the fore part of the day. If a previous candidate fails to appear, the board might be ready for you a bit early. By early afternoon an oral board is almost invariably behind schedule if there are many candidates, and you may have to wait. Take along a book or magazine to read, or your application to review, but leave any extraneous material in the waiting room when you go in for your interview. In any event, relax and compose yourself.

The matter of dress is important. The board is forming impressions about you – from your experience, your manners, your attitude, and your appearance. Give your personal appearance careful attention. Dress your best, but not your flashiest. Choose conservative, appropriate clothing, and be sure it is immaculate. This is a business interview, and your appearance should indicate that you regard it as such. Besides, being well groomed and properly dressed will help boost your confidence.

Sooner or later, someone will call your name and escort you into the interview room. *This is it.* From here on you are on your own. It is too late for any more preparation. But remember, you asked for this opportunity to prove your fitness, and you are here because your request was granted.

What happens when you go in?

The usual sequence of events will be as follows: The clerk (who is often the board stenographer) will introduce you to the chairman of the oral board, who will introduce you to the other members of the board. Acknowledge the introductions before you sit down. Do not be surprised if you find a microphone facing you or a stenotypist sitting by. Oral interviews are usually recorded in the event of an appeal or other review.

Usually the chairman of the board will open the interview by reviewing the highlights of your education and work experience from your application – primarily for the benefit of the other members of the board, as well as to get the material into the record. Do not interrupt or comment unless there is an error or significant misinterpretation; if that is the case, do not hesitate. But do not quibble about insignificant matters. Also, he will usually ask you some question about your education, experience or your present job – partly to get you to start talking and to establish the interviewing "rapport." He may start the actual questioning, or turn it over to one of the other members. Frequently, each member undertakes the questioning on a particular area, one in which he is perhaps most competent, so you can expect each member to participate in the examination. Because time is limited, you may also expect some rather abrupt switches in the direction the questioning takes, so do not be upset by it. Normally, a board member will not pursue a single line of questioning unless he discovers a particular strength or weakness.

After each member has participated, the chairman will usually ask whether any member has any further questions, then will ask you if you have anything you wish to add. Unless you are expecting this question, it may floor you. Worse, it may start you off on an extended, extemporaneous speech. The board is not usually seeking more information. The question is principally to offer you a last opportunity to present further qualifications or to indicate that you have nothing to add. So, if you feel that a significant qualification or characteristic has been overlooked, it is proper to point it out in a sentence or so. Do not compliment the board on the thoroughness of their examination – they have been sketchy, and you know it. If you wish, merely say, "No thank you, I have nothing further to add." This is a point where you can "talk yourself out" of a good impression or fail to present an important bit of information. Remember, *you close the interview yourself.*

The chairman will then say, "That is all, Mr. _____, thank you." Do not be startled; the interview is over, and quicker than you think. Thank him, gather your belongings and take your leave. Save your sigh of relief for the other side of the door.

How to put your best foot forward

Throughout this entire process, you may feel that the board individually and collectively is trying to pierce your defenses, seek out your hidden weaknesses and embarrass and confuse you. Actually, this is not true. They are obliged to make an appraisal of your qualifications for the job you are seeking, and they want to see you in your best light. Remember, they must interview all candidates and a non-cooperative candidate may become a failure in spite of their best efforts to bring out his qualifications. Here are 15 suggestions that will help you:

1) Be natural – Keep your attitude confident, not cocky

If you are not confident that you can do the job, do not expect the board to be. Do not apologize for your weaknesses, try to bring out your strong points. The board is interested in a positive, not negative, presentation. Cockiness will antagonize any board member and make him wonder if you are covering up a weakness by a false show of strength.

2) Get comfortable, but don't lounge or sprawl

Sit erectly but not stiffly. A careless posture may lead the board to conclude that you are careless in other things, or at least that you are not impressed by the importance of the occasion. Either conclusion is natural, even if incorrect. Do not fuss with your clothing, a pencil or an ashtray. Your hands may occasionally be useful to emphasize a point; do not let them become a point of distraction.

3) Do not wisecrack or make small talk

This is a serious situation, and your attitude should show that you consider it as such. Further, the time of the board is limited – they do not want to waste it, and neither should you.

4) Do not exaggerate your experience or abilities

In the first place, from information in the application or other interviews and sources, the board may know more about you than you think. Secondly, you probably will not get away with it. An experienced board is rather adept at spotting such a situation, so do not take the chance.

5) If you know a board member, do not make a point of it, yet do not hide it

Certainly you are not fooling him, and probably not the other members of the board. Do not try to take advantage of your acquaintanceship – it will probably do you little good.

6) Do not dominate the interview

Let the board do that. They will give you the clues – do not assume that you have to do all the talking. Realize that the board has a number of questions to ask you, and do not try to take up all the interview time by showing off your extensive knowledge of the answer to the first one.

7) Be attentive

You only have 20 minutes or so, and you should keep your attention at its sharpest throughout. When a member is addressing a problem or question to you, give him your undivided attention. Address your reply principally to him, but do not exclude the other board members.

8) Do not interrupt

A board member may be stating a problem for you to analyze. He will ask you a question when the time comes. Let him state the problem, and wait for the question.

9) Make sure you understand the question

Do not try to answer until you are sure what the question is. If it is not clear, restate it in your own words or ask the board member to clarify it for you. However, do not haggle about minor elements.

10) Reply promptly but not hastily

A common entry on oral board rating sheets is "candidate responded readily," or "candidate hesitated in replies." Respond as promptly and quickly as you can, but do not jump to a hasty, ill-considered answer.

11) Do not be peremptory in your answers

A brief answer is proper – but do not fire your answer back. That is a losing game from your point of view. The board member can probably ask questions much faster than you can answer them.

12) Do not try to create the answer you think the board member wants

He is interested in what kind of mind you have and how it works – not in playing games. Furthermore, he can usually spot this practice and will actually grade you down on it.

13) Do not switch sides in your reply merely to agree with a board member

Frequently, a member will take a contrary position merely to draw you out and to see if you are willing and able to defend your point of view. Do not start a debate, yet do not surrender a good position. If a position is worth taking, it is worth defending.

14) Do not be afraid to admit an error in judgment if you are shown to be wrong

The board knows that you are forced to reply without any opportunity for careful consideration. Your answer may be demonstrably wrong. If so, admit it and get on with the interview.

15) Do not dwell at length on your present job

The opening question may relate to your present assignment. Answer the question but do not go into an extended discussion. You are being examined for a *new* job, not your present one. As a matter of fact, try to phrase ALL your answers in terms of the job for which you are being examined.

Basis of Rating

Probably you will forget most of these "do's" and "don'ts" when you walk into the oral interview room. Even remembering them all will not ensure you a passing grade. Perhaps you did not have the qualifications in the first place. But remembering them will help you to put your best foot forward, without treading on the toes of the board members.

Rumor and popular opinion to the contrary notwithstanding, an oral board wants you to make the best appearance possible. They know you are under pressure – but they also want to see how you respond to it as a guide to what your reaction would be under the pressures of the job you seek. They will be influenced by the degree of poise you display, the personal traits you show and the manner in which you respond.

ABOUT THIS BOOK

This book contains tests divided into Examination Sections. Go through each test, answering every question in the margin. We have also attached a sample answer sheet at the back of the book that can be removed and used. At the end of each test look at the answer key and check your answers. On the ones you got wrong, look at the right answer choice and learn. Do not fill in the answers first. Do not memorize the questions and answers, but understand the answer and principles involved. On your test, the questions will likely be different from the samples. Questions are changed and new ones added. If you understand these past questions you should have success with any changes that arise. Tests may consist of several types of questions. We have additional books on each subject should more study be advisable or necessary for you. Finally, the more you study, the better prepared you will be. This book is intended to be the last thing you study before you walk into the examination room. Prior study of relevant texts is also recommended. NLC publishes some of these in our Fundamental Series. Knowledge and good sense are important factors in passing your exam. Good luck also helps. So now study this Passbook, absorb the material contained within and take that knowledge into the examination. Then do your best to pass that exam.

EXAMINATION SECTION

EXAMINATION SECTION
TEST 1

DIRECTIONS: Each question or incomplete statement is followed by several suggested answers or completions. Select the one that BEST answers the question or completes the statement. *PRINT THE LETTER OF THE CORRECT ANSWER IN THE SPACE AT THE RIGHT.*

1. Soft iron is MOST suitable for use in a   1.____

    A. permanent magnet B. natural magnet
    C. temporary magnet D. magneto

2. Static electricity is MOST often produced by   2.____

    A. pressure   B. magnetism   C. heat   D. friction

3. A fundamental law of electricity is that the current in a circuit is   3.____

    A. inversely proportional to the voltage
    B. equal to the voltage
    C. directly proportional to the resistance
    D. directly proportional to the voltage

4. A substance is classed as a magnet if it has   4.____

    A. the ability to conduct lines of force
    B. the property of high permeability
    C. the property of magnetism
    D. a high percentage of iron in its composition

5. If a compass is placed at the center of a bar magnet, the compass needle   5.____

    A. *points* to the geographic south pole
    B. *points* to the geographic north pole
    C. *alines* itself parallel to the bar
    D. *alines* itself perpendicular to the bar

6. When electricity is produced by heat in an iron-and-copper thermocouple, electrons move from   6.____

    A. north to south
    B. the hot junction, through the copper, across the cold junction to the iron, and then to the hot junction
    C. the hot junction, through the iron, across the cold junction to the copper, and then return through the copper to the hot junction
    D. east to west

7. The four factors affecting the resistance of a wire are its   7.____

    A. length, material, diameter, and temperature
    B. size, length, material, and insulation
    C. length, size, relative resistance, and material
    D. size, insulation, relative resistance, and material

1

8. Electricity in a battery is produced by

   A. chemical action
   B. chemical reaction
   C. a chemical acting upon metallic plates
   D. all of the above

9. Resistance is ALWAYS measured in

   A. coulombs   B. henrys   C. ohms   D. megohms

10. The magnetic pole that points northward on a compass

    A. is called the north pole
    B. is actually a south magnetic pole
    C. points to the north magnetic pole of the earth
    D. indicates the direction of the north geographic pole

11. Of the six methods of producing a voltage, which is the LEAST used?

    A. Chemical action   B. Heat
    C. Friction   D. Pressure

12. As the temperature of carbon is increased, its resistance will

    A. increase   B. decrease
    C. remain constant   D. double

13. Around a magnet, the external lines of force

    A. leave the magnet from the north pole and enter the south pole
    B. often cross one another
    C. leave the magnet from the south pole and enter the north pole
    D. may be broken by a piece of iron shielding

14. When a voltage is applied to a conductor, free electrons

    A. are forced into the nucleus of their atom
    B. are impelled along the conductor
    C. unite with protons
    D. cease their movement

15. When the molecules of a substance are altered, the action is referred to as

    A. thermal   B. photoelectric
    C. electrical   D. chemical

16. When matter is separated into individual atoms, it

    A. has undergone a physical change only
    B. has been reduced to its basic chemicals
    C. retains its original characteristics
    D. has been reduced to its basic elements

17. MOST permanent magnets and all electro-magnets are 17.____

    A. classed as natural magnets
    B. manufactured in various shapes from lodestone
    C. classed as artificial magnets
    D. manufactured in various shapes from magnetite

18. When a conductor moves across a magnetic field, 18.____

    A. a voltage is induced in the conductor
    B. a current is induced in the conductor
    C. both current and voltage are induced in the conductor
    D. neither a voltage nor a current is induced

19. The nucleus of an atom contains 19.____

    A. electrons and neutrons
    B. protons and neutrons
    C. protons and electrons
    D. protons, electrons, and neutrons

20. An alnico artificial magnet is composed of 20.____

    A. magnetite, steel, and nickel
    B. cobalt, nickel, and varnish
    C. aluminum, copper, and cobalt
    D. aluminum, nickel, and cobalt

21. A material that acts as an insulator for magnetic flux is 21.____

    A. glass   B. aluminum
    C. soft iron   D. unknown today

22. The force acting through the distance between two dissimilarly-charged bodies 22.____

    A. is a chemical force
    B. is referred to as a magnetic field
    C. constitutes a flow of ions
    D. is referred to as an electrostatic field

23. An atom that has lost or gained electrons 23.____

    A. is negatively charged   B. has a positive charge
    C. is said to be ionized   D. becomes electrically neutral

24. Which of the following is considered to be the BEST conductor? 24.____

    A. Zinc   B. Copper   C. Aluminum   D. Silver

25. As the temperature increases, the resistance of most conductors also increases. 25.____
    A conductor that is an EXCEPTION to this is

    A. aluminum   B. carbon   C. copper   D. brass

KEY (CORRECT ANSWERS)

1. C
2. D
3. D
4. C
5. C

6. B
7. A
8. D
9. C
10. A

11. C
12. B
13. A
14. B
15. D

16. D
17. C
18. A
19. B
20. D

21. D
22. D
23. C
24. D
25. B

TEST 2

DIRECTIONS: Each question or incomplete statement is followed by several suggested answers or completions. Select the one that BEST answers the question or completes the statement. *PRINT THE LETTER OF THE CORRECT ANSWER IN THE SPACE AT THE RIGHT.*

1. The dry cell battery is a _____ cell. 1.____
   A. secondary   B. polarized   C. primary   D. voltaic

2. The electrolyte of a lead-acid wet cell is 2.____
   A. sal ammoniac   B. manganese dioxide
   C. sulfuric acid   D. distilled water

3. A battery which can be restored after discharge is a _____ cell. 3.____
   A. primary   B. galvanic   C. dry   D. secondary

4. Lead-acid battery plates are held together by a 4.____
   A. glass wool mat   B. wood separator
   C. grid work   D. hard rubber tube

5. When mixing electrolyte, ALWAYS pour 5.____
   A. water into acid
   B. acid into water
   C. both acid and water into vat simultaneously
   D. first acid, then water into vat

6. When charging a battery, the electrolyte should NEVER exceed a temperature of 6.____
   A. 125° F.   B. 113° F.   C. 80° F.   D. 40° F.

7. The plates of a lead-acid battery are made of 7.____
   A. lead and lead dioxide   B. lead and lead oxide
   C. silver and peroxide   D. lead and lead peroxide

8. A battery is receiving a normal charge. It begins to gas freely. The charging current should 8.____
   A. be increased
   B. be decreased
   C. be cut off and the battery allowed to cool
   D. remain the same

9. A hydrometer reading is 1.265 at 92° F. The CORRECTED reading is 9.____
   A. 1.229   B. 1.261   C. 1.269   D. 1.301

10. In the nickel-cadmium battery, KOH is 10.____
    A. the positive plate   B. the negative plate
    C. the electrolyte   D. none of the above

11. When sulfuric acid, H_2SO_4, and water, H_2O, are mixed together, they form a

    A. gas
    B. compound
    C. mixture
    D. hydrogen solution

12. How many No. 6 dry cells are required to supply power to a load requiring 6 volts if the cells are connected in series?

    A. Two   B. Four   C. Five   D. Six

13. The ordinary 6-volt lead-acid storage battery consists of how many cells?

    A. Two   B. Three   C. Four   D. Six

14. A fully-charged aircraft battery has a specific gravity reading of

    A. 1.210 to 1.220
    B. 1.250 to 1.265
    C. 1.285 to 1.300
    D. 1.300 to 1.320

15. What is the ampere-hour rating of a storage battery that can deliver 20 amperes continuously for 10 hours?
    _____ ampere-hour.

    A. 20   B. 40   C. 200   D. 400

16. The normal cell voltage of a fully-charged nickel-cadmium battery is _____ volts.

    A. 2.0   B. 1.5   C. 1.4   D. 1.0

17. The electrolyte in a mercury cell is

    A. sulfuric acid
    B. KOH
    C. potassium hydroxide, zincate, and mercury
    D. potassium hydroxide, water, and zincate

18. Concentrated sulfuric acid has a specific gravity of

    A. 1.285   B. 1.300   C. 1.830   D. 2.400

19. The number of negative plates in a lead-acid cell is ALWAYS _____ of positive plates.

    A. one greater than the number
    B. equal to the number
    C. one less than the number
    D. double the number

20. A lead-acid battery is considered fully charged when the specific gravity readings of all cells taken at half-hour intervals show no change for _____ hour(s).

    A. four   B. three   C. two   D. one

KEY (CORRECT ANSWERS)

1. C
2. C
3. D
4. C
5. B

6. A
7. D
8. B
9. C
10. C

11. C
12. B
13. B
14. C
15. C

16. C
17. D
18. C
19. A
20. A

TEST 3

DIRECTIONS: Each question or incomplete statement is followed by several suggested answers or completions. Select the one that BEST answers the question or completes the statement. *PRINT THE LETTER OF THE CORRECT ANSWER IN THE SPACE AT THE RIGHT.*

1. In which direction does current flow in an electrical circuit? 1.___

    A. - to + externally, + to - internally
    B. + to - externally, + to - internally
    C. - to + externally, - to + internally
    D. + to - externally, - to + internally

2. Given the formula $P = E^2/R$, solve for E. 2.___

    A. $E = \sqrt{ER}$ B. $E = \sqrt{PR}$ C. $E = IR$ D. $E = \sqrt{P/R}$

3. Resistance in the power formula equals 3.___

    A. $R = \sqrt{I/P}$ B. $R = E/I$ C. $R = \sqrt{P \times I}$ D. $R = E^2/P$

4. One joule is equal to 4.___

    A. 1 watt second
    B. 10 watt seconds
    C. 1 watt minute
    D. 10 watt minutes

5. A lamp has a source voltage of 110 v. and a current of 0.9 amps. What is the resistance of the lamp? 5.___

    A. 12.22 Ω   B. 122.2 Ω   C. 0.008 Ω   D. 0.08 Ω

6. In accordance with Ohm's law, the relationship between current and voltage in a simple circuit is that the 6.___

    A. current varies inversely with the resistance if the voltage is held constant
    B. voltage varies as the square of the applied e.m.f.
    C. current varies directly with the applied voltage if the resistance is held constant
    D. voltage varies inversely as the current if the resistance is held constant

7. The current needed to operate a soldering iron which has a rating of 600 watts at 110 volts is 7.___

    A. 0.182 a.   B. 5.455 a.   C. 18.200 a.   D. 66.000 a.

8. In electrical circuits, the time rate of doing work is expressed in 8.___

    A. volts   B. amperes   C. watts   D. ohms

9. If the resistance is held constant, what is the relationship between power and voltage in a simple circuit? 9.___

    A. Resistance must be varied to show a true relationship.
    B. Power will vary as the square of the applied voltage.
    C. Voltage will vary inversely proportional to power.
    D. Power will vary directly with voltage.

10. How many watts are there in 1 horsepower?

    A. 500 B. 640 C. 746 D. 1,000

11. What formula is used to find watt-hours?

    A. E x T B. E x I x T C. E x I x $\sqrt{\theta}$ D. E x I²

12. What is the resistance of the circuit shown at the right?

    A. 4.8 Ω
    B. 12.0 Ω
    C. 48 Ω
    D. 120 Ω

    I_T = 0.2 AMP., 24V, R = ?

13. In the figure at the right, solve for I_T.

    A. 0.5 a.
    B. 1 a.
    C. 13 a.
    D. 169 a.

    13 Ω, E = ?, P = 13 Watts

14. A simple circuit consists of one power source,

    A. and one power consuming device
    B. one power consuming device, and connecting wiring
    C. protective device, and control device
    D. one power consuming device, and protective device

15. The device used in circuits to prevent damage from overloads is called a

    A. fuse B. switch C. resistor D. connector

16. What happens in a series circuit when the voltage remains constant and the resistance increases?
    Current

    A. increases   B. decreases
    C. remains the same   D. increases by the square

17. Other factors remaining constant, what would be the effect on the current flow in a given circuit if the applied potential were doubled?
It would

    A. double
    B. remain the same
    C. be divided by two
    D. be divided by four

17.____

18. Which of the following procedures can be used to calculate the resistance of a load?

    A. *Multiply* the voltage across the load by the square of the current through the load
    B. *Divide* the current through the load by the voltage across the load
    C. *Multiply* the voltage across the load by the current through the load
    D. *Divide* the voltage across the load by the current through the load

18.____

19. A cockpit light operates from a 24-volt d-c supply and uses 72 watts of power. The current flowing through the bulb is _____ amps.

    A. 0.33   B. 3   C. 600   D. 1,728

19.____

20. If the resistance is held constant, what happens to power if the current is doubled?
Power is

    A. doubled
    B. multiplied by 4
    C. halved
    D. divided by 4

20.____

KEY (CORRECT ANSWERS)

1. A
2. B
3. D
4. A
5. B

6. C
7. B
8. C
9. B
10. C

11. B
12. D
13. B
14. B
15. A

16. B
17. A
18. D
19. B
20. B

TEST 4

DIRECTIONS: Each question or incomplete statement is followed by several suggested answers or completions. Select the one that BEST answers the question or completes the statement. *PRINT THE LETTER OF THE CORRECT ANSWER IN THE SPACE AT THE RIGHT.*

1. If a circuit is constructed so as to allow the electrons to follow only one possible path, the circuit is called a(n) _____ circuit.   1.____

    A. series-parallel
    B. incomplete
    C. series
    D. parallel

2. According to Kirchhoff's Law of Voltages, the algebraic sum of all the voltages in a series circuit is equal to   2.____

    A. zero
    B. source voltage
    C. total voltage drop
    D. the sum of the IR drop of the circuit

3. In a series circuit, the total current is   3.____

    A. always equal to the source voltage
    B. determined by the load only
    C. the same through all parts of the circuit
    D. equal to zero at the positive side of the source

4.   4.____

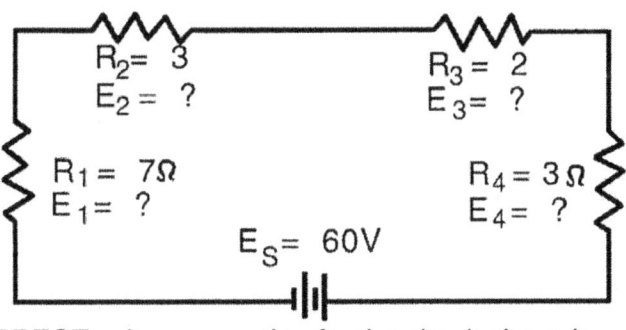

    The CORRECT voltage equation for the circuit above is

    A. $E_S + E_1 + E_2 + E_3 + E_4 = 0$
    B. $E_S - E_1 - E_2 - E_3 - E_4 = 0$
    C. $E_S = -E_1 - E_2 - E_3 - E_4$
    D. $-E_S = E_1 + E_2 + E_3 + E_4$

5. Referring to the circuit shown in Question 4 above, after expressing the voltage drops around the circuit in terms of current and resistance and the given values of source voltage, the equation becomes   5.____

    A. $-60 - 7I - 3I - 2I - 3I = 0$
    B. $-60 + 7I + 3I + 2I + 3I = 0$
    C. $60 - 7I - 3I - 2I - 3I = 0$
    D. $60 + 7I + 3I + 2I + 3I = 0$

11

6. By the use of the correct equation, it is found that the current (I) in the circuit shown in Question 4 is of positive value. This indicates that the

    A. assumed direction of current flow is correct
    B. assumed direction of current flow is incorrect
    C. problem is not solvable
    D. battery polarity should be reversed

7.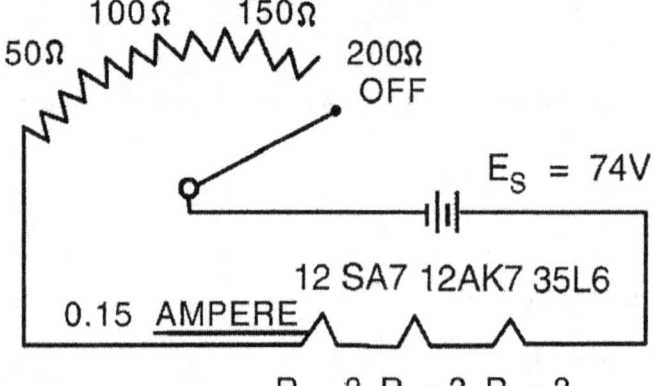

In what position would the variable rheostat in the circuit above be placed in order that the filaments of the tubes operate properly with a current flow of 0.15 ampere? _____ position.

    A. 50 Ω   B. 100 Ω   C. 150 Ω   D. 200 Ω

8. The power absorbed by the variable rheostat in the circuit used in Question 7 above, when placed in its proper operating position, would be _____ watts.

    A. 112.50   B. 2.25   C. 337.50   D. 450.00

9.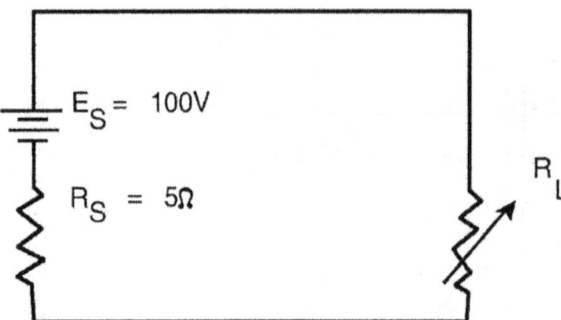

In the circuit above, maximum power would be transferred from the source to the load (R_L) if R_L were set at _____ ohms.

    A. 2   B. 5   C. 12   D. 24

10.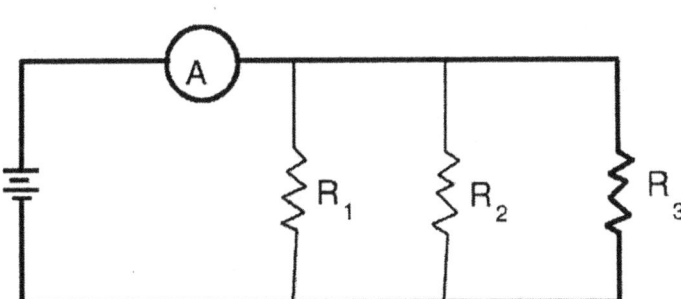

In the circuit above, if an additional resistor were placed in parallel to R_3, the ammeter reading would

A. increase
B. decrease
C. remain the same
D. drop to zero

11. In a parallel circuit containing a 4-ohm, 5-ohm, and 6-ohm resistor, the current flow is

A. *highest* through the 4-ohm resistor
B. *lowest* through the 4-ohm resistor
C. *highest* through the 6-ohm resistor
D. *equal* through all three resistors

12. Three resistors of 2, 4, and 6 ohms, respectively, are connected in parallel. Which resistor would absorb the GREATEST power?

A. The 2-ohm resistor
B. The 4-ohm resistor
C. The 6-ohm resistor
D. It will be the same for all resistors

13. If three lamps are connected in parallel with a power source, connecting a fourth lamp in parallel will

A. decrease E_T
B. decrease I_T
C. increase E_T
D. increase I_T

14.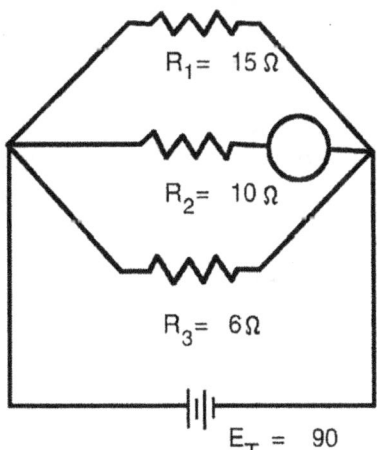

What is the current flow through the ammeter in the circuit shown above?
_____ amps.

A. 4
B. 9
C. 15
D. 28

15.

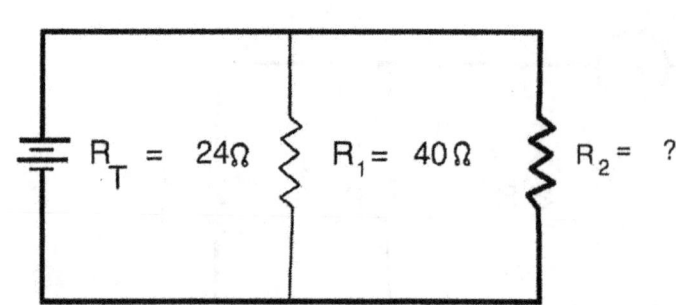

In the circuit shown above, the TOTAL resistance is 24 ohms. What is the value of R_2?
_____ ohms.

A. 16   B. 40   C. 60   D. 64

16.

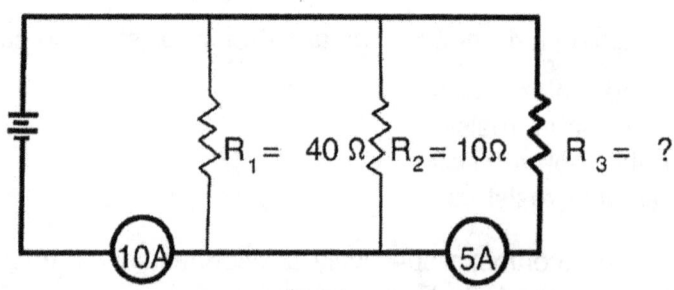

What is the source voltage of the circuit shown above?
_____ volts.

A. 40   B. 50   C. 100   D. 500

17. What is the value of R_3 in the circuit shown in Question 16 above?
_____ ohms.

A. 8   B. 10   C. 20   D. 100

18.

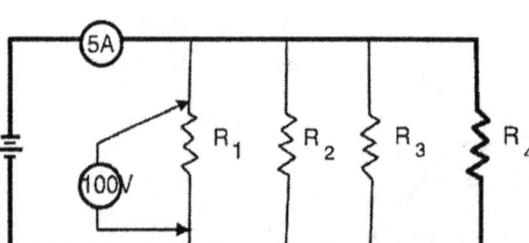

If all 4 resistors in the circuit above are of equal ohmic resistances, what is the value of R_3?
_____ ohms.

A. 5   B. 20   C. 60   D. 80

19.

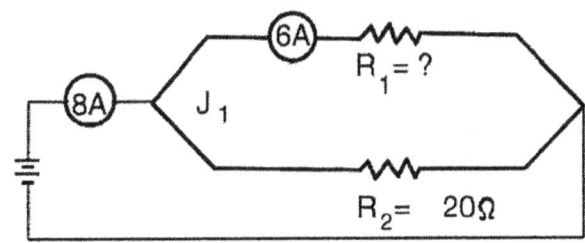

What is the value of the source voltage in the circuit above?
_____ volts

A. 20   B. 40   C. 120   D. 160

20.

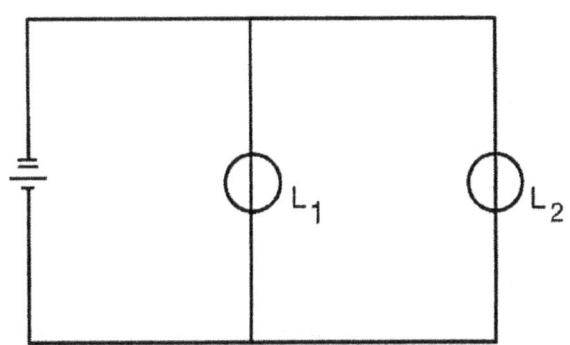

If Lamp L_2 in the circuit above should suddenly burn out, which of the statements below is CORRECT?

A. More current would flow through lamp L_1.
B. Source voltage would decrease.
C. The filament resistance of lamp L_1 would decrease.
D. Lamp L_1 would still burn normal.

21. When referring to a circuit's conductance, you visualize the degree to which the circuit

A. *permits* or conducts voltage
B. *opposes* the rate of voltage changes
C. *permits* or conducts current flow
D. *opposes* the rate of current flow

22.

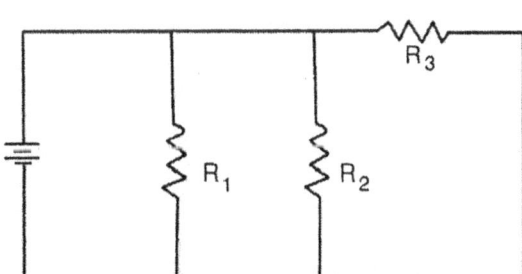

The TOTAL conductance of the circuit above would be solved by which of the equations?

A. $G_T - G_1 - G_2 - G_3 = 0$
B. $G_T + G_1 + G_2 + G_3 = 0$
C. $G_T = G_1 - G_2 - G_3$
D. $G_T = G_1 + G_2 + G_3$

23.

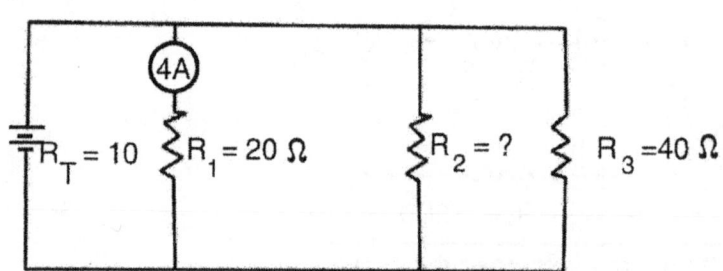

If the resistors in the circuit above are all rated at 250 watts, which resistor or resistors would overheat?

   A. R_1 B. R_2 C. R_3 D. All

24.

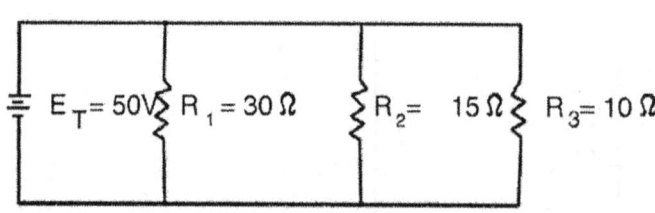

The TOTAL conductance of the circuit above is

   A. 0.15G   B. 0.20G   C. 0.50G   D. 0.75G

KEY (CORRECT ANSWERS)

1. C   11. A
2. A   12. A
3. C   13. D
4. B   14. B
5. C   15. C

6. A   16. A
7. B   17. A
8. B   18. D
9. B   19. B
10. A   20. D

21. C
22. D
23. A
24. B

TEST 5

DIRECTIONS: Each question or incomplete statement is followed by several suggested answers or completions. Select the one that BEST answers the question or completes the statement. *PRINT THE LETTER OF THE CORRECT ANSWER IN THE SPACE AT THE RIGHT.*

1. The MINIMUM number of resistors in a compound circuit is (are) 1.____
   A. four   B. three   C. two   D. one

2.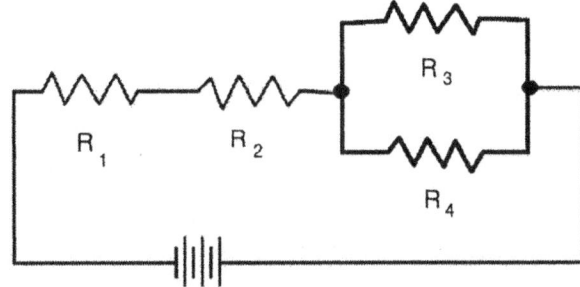
   Total resistance of the circuit shown is determined by the formula 2.____

   A. $R_1 R_2 + \dfrac{R_3 R_4}{R_4 + R_3}$

   B. $R_1 + R_2 + \dfrac{R_3 + R_4}{R_3 R_4}$

   C. $R_1 + R_2 + \dfrac{R_3 R_4}{R_3 + R_4}$

   D. $R_1 + R_2 + (\dfrac{R_3 R_4}{R_3 + R_4})$

3.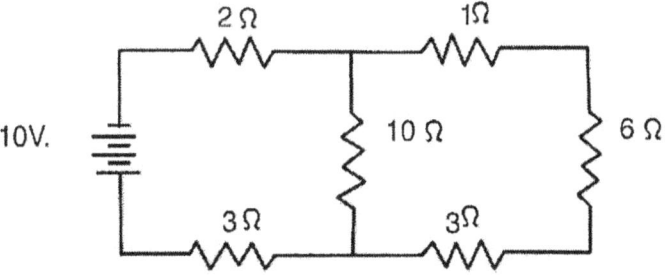

   In the circuit above, what is the value of I_t? 3.____
   $I_t =$ _____ amp.

   A. 1.14   B. 0.4   C. 0.667   D. 1

4. In the circuit in Question 3 above, how much power is consumed by the 6-ohm resistor? 4.____
   _____ watts.

   A. 15   B. 1.5   C. 60   D. 6

5. A voltage divider is used to 5.____

   A. provide different voltage values for multiple loads from a single source
   B. provide several voltage drops in parallel
   C. increase the voltage to the load at several taps
   D. provide tap points to alter power supplied

17

6. The total power supplied to the entire circuit by a voltage divider and 4 loads is the

   A. sum of the 4 loads
   B. voltage divider minus 4 loads
   C. voltage divider plus the 4 loads
   D. voltage divider only

7. The total voltage of a voltage divider is the

   A. input voltage minus the load's voltages
   B. the load's voltages only
   C. sum of the input and load voltage
   D. sum of the voltages across the divider

8. An attenuator is

   A. a network of resistors used to reduce power, voltage, or current
   B. a network of resistors to change the input voltage
   C. also called a pad
   D. used in every power circuit

9. In an attenuator, the resistors are

   A. adjusted separately
   B. connected in parallel with the load
   C. connected in series with the load
   D. ganged

10. What two conditions may be observed in a bridge circuit?

    A. T and L network characteristics
    B. No-load and full-load bridge current
    C. Unequal potential and unequal current
    D. Balance and unbalance

11.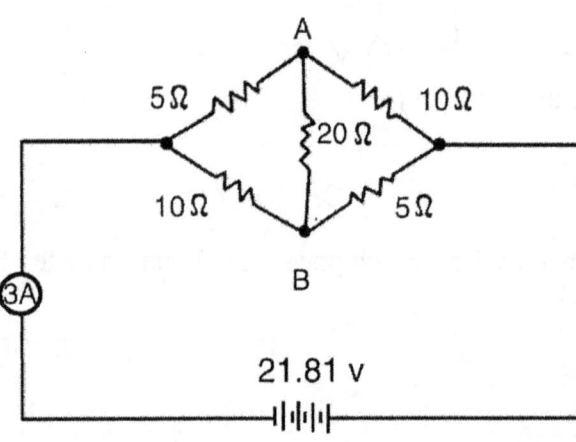

    In the circuit above, how much current flows in the resistor and what is its direction?

    A. 26 a.; B to A
    B. 1a.; A to B
    C. 0.273 a.; A to B
    D. 1a.; B to A

12. In a three-wire distribution system, an unbalanced situation is indicated by the

    A. potential of the positive wire being equal to the negative wire
    B. positive wire carrying more amperage than the negative wire
    C. current in the neutral wire
    D. neutral wire carrying the total current

12.____

13.

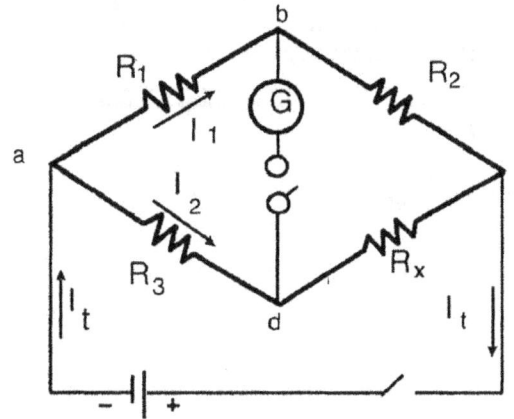

SCHEMATIC WHEATSTONE-BRIDGE CIRCUIT

In the figure above, the galvanometer will show zero deflection when

A. $\dfrac{R_1}{R_2} + \dfrac{R_3}{R_x}$

B. $R_x = \dfrac{R_1 R_3}{R_2}$

C. $\dfrac{I_1 R_1}{I_2 R_x} = \dfrac{I_2 R_3}{I_1 R_2}$

D. $R_x = \dfrac{R_1 R_2}{R_3}$

13.____

14. In the Wheatstone Bridge type circuit shown at the right, the bridge current is toward Point A.
    The resistance of R_X is

    A. 30Ω
    B. greater than 45Ω
    C. 20Ω
    D. less than 15Ω

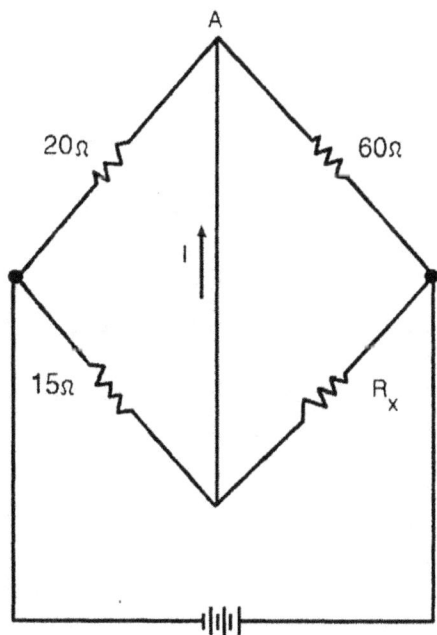

14.____

15.

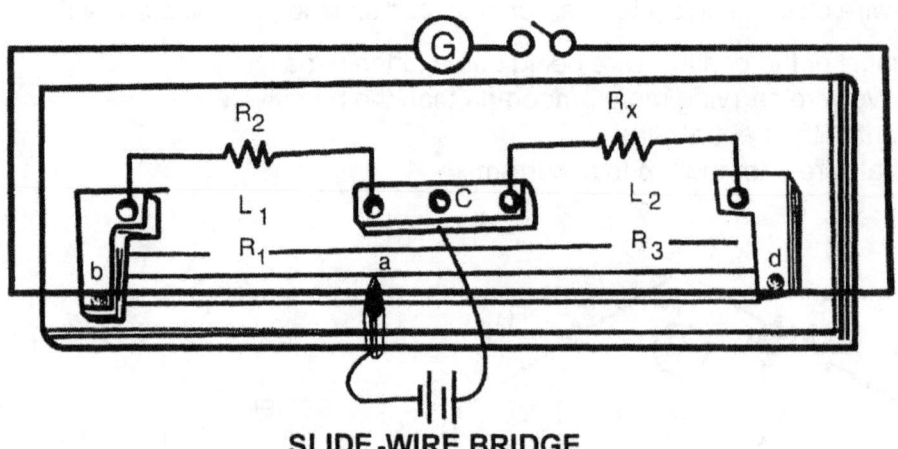

SLIDE-WIRE BRIDGE

In the slide-wire bridge shown above, L_1 is equal to

A. $L_1 = \dfrac{R_2 L_2}{R_1}$

B. $L_1 = \dfrac{R_1 + L_2}{R_2}$

C. $\dfrac{R_2}{R_1 L_2} = L_1$

D. $\dfrac{R_2 L_2}{R_x} = L_1$

16.

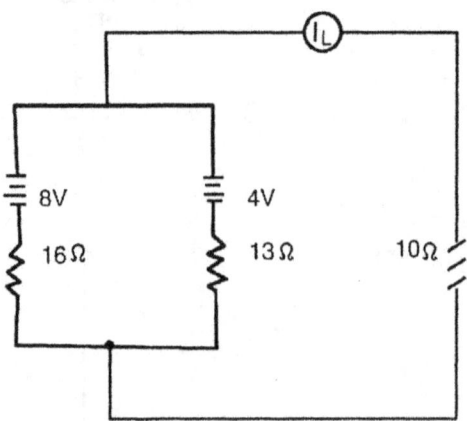

In the circuit above, I line is

A. 4.44 a.   B. 0.444 a.   C. 0.337 a.   D. 5.22 a.

17. When checking a 3-wire distribution circuit going against the direction of current flow, the IR drop is ALWAYS

    A. negative
    B. positive
    C. not used
    D. always in direction of current flow

18.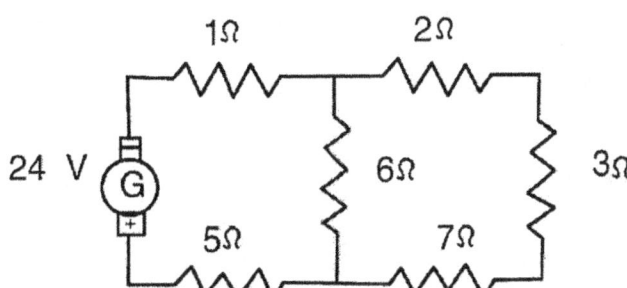

In the circuit above, the voltage drop across the 3-ohm resistor is _____ volts.

A. 2.4 B. 24 C. 9.6 D. 0.96

19. The resistance of the wire is taken into consideration in the 2- and 3-wire distribution systems because the

A. source and load are very close
B. resistance of the wire is the same throughout
C. load and source are at a considerable distance from each other
D. load must be decreased in order to determine accurate circuit values

20. What is Kirchhoff's second law as applied to 3-wire distribution circuits?

A. Sum of all the voltages is zero.
B. Algebraic sum of all the voltages about closed path is zero.
C. Algebraic sum of all voltage is zero.
D. All IR drops in the circuit are negative.

KEY (CORRECT ANSWERS)

1. B
2. C
3. D
4. B
5. A

6. C
7. D
8. A
9. D
10. D

11. C
12. C
13. A
14. B
15. D

16. C
17. B
18. A
19. C
20. B

TEST 6

DIRECTIONS: Each question or incomplete statement is followed by several suggested answers or completions. Select the one that BEST answers the question or completes the statement. *PRINT THE LETTER OF THE CORRECT ANSWER IN THE SPACE AT THE RIGHT.*

1. A mil is what part of an inch?

    A. 1/10
    B. 1/100
    C. 1/1000
    D. 1/1,000,000

2. The discharge (electrical leakage) that MIGHT occur from a wire carrying a high potential is called

    A. arcing
    B. sparking
    C. static discharge
    D. corona

3. Bare wire ends are spliced by the

    A. western union method
    B. rat-tail joint method
    C. fixture joint method
    D. all of the above

4. What is a unit conductor called that has a length of one foot and a cross-sectional area of one circular mil?

    A. Square mil
    B. Circular mil
    C. Circular mil foot
    D. Square mil foot

5. The induction-type soldering iron is commonly known as the

    A. soldering copper
    B. pencil iron
    C. soldering gun
    D. resistance gun

6. All good quality soldering irons operate at what temperature?

    A. 400 - 500° F.
    B. 500 - 600° F.
    C. 600 - 700° F.
    D. 300 - 600° F.

7. A No. 12 wire has a diameter of 80.81 mils. What is the area in circular mils? _____ cm.

    A. 6,530 B. 5,630 C. 4,530 D. 3,560

8. Dielectric strength is the

    A. opposite of potential difference
    B. ability of a conductor to carry large amounts of current
    C. ability of an insulator to withstand a potential difference
    D. strength of a magnetic field

9. To readily transfer the heat from the soldering iron tip, it FIRST should be

    A. tinned with solder
    B. allowed to form an oxide film
    C. cleaned with carbon tetrachloride
    D. allowed to heat for 25 minutes

10. A No. 12 wire has a diameter of 80.81 mils. What is the area in square mils? _____ square mils.

   A. 2,516.8   B. 5,128.6   C. 6,530   D. 8,512.6

11. Varnished cambric insulation is used to cover conductors carrying voltages above _____ volts.

   A. 1,000   B. 1,500   C. 15,000   D. 5,000

12. The solder splicer is used to

   A. prevent the waste of rosin core solder
   B. connect together small lengths of solder
   C. connect two conductors together
   D. none of the above

13. The conductance of a conductor is the ease with which current will flow through it. It is measured in

   A. ohms   B. mhos   C. henrys   D. amperes

14. Asbestos insulation loses its insulating properties when it becomes

   A. overaged
   B. overheated
   C. used over a long period of time
   D. wet

15. How are solderless connectors installed on conductors?

   A. Bolted on   B. Chemical compound
   C. Crimped on   D. All of the above

16. The factor(s) governing the selection of wire size is (are)

   A. (I^2R loss) in the line
   B. (IR drop) in the line
   C. current-carrying ability of the line
   D. all of the above

17. Enamel insulated conductors are USUALLY called

   A. magnet wire   B. high voltage wire
   C. low voltage wire   D. transmission lines

18. The advantage of solderless connectors over soldered-type connectors is that they are

   A. mechanically stronger   B. easier to install
   C. free of corrosion   D. all of the above

19. The basic requirement of any splice is that it be

    A. soldered
    B. mechanically and electrically as strong as the conductor that is spliced
    C. made with a splicer
    D. taped

20. The type of tape that is used for electrical circuits having a temperature of 175° F. or above is

    A. glass cloth
    B. plastic
    C. synthetic rubber compound
    D. impregnated cloth

KEY (CORRECT ANSWERS)

1.	C	11.	C
2.	D	12.	C
3.	D	13.	B
4.	C	14.	D
5.	A	15.	C
6.	B	16.	D
7.	A	17.	A
8.	C	18.	B
9.	A	19.	B
10.	B	20.	A

EXAMINATION SECTION
TEST 1

DIRECTIONS: Each question or incomplete statement is followed by several suggested answers or completions. Select the one that BEST answers the question or completes the statement. *PRINT THE LETTER OF THE CORRECT ANSWER IN THE SPACE AT THE RIGHT.*

1. The cathode of a phototube is USUALLY coated with a thin layer of _____ oxide. 1._____

   A. magnesium   B. cesium   C. titanium   D. zinc

2. The capacitor on a capacitor motor is connected in _____ winding. 2._____

   A. parallel with the starting
   B. series with the running
   C. parallel with the running
   D. series with the starting

3. The refrigerant used in MOST modern home electric cooling appliances is 3._____

   A. neon   B. argon   C. zenon   D. freon

4. Splicing compound is USUALLY referred to as 4._____

   A. cable varnish   B. friction tape
   C. rubber tape   D. varnish cambric

5. The filament supports of an incandescent lamp are affixed to the 5._____

   A. button rod   B. lead-in wires
   C. steam seal   D. ceramic insulator

6. A non-tamperable fuse is known as a 6._____

   A. fusetron   B. fusetat
   C. circuit breaker   D. Kirkman tamp-lock

7. The wall plate used to cover two toggle switches mounted side by side in a wall box is known as a _____ plate. 7._____

   A. multiple toggle   B. duplex
   C. two gang   D. double

8. Building wire with a thermoplastic insulation is called type 8._____

   A. T.P.   B. R.H.   C. T.W.   D. RH-RW

9. A repulsion-start induction motor operates on 9._____

   A. 4 wire A.C.   B. single phase A.C.
   C. D.C. - 110V-220V   D. A.C. - D.C.

10. A *fish tape* is used to 10._____

    A. pull wires through a conduit   B. weatherproof a splice
    C. test a grounded circuit   D. support long cable runs

11. The color code of a 3 wire #12 cable is

    A. white black green
    B. blue black red
    C. white black red
    D. red white green

12. The motor that has no brushes or commutator is known as a _____ motor.

    A. split phase
    B. capacitor
    C. compound
    D. shunt

13. The temperature of a well-designed continuously run motor, delivering its full rated horsepower, should NOT increase by more than _____ Fahrenheit.

    A. 40°
    B. 52°
    C. 60°
    D. 72°

14. A floodlight operating at a point 500 feet from the meter, wired with #14 wire whose resistance is 2.575 ohms per 1000', has a voltage drop of *approximately* _____ volts.

    A. 5.7
    B. 11.33
    C. 12.74
    D. 15.37

15. The grid in the vacuum tube was introduced by

    A. Fauere
    B. Oersted
    C. De Forest
    D. Le Lanche

16. In an element for an electric range, the material that insulates the wire from the tube is

    A. magnesium oxide
    B. asbestos
    C. high temperature fibre glass
    D. titanium oxide

17. Most thermostats and relays that are used to activate and control a home heating system operate on _____ volts.

    A. 6
    B. 24
    C. 32
    D. 46

18. The revolutions per minute of an electric motor can be determined by using a(n)

    A. hydrometer
    B. tachometer
    C. pulse indicator
    D. prony brake

19. A record player pick-up arm, equipped with a phono cartridge that contains Rochelle-Salts, will produce a voltage known as

    A. phono-electric
    B. bio-electric
    C. piezoelectric
    D. pyrometric

20. The device that controls the flow of electrons in a solid is the

    A. electron tube
    B. transistor
    C. anode
    D. cathode

21. Fluorescent lamps are designed to operate on

    A. the rated voltage that appears on the lamp
    B. a rectifier controlled voltage
    C. a 115 volt or 230 volt circuit
    D. a circuit where the voltage fluctuation does not exceed 5%

22. The efficiency of a 3 horsepower motor that requires 2.4 kilowatts to drive it is

   A. 74%   B. 82%   C. 90%   D. 94%

23. The magnetic resistance that opposes the flow of magnetic current is

   A. inductance
   C. reactance
   B. reluctance
   D. impedance

24. The output in lumens per watt for an incandescent lamp (filament type) is _____ to _____ lumens.

   A. 14; 23   B. 30; 55   C. 50; 57   D. 58; 75

25. The voltage of a battery cell depends upon

   A. the number of lines cut per second
   B. the size of the plates and the distance they are set apart
   C. material that the plate is made of and the electrolyte used
   D. area of the zinc container

26. Most window-type air conditioners, such as used in the home, are equipped with a(n) _____ motor.

   A. synchronous
   C. seal-vac
   B. R-I
   D. hermetically sealed

27. Light that contains only a single color and also a single wave length is known as the _____ light.

   A. spectrum
   C. aurora
   B. laser
   D. sodium vapor

28. The *Edison effect* led to the development of the

   A. mercury vapor lamp
   C. phonograph
   B. radio tube
   D. fluorescent lamp

29. A device for producing high tension induced current is the _____ coil.

   A. Ruhmkorff   B. Solenoid   C. Thury   D. Choke

30. In a triode tube, the element placed between the cathode and the plate is called

   A. rectifier
   C. S C C
   B. controlled grid
   D. D C C

KEY (CORRECT ANSWERS)

1.	B	11.	C	21.	C
2.	D	12.	A	22.	D
3.	D	13.	D	23.	B
4.	C	14.	C	24.	A
5.	A	15.	C	25.	C
6.	B	16.	A	26.	D
7.	C	17.	B	27.	B
8.	C	18.	B	28.	B
9.	B	19.	C	29.	A
10.	A	20.	B	30.	B

TEST 2

DIRECTIONS: Each question or incomplete statement is followed by several suggested answers or completions. Select the one that BEST answers the question or completes the statement. *PRINT THE LETTER OF THE CORRECT ANSWER IN THE SPACE AT THE RIGHT.*

1. A fixture hickey is used to 1.____

    A. bend pipe
    B. suspend a ceiling light
    C. make a 60° offset in BX
    D. ground a fixture

2. Nichrome wire is used in electrical heating devices because it 2.____

    A. is non-magnetic
    B. has a low melting point
    C. is cheaper than copper wire
    D. has a high resistance

3. The letters *E M T* in conduit work refer to 3.____

    A. underwriters approval   B. thin wall conduit
    C. A.C. use only   D. ready for first inspection

4. A 120 volt three-way incandescent lamp bulb has 4.____

    A. one filament   B. two filaments
    C. three filaments   D. a variable resistor

5. When an object to be copperplated is immersed in its electrolyte, it should be connected to the 5.____

    A. anode   B. cathode
    C. right terminal   D. electrolyte

6. A voltmeter consists of a milliammeter and a high resistance which are connected in 6.____

    A. multiple   B. parallel   C. series   D. shunt

7. A device for producing electricity directly from heat is called a 7.____

    A. turbine   B. thermocouple
    C. transformer   D. rheostat

8. The combined resistance of a circuit containing five 40 ohm resistances in parallel is _____ ohms. 8.____

    A. 8   B. 20   C. 40   D. 200

9. An alternator differs from a D.C. generator because it has no 9.____

    A. brushes   B. commutator
    C. field poles   D. rotor

10. The resistance of a wire 1/16 inch in diameter is one OHM. A wire of the same length, but twice the diameter, has a resistance of ohms. 10.____

    A. 1/4   B. 1/2   C. 1   D. 2

29

11. A device that measures energy consumption of electricity is called a

    A. wattmeter   B. kilowatthourmeter
    C. kilowatt meter   D. ammeter

12. A *universal* motor is a(n) _____ motor.

    A. shunt   B. induction   C. series   D. synchronous

13. In a three phase, four wire, 208 volt distribution system, the voltage between any phase wire and the neutral is _____ volts.

    A. 0   B. 120   C. 208   D. 240

14. Of the following, the motor that does NOT have a commutator is

    A. universal   B. series
    C. repulsion induction D. split phase

15. An incandescent lamp rated at 130 volts-100 watts, and operated at 115 volts will

    A. consume more wattage and impair the life of the filament
    B. increase lamp life and reduce wattage consumed
    C. produce fewer lumens per watt and increase lamp efficiency
    D. have no effect on the lamp

16. A 2 horsepower 75% efficient D.C. motor operating at full load draws *approximately* _____ watts.

    A. 1000   B. 1500   C. 2000   D. 3000

17. An insulating material that withstands heat better than wire with more ordinary insulation is

    A. rubber   B. plastic
    C. rubber with cotton covering D. varnished cambric

18. Electrical resistance can be measured with a(n)

    A. voltmeter and an ammeter   B. A.C. wattmeter
    C. thermocouple   D. induction coil

19. The property of a circuit that enables it to store electrical energy in the form of an electrostatic field is called

    A. inductance   B. reactance
    C. resistance   D. capacitance

20. If a 50 ohm resistance draws two amperes from a circuit, the power it uses is

    A. 0.2 KW   B. 25 watts
    C. 100 watts   D. none of the above

21. The world's FIRST central light and power plant was developed by
    A. Samuel F.B. Morse   B. Lee De Forest
    C. Edwin H. Armstrong   D. Thomas A. Edison

22. A *tuner* circuit consists of a
    A. zener diode and tunnel transistor
    B. capacitor and inductance coil
    C. resistor and R.F. amplifier tube
    D. resistor and capacitor

23. A hotplate having a resistance of 30 ohms, connected to a 120 volt outlet, would draw a current of _____ amperes.
    A. 4   B. 90   C. 150   D. 3600

24. Of the following, the term that does NOT relate to magnetism is
    A. reluctance   B. oersted
    C. coulomb   D. magneto-motive force

25. A basic difference between radio waves and sound waves is that radio waves are
    A. of a different frequency   B. electrical currents
    C. molecules of air in motion D. electromagnetic waves

26. An object that has a positive electrostatic charge would have an excess of
    A. electrons   B. protons
    C. neutrons   D. omega minus particles

27. Of the following, the statement that does NOT apply to a capacitor is that it can
    A. store electrons
    B. pass alternating current
    C. pass direct current
    D. be used to smooth out pulsating direct current

28. The section of a radio transmitter or receiver that causes a stream of electrons to vibrate back and forth at high frequencies is known as a(n)
    A. modulator   B. oscillator   C. amplifier   D. detector

29. The separation of speech or music from a radio wave carrying music or speech is referred to as
    A. audio filtration   B. separation
    C. demodulation   D. tracing

30. A circuit used to smooth out the surges of pulsating direct current from a rectifier is called a
    A. filter   B. multiplexer
    C. demodulator   D. local oscillator

KEY (CORRECT ANSWERS)

1.	B	11.	B	21.	D
2.	D	12.	C	22.	B
3.	B	13.	B	23.	A
4.	B	14.	D	24.	C
5.	B	15.	B	25.	D
6.	C	16.	C	26.	B
7.	B	17.	D	27.	C
8.	A	18.	A	28.	B
9.	B	19.	D	29.	C
10.	A	20.	A	30.	A

TEST 3

DIRECTIONS: Each question or incomplete statement is followed by several suggested answers or completions. Select the one that BEST answers the question or completes the statement. *PRINT THE LETTER OF THE CORRECT ANSWER IN THE SPACE AT THE RIGHT.*

1. The simple motor found in an electric clock is called a(n) _____ motor. 1.____

    A. synchronous
    B. induction
    C. rotor
    D. D.C.

2. The amperage of a fully charged car storage battery is USUALLY near _____ amps. 2.____

    A. 10
    B. 100
    C. 1000
    D. 10,000

3. To prevent the initial surge of current drawn by an electric motor from *burning out* the fuse in the circuit, one uses a 3.____

    A. cartridge fuse
    B. circuit breaker
    C. plug fuse
    D. fusetron

4. The many radio waves striking the antenna of a receiver are tuned-in with the 4.____

    A. transformer
    B. choke coil
    C. variable condenser
    D. diode detector

5. The starting motor of an automobile engine is shifted into mesh with the flywheel gear by a 5.____

    A. vibrator
    B. solenoid
    C. bendix
    D. starter button

6. The picture tube of a television set is also referred to as a _____ tube. 6.____

    A. cathode-ray
    B. power beam
    C. oscilliscope
    D. photo-electric

7. Generators that have two or more sets of field poles and require fewer revolutions to generate a 60-cycle-per second current are called 7.____

    A. duo-dynamos
    B. vibrators
    C. poly-phase generators
    D. alternators

8. A bar that has been artificially magnetized can be demagnetized by 8.____

    A. quenching it in hot oil
    B. pounding it with a heavy hammer
    C. bending it into a *U* shape
    D. wrapping it in insulating tape

9. The part of a generator which determines if it is a direct current generator is the 9.____

    A. stator
    B. field
    C. commutator
    D. brush

10. The term which refers to pressure or force in electric current is 10.____

    A. amperage
    B. voltage
    C. ohms
    D. electrons

11. Nichrome wire is MOST likely to be found in a(n)

    A. T.V. circuit
    B. electric motor
    C. electric clock
    D. electric heater

12. Electromagnetic waves are changed into pulses capable of producing sound waves in a radio by means of a

    A. transformer
    B. speaker
    C. detector
    D. oscillator

13. The SIMPLEST form of electronic tube is called

    A. cathode B. diode C. plate D. triode

14. Of the following, the one that is NOT a part of a radio tube is the

    A. envelope B. plate C. condenser D. filament

15. The speed of a simple electric motor can be controlled with the use of a

    A. variable resistor
    B. electrolytic condenser
    C. variable condenser
    D. prony-brake

16. A single wet cell can be made from a copper penny and a *zinc* penny attached to two copper leads immersed in

    A. mineral oil
    B. salt-water solution
    C. distilled water
    D. chromate of soda

17. The MINIMUM gauge wire for house circuits should be

    A. 10 B. 18 C. 14 D. 22

18. The safety device used in a house wiring circuit to protect against an overload is a

    A. circuit breaker
    B. knife switch
    C. cut-off
    D. mercury switch

19. To prevent the generator from burning out at high speeds, the battery circuit of the automobile employs a

    A. choke coil
    B. variable resistor
    C. voltage regulator
    D. current trap

20. An interrupted current of 6 volts flows in the primary circuit of an induction coil of 100 turns of wire. If the secondary coil has 1,000 turns, the theoretical voltage output is

    A. .6 B. 60 C. 600 D. .06

21. A 200 watt bulb in a 100 volt circuit uses _____ ampere(s).

    A. .2 B. .02 C. 2 D. 20

22. A 220 volt air conditioner drawing 15 amperes of current operates 10 hours a day. The total cost of operation for four weeks at the rate of 4 cents per kilowatt hour would be

    A. $18.48 B. $55.44 C. $26.40 D. $36.96

23. If a dry cell battery is capable of supplying a force of two volts and ten amperes of current, connecting five such batteries in parallel will result in a total capacity of _____ volts with _____ amperes.

    A. 2; 50   B. 20; 10   C. 10; 50   D. 10; 10

24. To calculate the number of turns of wire needed to make a step-up or step-down transformer when the voltages are known, and one set of windings is determined, we use the following formula:

    A. $\dfrac{\text{Primary turns}}{\text{Secondary turns}} = \dfrac{\text{Primary volts}}{\text{Secondary volts}}$

    B. $\dfrac{\text{Primary turns}}{\text{Primary volts}} = \dfrac{\text{Secondary volts}}{\text{Secondary turns}}$

    C. $\dfrac{\text{Primary turns}}{\text{Secondary volts}} = \dfrac{\text{Primary volts}}{\text{Secondary turns}}$

    D. $\dfrac{\text{Primary turns}}{\text{Secondary volts}} = \dfrac{\text{Primary volts}}{\text{Secondary turns}}$

25. To measure the specific gravity of the contents of a storage battery, one uses a

    A. hygrometer   B. galvanometer
    C. ammeter   D. hydrometer

26. Lightning is _____ electricity.

    A. induced   B. ionized   C. static   D. magnetic

27. A lodestone is related to

    A. magnetism   B. resistance
    C. conductivity   D. reluctance

28. The term related to a storer of electricity is

    A. milliampere   B. microfarad
    C. megohm   D. microvolt

29. The thermostat as a switch employs the use of a

    A. diode tube   B. tungsten filament
    C. bimetallic strip   D. thermocouple

30. In servicing electrical apparatus, it is necessary to know the values of amperage, voltage, and resistance. When two of the factors are known, the third may be found by applying *Ohm's Law.*
Of the following formulas, the one that does NOT apply is

    A. I = R/E   B. R = E/I   C. E = IR   D. I = E/R

KEY (CORRECT ANSWERS)

1.	A	11.	D	21.	C
2.	B	12.	C	22.	D
3.	D	13.	B	23.	A
4.	C	14.	C	24.	A
5.	B	15.	A	25.	D
6.	A	16.	B	26.	C
7.	D	17.	C	27.	A
8.	B	18.	A	28.	B
9.	C	19.	C	29.	C
10.	B	20.	B	30.	A

TEST 4

DIRECTIONS: Each question or incomplete statement is followed by several suggested answers or completions. Select the one that BEST answers the question or completes the statement. *PRINT THE LETTER OF THE CORRECT ANSWER IN THE SPACE AT THE RIGHT.*

1. The effect of a capacitor on direct current is to _____ it. 1.____

   A. modulate
   B. block
   C. pass
   D. demodulate

2. Factors which determine the resistance of a wire are: 2.____

   A. Diameter, insulating material, length, strands
   B. Length, diameter, material, temperature
   C. Material, light factor, pressure, circumference
   D. Pressure, magnetism, binding, length

3. Current flow in a triode vacuum tube may be controlled by the 3.____

   A. plate and the grid
   B. filament and the plate
   C. grid and the heater
   D. cathode and the filament

4. If the resistance in a parallel circuit is *increased,* the voltage drop across a resistor would 4.____

   A. *increase*
   B. vary proportionally
   C. *decrease*
   D. remain the same

5. In parallel and series circuits, current is 5.____

   A. inversely proportional to resistance and directly proportional to voltage
   B. directly proportional to resistance and inversely proportional to voltage
   C. not affected by voltage
   D. not affected by resistance

6. The process of mixing audio waves with radio waves is called 6.____

   A. rectification
   B. attenuation
   C. modulation
   D. superimposition

7. Transistors are made of three parts: a base, a collector, and an emitter. When compared to a vacuum tube, the collector is comparable to the 7.____

   A. grid   B. plate   C. cathode   D. filament

8. Resistance wire used in electrical appliances is *usually* an alloy of 8.____

   A. tungsten, chromium, brass
   B. nickel, chromium, iron
   C. copper, nickel, tungsten
   D. iron, copper, molybdenum

9. A meter with terminals connected in series and across the line is a 9.____

   A. voltmeter   B. ammeter   C. ohmmeter   D. wattmeter

10. One hundred volts will push _____ milliamperes through 20k ohms of resistance. 10.____

    A. 2   B. 5   C. 50   D. 2000

37

11. A resistor having bands of orange, red, yellow, and silver would have a resistance value of _____ ohms. 11._____

    A. 32k   B. 320k   C. 2.3 meg   D. 43 meg

12. A flashbulb used for photographic purposes contains 12._____

    A. aluminum and oxygen   B. tungsten and helium
    C. aluminum and hydrogen   D. tungsten and argon

13. A generator having a cummutator produces _____ current. 13._____

    A. alternating   B. direct
    C. synchronous   D. modulating

14. A step-down transformer has 1,200 turns on the primary. 90 volts is applied to the primary, and the second is to produce 15 volts. 14._____
    How many turns should be wound on the secondary?

    A. 200   B. 600   C. 7,200   D. 108,000

15. In a radio circuit, a transformer CANNOT be used to 15._____

    A. step-up a-c voltage
    B. isolate part of a circuit
    C. step-down d-c voltage
    D. couple part of a circuit to another

16. A transformer has 200 turns of #14 wire wound on primary and 1,000 turns of #14 wire wound on the secondary. 16._____
    A voltmeter attached to the secondary terminals would indicate _____ volts if 50 volts were attached to the primary.

    A. 0   B. 10   C. 250   D. 600

17. Service entrance cable for the typical home is usually made up of three wires. 17._____
    The *hot* wires are usually No.

    A. 4 or No. 6   B. 8 or No. 10
    C. 12 or No. 14   D. 16 or No. 18

18. In the PNP type transistor, the collector is *normally* 18._____

    A. negative   B. positive
    C. shorted out   D. not needed

19. In a beam power tube, the screen grid is 19._____

    A. the plate   B. positive
    C. the suppressor   D. negative

20. A silicon controlled rectifier is 20._____

    A. a nuvistor   B. a CRT
    C. thermally operated   D. a semi-conductor

21. In copper plating a metallic object, it should be placed at the   21.____

    A. anode   B. switch   C. cathode   D. electrolyte

22. At five cents per kilowatt hour, a 100-watt lamp which is operated for one hundred (100)   22.____
    hours would use energy that would cost

    A. 5 cents   B. less than 10 cents
    C. 50 cents   D. 5 dollars

23. A galvanometer may be converted to a voltmeter by adding a   23.____

    A. shunt in series   B. multiplier in series
    C. multiplier in parallel D. shunt in parallel

24. The counter emf of an inductance coil is measured in   24.____

    A. milliamperes   B. microfarads
    C. henrys   D. millivolts

25. A fluorescent lamp lights when the   25.____

    A. ballast coil produces a high-voltage charge
    B. starter switch is placed in parallel with the filament
    C. mercury forms minute droplets on the filament
    D. ballast changes the A.C. to D.C. in the tube

26. The electrolyte used in a dry cell is composed of   26.____

    A. carbon, magnesium oxide, ammonia, sodium chloride
    B. sodium, manganese dioxide, alumina, zinc sulphate
    C. carbon, manganese dioxide, sal ammoniac, zinc chloride
    D. sodium, magnesium sulphate, arsenic, zinc oxide

27. A variable capacitor has its capacitance *increased* when the   27.____

    A. plates are open
    B. rotor is attached to the stator
    C. plates are meshed
    D. dielectric is given a full charge

28. The gas mixture commonly used in incandescent lamps is   28.____

    A. nitrogen and argon   B. nitrogen and helium
    C. helium and argon   D. hydrogen and oxygen

29. A motor with a high-starting torque and rapid acceleration is a(n) _____ motor.   29.____

    A. D.C. shunt wound   B. D.C. series wound
    C. A.C. synchronous   D. A.C. split phase

30. Bry cells used for powering cordless electric razors are usually _____ cells.   30.____

    A. manganese alkaline   B. nickel cadmium
    C. nickel silver   D. zinc carbon

KEY (CORRECT ANSWERS)

1.	B	11.	B	21.	C
2.	B	12.	A	22.	C
3.	A	13.	B	23.	B
4.	D	14.	A	24.	C
5.	A	15.	C	25.	A
6.	C	16.	A	26.	C
7.	B	17.	A	27.	C
8.	B	18.	A	28.	A
9.	D	19.	B	29.	B
10.	B	20.	D	30.	B

EXAMINATION SECTION
TEST 1

DIRECTIONS: Each question or incomplete statement is followed by several suggested answers or completions. Select the one that BEST answers the question or completes the statement. *PRINT THE LETTER OF THE CORRECT ANSWER IN THE SPACE AT THE RIGHT.*

1. Which of the following capacitors could be damaged by a reversal in polarity? A(n) _____ capacitor.
    - A. ceramic
    - B. paper
    - C. mica
    - D. electrolytic
    - E. vacuum

    1._____

2. If the current through a resistor is 6 amperes and the voltage drop across it is 100 volts, what is the approximate value of the resistor in ohm(s)?
    - A. 1660
    - B. 166
    - C. 16.6
    - D. 1.66
    - E. 0.0166

    2._____

3. What is the CORRECT use for an arbor press?
    - A. Bending sheet metal
    - B. Driving self-tapping screws
    - C. Removing screws
    - D. Removing "C" rings
    - E. Removing bearings from shafts

    3._____

4. Which one of the following is a tensioning device in bulk-belt-type conveyor systems? _____ take-up.
    - A. Spring
    - B. Power
    - C. Hydraulic
    - D. Fluid coupled
    - E. Flexible coupled

    4._____

5. When $X_L = X_C$ in a series circuit, what condition exists?
    - A. The circuit impedance is increasing
    - B. The circuit is at resonant frequency
    - C. The circuit current is minimum
    - D. The circuit has no e.m.f. at this time
    - E. None of the above

    5._____

6. Which of the following pieces of information is NOT normally found on a schematic diagram?
    - A. Functional stage name
    - B. Supply voltages
    - C. Part symbols
    - D. Part values
    - E. Physical location of parts

    6._____

7. When a single-phase induction motor drawing 24 amps at 120 VAC is reconnected to 240 VAC, what will be the amperage at 240 VAC? _____ amps.
    - A. 6
    - B. 8
    - C. 12
    - D. 24
    - E. 36

    7._____

8. Which one of the following meters measures the SMALLEST current?

   A. Kilometer B. Milliammeter C. Microvoltmeter
   D. Millivoltmeter E. Kilovoltmeter

9. If the current through a 1000-ohm resistor is 3 milliamperes, the voltage drop across the resistor is _____ volt(s).

   A. 1 B. 2.5 C. 3 D. 30 E. 300

10. The normally closed contacts of a relay are open when its solenoid is energized with VDC. The voltage at which the contacts re-close will be

    A. dependent upon the current through the contacts
    B. dependent upon the voltage applied to the contacts
    C. 24 VDC through the coil
    D. more than 24 VDC through the contacts
    E. less than 24 VDC through the coil

11. Electrical energy is converted to mechanical rotation by what component in the electric motor?

    A. Armature B. Commutator C. Field
    D. Start windings E. Stator

12. Ohm's Law expresses the basic relationship of

    A. current, voltage, and resistance
    B. current, voltage, and power
    C. current, power, and resistance
    D. resistance, impedance, and voltage
    E. resistance, power, and impedance

13. In parallel circuits, the voltage is *always*

    A. variable B. constant C. alternating
    D. fluctuating E. sporadic

14. Which one of the following is used as a voltage divider?

    A. Rotary converter B. Potentiometer C. Relay
    D. Circuit breaker E. Voltmeter

Question 15.

Question 15 is based on the following diagram.

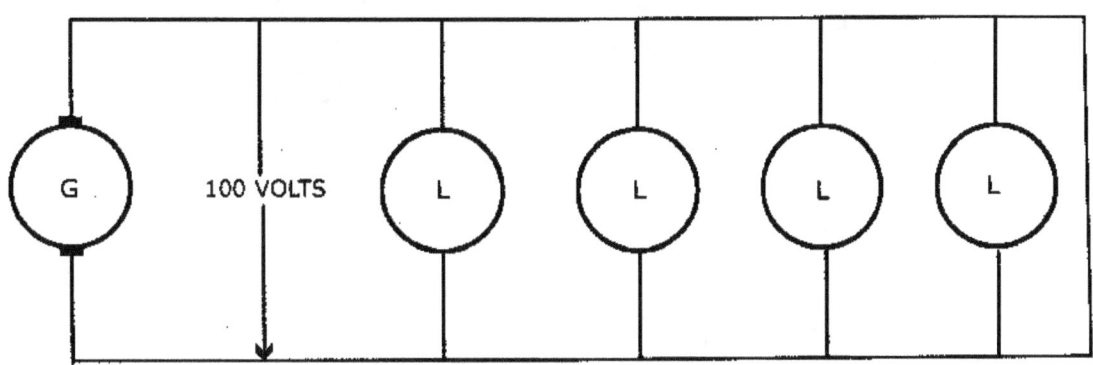

15. What is the resistance of the entire circuit? _____ ohms. 15.____
    A. 15   B. 25   C. 35   D. 45   E. 50

16. Which one of the following tools is used to bring a bore to a specified tolerance? 16.____
    A. Tap
    B. Reamer
    C. Countersink
    D. Counterbore
    E. Center drill

17. The primary function of a take-up pulley in a belt conveyor is to 17.____
    A. carry the belt on the return trip
    B. track the belt
    C. maintain the proper belt tension
    D. change the direction of the belt
    E. regulate the speed of the belt

Question 18.

Question 18 is based on the following diagram.

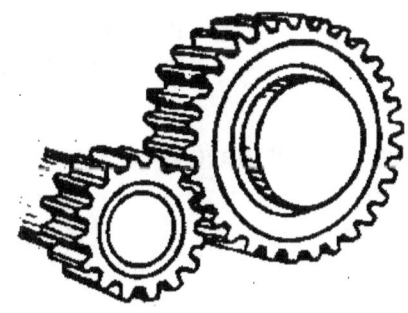

18. What is the name of the gears? 18.____
    A. Spur external
    B. Spur internal
    C. Helical
    D. Herringbone
    D. Worm

Question 19.

Question 19 is based on the following diagram.

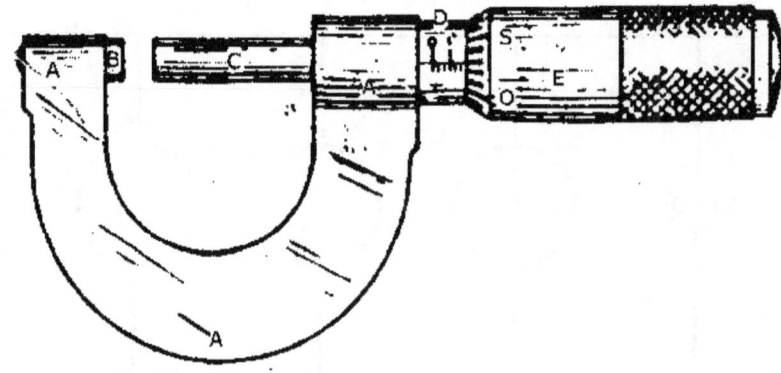

19. The part labeled D is the 19.____
   A. sleeve B. thimble C. frame
   D. anvil E. pindle

Question 20.

Question 20 is based on the following symbol.

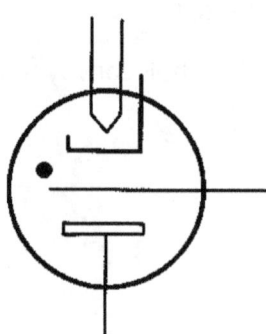

20. This symbol represents a _____ tube. 20.____
   A. thyratron vacuum B. thyratron gas
   C. variable-mu vacuum D. variable-mu gas
   E. vacuum photo

21. A diode can be substituted for which one of the following? 21.____
   A. Transformer B. Relay C. Rectifier
   D. Condenser E. Rheostat

Question 22.

Question 22 is based on the following diagram.

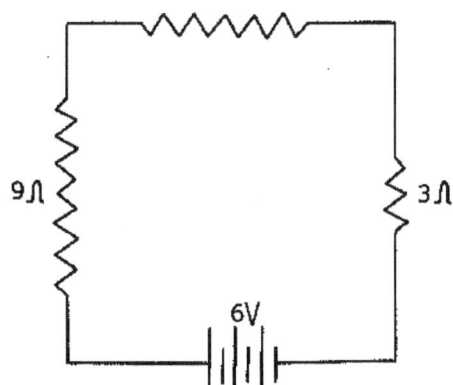

22. The rate of amperes flowing in the circuit is: 22.____

    A. .03 1/3   B. .18   C. .24
    D. .30 1/3   E. .33 1/3

23. The firing point in a thyratron tube is *most usually* controlled by the 23.____

    A. cathode   B. grid   C. plate
    D. heater   E. envelope

Questions 24-25.

Questions 24 and 25 shall be answered in accordance with the diagram below.

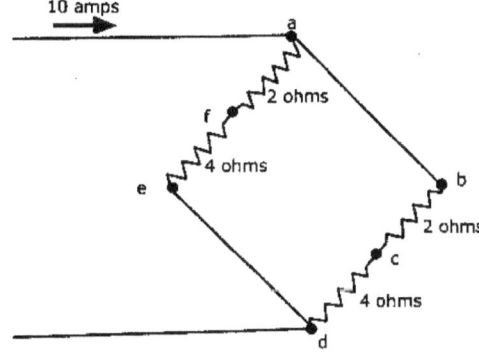

24. With reference to the above diagram, the voltage difference between points c and f is, *most nearly*, in volts, 24.____

    A. 40   B. 20   C. 10   D. 5   E. 0

25. With reference to the above diagram, the current flowing through the resistance c d is, *most nearly*, in amperes, 25.____

    A. 10   B. 5   C. 4   D. 2   E. 1

KEY (CORRECT ANSWERS)

1. D	6. E	11. A	16. B	21. C
2. C	7. C	12. A	17. C	22. E
3. E	8. B	13. B	18. A	23. B
4. A	9. C	14. B	19. A	24. E
5. B	10. E	15. E	20. B	25. B

EXAMINATION SECTION
TEST 1

DIRECTIONS: Each question or incomplete statement is followed by several suggested answers or completions. Select the one that BEST answers the question or completes the statement. *PRINT THE LETTER OF THE CORRECT ANSWER IN THE SPACE AT THE RIGHT.*

1. Two gears are meshed. The first gear has 20 teeth per inch and is rotating at 500 rpms. What is the speed of the second gear if it has 40 teeth per inch? _____ rpms.

    A. 500   B. 400   C. 250   D. 200

2. With two meshed gears, the first gear rotates at 100 rpms, the second gear rotates at 2000 rpms and has 10 teeth per inch.
   The first gear has _____ number of teeth per inch.

    A. 200   B. 100   C. 50   D. 150

3. Two pulleys are connected. The first pulley has a diameter of 5 inches; the second pulley has a diameter of 15 inches and rotates at 25 rpms.
   The speed of the first pulley is _____ rpms.

    A. 30   B. 75   C. 200   D. 400

4. Of two connected pulleys, the first has a radius of 10 inches and rotates at 50 rpms; the second rotates at 25 rpms.
   The diameter of the second pulley is _____ inches.

    A. 40   B. 30   C. 20   D. 10

5. Two pulleys are connected. The first pulley rotates at 75 rpms; the second pulley rotates at 100 rpms and has a diameter of 9 inches.
   The diameter of the first pulley is _____ inches.

    A. 10   B. 12   C. 15   D. 20

6. Of two connected pulleys, the first pulley has a radius of 12 inches and rotates at 60 rpms; the second pulley has a diameter of 16 inches.
   The speed of the second pulley is _____ rpms.

    A. 1000   B. 1020   C. 1040   D. 1080

7. If 16_{10} were converted to base 2, 8, and 16, the results would be _____ base 2, _____ base 8, and _____ base 16, respectively.

    A. 10000; 20; 10
    B. 1000; 2000; 20
    C. 20000; 200; 20
    D. 2000; 100; 10

8. Converting CAF_{16} to base 10 and base 8, the results would be _____ base 10 and _____ base 8, respectively.

    A. 2437; 2567
    B. 3247; 6257
    C. 4327; 5267
    D. 3427; 2657

9. Converting 101011001_2 to base 8, 10, and 16, the results would be _____ base 8, _____ base 10, and _____ base 16, respectively.

   A. 135; 45; 59
   B. 567; 435; 259
   C. 315; 245; 135
   D. 531; 345; 159

10. If 136_8 were converted to base 2, 10, and 16, the results would be _____ base 2, _____ base 10, and _____ base 16, respectively.

    A. 001011110; 94, 5E
    B. 010100110; 92; 10E
    C. 00100000; 90; 15E
    D. 011001110; 96; 20E

11. It may be correctly stated that 1000 picofarads are equal to _____ microfarads.

    A. .0001   B. .001   C. .01   D. .1

12. If 5 megohms were converted to kohms, the result would be _____ kohms.

    A. 1000   B. 2000   C. 4000   D. 5000

13. 1 nanohenry would convert to _____ millihenries.

    A. .001   B. .0001   C. .00001   D. .0000001

14. If 7 milliamps were converted to microamps, the answer would be _____ microamps.

    A. 7000   B. 700   C. 70   D. 7

15. If two resistors are in parallel and are 100 ohms each, the total resistance is

    A. 100   B. 150   C. 50   D. 10

16. In reference to the circuit in Question 15, if the first resistor has 25 volts DC, (VDC) across it, the second resistor also has 25 VDC across it, and there are no other components in the circuit except for the power source, the total circuit voltage is _____ VDC.

    A. 25   B. 50   C. 250   D. 500

17. In reference to the circuit in Question 15, if the first resistor has 1 amp on it, and the second resistor also has 1 amp on it, the total circuit amperage is _____ amps.

    A. 1   B. 2   C. 3   D. 4

18. If two resistors are in series and are 100 ohms each, the total resistance is

    A. 50   B. 100   C. 150   D. 200

19. In reference to the circuit in Question 18, if the first resistor has 25 VDC across it and the second resistor also has 25 VDC across it, the total circuit voltage is

    A. 50   B. 100   C. 200   D. 500

20. In reference to the circuit in Question 18, if the first resistor has 1 amp across it and the second resistor also has 1 amp on it, the total circuit amperage is

    A. 1   B. 5   C. 10   D. 15

21. Where two resistors are in parallel, one is 100 ohms and the other is 300 ohms.   21.____
    The total resistance is _____ ohms.

    A. 25   B. 35   C. 55   D. 75

22. Three resistors in series are 25 ohms, 50 ohms, and 75 ohms, respectively.   22.____
    The total resistance is _____ ohms.

    A. 25   B. 50   C. 100   D. 150

23. Two inductors are in parallel; the first is 50 henries and the second is also 50 henries.   23.____
    The total inductance is _____ henries.

    A. 25   B. 50   C. 55   D. 60

24. Two inductors are in series and the first is 50 henries; the second is 50 henries.   24.____
    The total inductance is _____ henries.

    A. 25   B. 50   C. 75   D. 100

25. Where two inductors are in parallel, the first is 100 henries and the second is 200 henries.   25.____
    The total inductance is _____ henries.

    A. 50   B. 75   C. 65   D. 100

KEY (CORRECT ANSWERS)

1. C	6. D	11. B	16. A	21. D
2. A	7. A	12. D	17. B	22. D
3. B	8. B	13. D	18. D	23. A
4. A	9. D	14. A	19. A	24. D
5. B	10. A	15. C	20. A	25. B

TEST 2

DIRECTIONS: Each question or incomplete statement is followed by several suggested answers or completions. Select the one that BEST answers the question or completes the statement. *PRINT THE LETTER OF THE CORRECT ANSWER IN THE SPACE AT THE RIGHT.*

1. Two inductors are in series; the first inductor is 100 henries and the second is 200 henries.
   The total inductance is _____ henries.

   A. 200   B. 300   C. 400   D. 500

   1._____

2. Two capacitors are in parallel; each capacitor is 30 farads.
   The total capacitance is _____ farads.

   A. 60   B. 80   C. 100   D. 200

   2._____

3. Two capacitors are in series; each capacitor is 30 farads. The total capacitance is _____ farads.

   A. 10   B. 15   C. 20   D. 25

   3._____

4. Two capacitors are in parallel; the first is 50 farads and the second is 100 farads.
   The total capacitance is _____ farads.

   A. 50   B. 100   C. 125   D. 150

   4._____

5. Two capacitors are in series; the first is 50 farads and the second is 100 farads.
   The total capacitance is _____ farads.

   A. 33.333   B. 49.999   C. 13.333   D. 25.555

   5._____

6. A resistor's color codes are orange, blue, yellow, and gold, in that order.
   The value of the resistor is _____ kohms ± _____ %.

   A. 200; 2   B. 300; 4   C. 360; 5   D. 400; 7

   6._____

7. If a resistors color codes are red, black, and blue, the value of this resistor is _____ megohms ± _____ %.

   A. 20; 20   B. 40; 80   C. 30; 30   D. 50; 50

   7._____

8. If a resistor's color codes are gray, green, black, and silver, the resistor's value is _____ ohms ± _____ %.

   A. 55; 5   B. 75; 15   C. 85; 10   D. 100; 25

   8._____

9. One complete cycle of a sinewave takes 1000 microseconds. Its frequency is _____ hertz.

   A. 500   B. 1000   C. 2000   D. 5000

   9._____

10. If one complete cycle of a squarewave takes 5 microseconds, its frequency is _____ khertz.

    A. 200   B. 500   C. 700   D. 1000

    10._____

11. What is the PRT (pulse repetition time) of a 50 hertz (hz) sinewave? _____ milliseconds. 11.____

    A. 10   B. 20   C. 40   D. 60

12. The PRT of a 20 khz sawtooth signal is _____ megahertz. 12.____

    A. 50   B. 100   C. 200   D. 500

13. If a resistor measures 10 volts and 2 amps across it, the resistance is _____ ohms. 13.____

    A. 0   B. 2   C. 5   D. 10

14. If a 30 ohm resistor measures 10 volts, the power consumed by the resistor is _____ watts. 14.____

    A. 3000   B. 5000   C. 6500   D. 7000

15. If a 50 ohm resistor measures 4 amps across, the power consumed by it is _____ watts. 15.____

    A. 200   B. 400   C. 600   D. 800

16. If a 100 ohm resistor measures 25 volts across, the current on it is _____ amps. 16.____

    A. .15   B. .25   C. .55   D. .65

Questions 17-23.

DIRECTIONS: Questions 17 through 23 are to be answered on the basis of the following diagram.

SERIES CIRCUIT

$V_{supply} = V_A + V_B + V_C$
$I_{total} = I_A = I_B = I_C$

PARALLEL CIRCUIT

$V_{supply} = V_A = V_B = V_C$
$I_{total} = I_A + I_B + I_C$

17. In the series circuit above, if Vsupply = 100 VDC, resistor A is 10 ohms, resistor B is 50 ohms, and resistor C is 5 ohms, the total circuit current is _____ amps. 17.____

    A. 1.538   B. 1.267   C. 1.358   D. 1.823

18. In the series circuit shown above, the current across each individual resistor is _____ amps. 18.____

    A. .5   B. 1.5   C. 2.5   D. 3.5

19. In the series circuit shown above, the total power drawn by the circuit is _____ watts. 19.___

    A. 140.25   B. 150.75   C. 153.38   D. 173.38

20. In the series circuit shown above, the power drawn from each individual resistor is _____, _____, and _____ watts, respectively. 20.___

    A. 23.65; 118.27; 11.827
    B. 17.567; 123.27; 11.27
    C. 18.627; 145.27; 12.27
    D. 21.735; 116.87; 11.83

21. In the parallel circuit shown above, if Vsupply = 100 VDC, resistor A is 10 ohms, resistor B is 50 ohms, and resistor C is 5 ohms, the total circuit current is _____ amps. 21.___

    A. 21   B. 27   C. 32   D. 45

22. In the parallel circuit shown above, the total power drawn by the circuit is _____ watts. 22.___

    A. 1200   B. 2300   C. 2700   D. 3200

23. In the parallel circuit above, the power drawn by each individual resistor is _____ watts, respectively. 23.___

    A. 100; 200; 2000
    B. 200; 400; 5000
    C. 300; 500; 750
    D. 450; 600; 1500

24. On an 0-scope display, one cycle of a signal takes up 4 1/2 divisions and the peak-to-peak amplitude of the signal takes up 3 3/4 divisions. 24.___
    With the volts/division knob set on 5 volts and the time/division knob set to 5 microseconds, the peak-to-peak amplitude and the frequency of the signal are _____ volts and _____ khz, respectively.

    A. 15.75; 100
    B. 22.5; 200
    C. 37.5; 350
    D. 45.75; 570

25. If a signal that has a peak-to-peak amplitude of 15 volts and a frequency of 5 megaherz is to be observed on an 0-scope with one complete cycle shown, the time/division knob and volts/division knob should be set on _____ microseconds and _____ volts per division, respectively. 25.___

    A. .02; 2   B. .05; 4   C. .07; 3.5   D. 10; 7.5

KEY (CORRECT ANSWERS)

1. B	6. C	11. B	16. B	21. C
2. A	7. A	12. A	17. A	22. D
3. B	8. C	13. C	18. B	23. A
4. D	9. B	14. A	19. C	24. B
5. A	10. A	15. D	20. A	25. A

EXAMINATION SECTION
TEST 1

DIRECTIONS: Each question or incomplete statement is followed by several suggested answers or completions. Select the one that BEST answers the question or completes the statement. *PRINT THE LETTER OF THE CORRECT ANSWER IN THE SPACE AT THE RIGHT.*

Questions 1-6.

DIRECTIONS: Questions 1 through 6 are to be answered on the basis of the circuit diagram below. All switches are initially open.

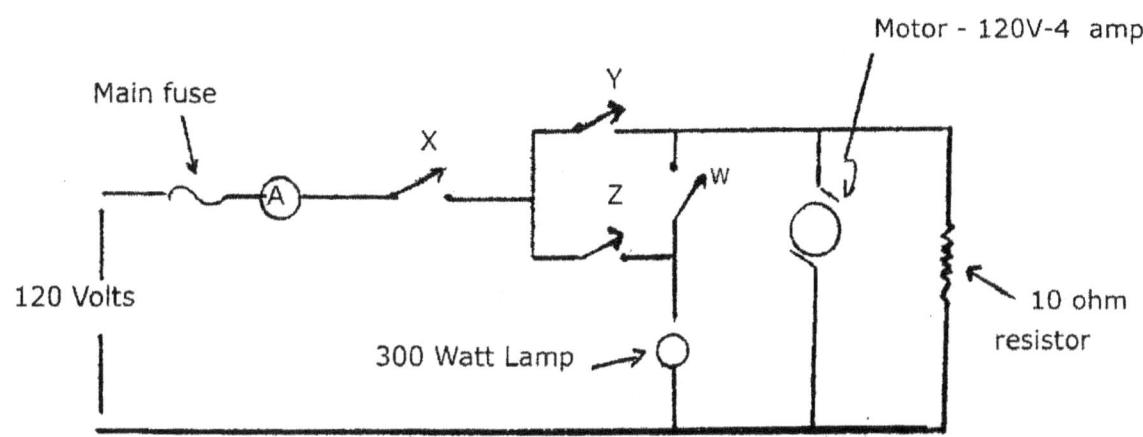

1. To light the 300 watt lamp, the following switches MUST be closed: 1.____

    A. X and Y   B. Y and Z   C. X and Z   D. X and W

2. If all of the switches W, X, Y, and Z are closed, the following will happen: 2.____

    A. The lamp will light and the motor will rotate
    B. The lamp will light and the motor will not rotate
    C. The lamp will not light and the motor will not rotate
    D. A short circuit will occur and the main fuse will blow

3. With 120 volts applied across the 10 ohm resistor, the current drawn by the resistor is _____ amp(s).   3.____

    A. 1/12   B. 1.2   C. 12   D. 1200

4. With 120 volts applied to the 10 ohm resistor, the power used by the resistor is _____ kw.   4.____

    A. 1.44   B. 1.2   C. .144   D. .12

5. The current drawn by the 300 watt lamp when lighted should be APPROXIMATELY _____ amps.   5.____

    A. 2.5   B. 3.6   C. 25   D. 36

6. In the circuit shown, the symbol A is used to indicate a (n)
   A. ammeter
   B. *and* circuit
   C. voltmeter
   D. wattmeter

7. Of the following materials, the BEST conductor of electricity is
   A. iron
   B. copper
   C. aluminum
   D. glass

8. The sum of 6'6", 5'9", and 2' 1 1/2" is
   A. 13'4 1/2"
   B. 13'6 1/2"
   C. 14'4 1/2"
   D. 14'6 1/2"

9.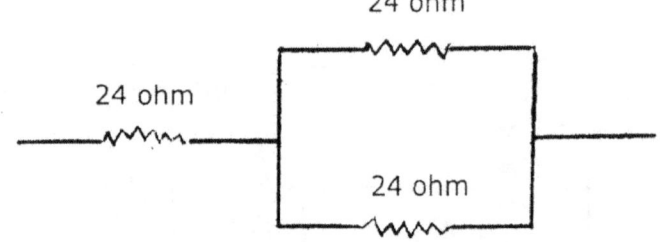

   The equivalent resistance of the three resistors shown in the sketch above is _____ ohms.

   A. 8
   B. 24
   C. 36
   D. 72

10.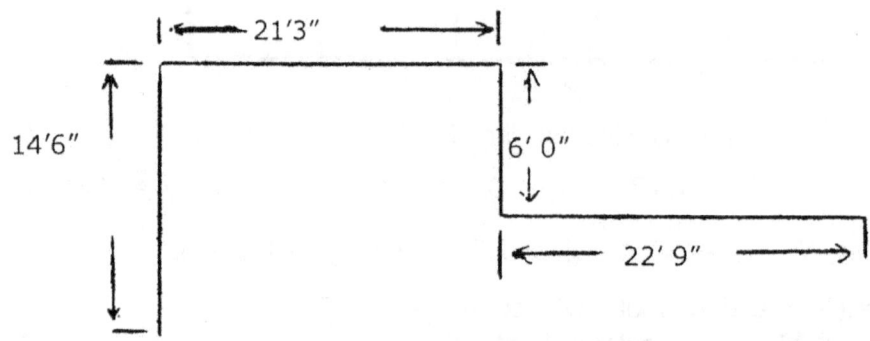

    The TOTAL length of electrical conduit that must be run along the path shown on the diagram above is

    A. 63'8"
    B. 64'6"
    C. 65'6"
    D. 66'8"

11. Of the following electrical devices, the one that is NOT normally used in direct current electrical circuits is a (n)
    A. circuit breaker
    B. double-pole switch
    C. transformer
    D. inverter

12. The number of 120-volt light bulbs that should NORMALLY be connected in series across a 600-volt electric line is
    A. 1
    B. 2
    C. 3
    D. 5

13. Of the following motors, the one that does NOT have any brushes is the _____ motor.

    A. d.c. shunt
    B. d.c. series
    C. squirrel cage induction
    D. compound

14. Of the following materials, the one that is COMMONLY used as an electric heating element in an electric heater is

    A. zinc
    B. brass
    C. terne plate
    D. nichrome

Questions 15-25.

DIRECTIONS: Questions 15 through 25 are to be answered on the basis of the instruments listed below. Each instrument is listed with an identifying number in front of it.

    1 - Hygrometer
    2 - Ammeter
    3 - Voltmeter
    4 - Wattmeter
    5 - Megger
    6 - Oscilloscope
    7 - Frequency meter
    8 - Micrometer
    9 - Vernier caliper
    10 - Wire gage
    11 - 6-foot folding rule
    12 - Architect's scale
    13 - Planimeter
    14 - Engineer's scale
    15 - Ohmmeter

15. The instrument that should be used to accurately measure the resistance of a 4,700 ohm resistor is Number

    A. 3   B. 4   C. 7   D. 15

16. To measure the current in an electrical circuit, the instrument that should be used is Number

    A. 2   B. 7   C. 8   D. 15

17. To measure the insulation resistance of a rubber-covered electrical cable, the instrument that should be used is Number

    A. 4   B. 5   C. 8   D. 15

18. An AC motor is hooked up to a power distribution box.
    In order to check the voltage at the motor terminals, the instrument that should be used is Number

    A. 2   B. 3   C. 4   D. 7

19. To measure the shaft diameter of a motor accurately to one-thousandth of an inch, the instrument that should be used is Number

    A. 8   B. 10   C. 11   D. 14

20. The instrument that should be used to determine whether 25 Hz. or 60 Hz. is present in an electrical circuit is Number

    A. 4   B. 5   C. 7   D. 8

21. Of the following, the PROPER instrument to use to determine the diameter of the conductor of a piece of electrical hook-up wire is Number

    A. 10   B. 11   C. 12   D. 14

22. The amount of electrical power being used in a balanced three-phase circuit should be measured with Number

    A. 2   B. 3   C. 4   D. 5

23. The electrical wave form at a given point in an electronic circuit can be observed with Number

    A. 2   B. 3   C. 6   D. 7

24. The PROPER instrument to use for measuring the width of a door is Number

    A. 11   B. 12   C. 13   D. 14

25. A one-inch hole with a tolerance of plus or minus three-thousandths is reamed in a steel block.
    The PROPER instrument to use to accurately check the diameter of the hole is Number

    A. 8   B. 9   C. 11   D. 14

KEY (CORRECT ANSWERS)

1. C
2. A
3. C
4. A
5. A

6. A
7. B
8. C
9. C
10. B

11. C
12. D
13. C
14. D
15. D

16. A
17. B
18. B
19. A
20. C

21. A
22. C
23. C
24. A
25. B

TEST 2

DIRECTIONS: Each question or incomplete statement is followed by several suggested answers or completions. Select the one that BEST answers the question or completes the statement. *PRINT THE LETTER OF THE CORRECT ANSWER IN THE SPACE AT THE RIGHT.*

1. The number of conductors required to connect a 3-phase delta connected heater bank to an electric power panel board is   1._____

    A. 2   B. 3   C. 4   D. 5

2. Of the following, the wire size that is MOST commonly used for branch lighting circuits in homes is _____ A.W.G.   2._____

    A. #12   B. #8   C. #6   D. #4

3. When installing electrical circuits, the tool that should be used to pull wire through a conduit is a   3._____

    A. mandrel B. snake
    C. rod   D. pulling iron

4. Of the following AC voltages, the LOWEST voltage that a neon test lamp can detect is _____ volts.   4._____

    A. 6   B. 12   C. 80   D. 120

5. Of the following, the BEST procedure to use when storing tools that are subject to rusting is to   5._____

    A. apply a thin coating of soap onto the tools
    B. apply a light coating of oil to the tools
    C. wrap the tools in clean cheesecloth
    D. place the tools in a covered container

6. If a 3 1/2 inch long nail is required to nail wood framing members together, the nail size to use should be   6._____

    A. 2d   B. 4d   C. 16d   D. 60d

7. Of the four motors listed below, the one that can operate only on alternating current is a(n) _____ motor.   7._____

    A. series   B. shunt
    C. compound D. induction

8. The sum of 1/3 + 2/5 + 5/6 is   8._____

    A. 1 17/30   B. 1 3/5   C. 1 15/24   D. 1 5/6

9. Of the following instruments, the one that should be used to measure the state of charge of a lead-acid storage battery is a(n)   9._____

    A. ammeter   B. ohmmeter
    C. hydrometer D. thermometer

10. If three 1 1/2 volt dry cell batteries are wired in series, the TOTAL voltage provided by the three batteries is _____ volts.

    A. 1.5   B. 3   C. 4.5   D. 6.0

11. Taking into account time and one-half payment for time over 40 hours of work, the gross pay of an employee who works 43 hours in a week at a rate of pay of $10.68 per hour is

    A. $427.20   B. $459.24   C. $475.26   D. $491.28

12. The sum of 0.365 + 3.941 + 10.676 + 0.784 is

    A. 13.766   B. 15.666   C. 15.756   D. 15.766

13. In order to transmit mechanical power between two rotating shafts at right angles to each other, two gears are used. Of the following, the type of gears that should be used are _____ gears.

    A. herringbone   B. spur
    C. bevel   D. rack and pinion

14. To properly ground the service electrical equipment in a building, a ground connection should be made to _____ the building.

    A. the waste or soil line leaving
    B. the vent line going to the exterior of
    C. any steel beam in
    D. the cold water line entering

15. The area of the triangle shown at the right is _____ square inches.
    A. 120
    B. 240
    C. 360
    D. 480

Questions 16-25.

DIRECTIONS: Questions 16 through 25 are to be answered on the basis of the tools shown on the next page. The tools are not shown to scale. Each tool is shown with an identifying number alongside it.

3 (#2)

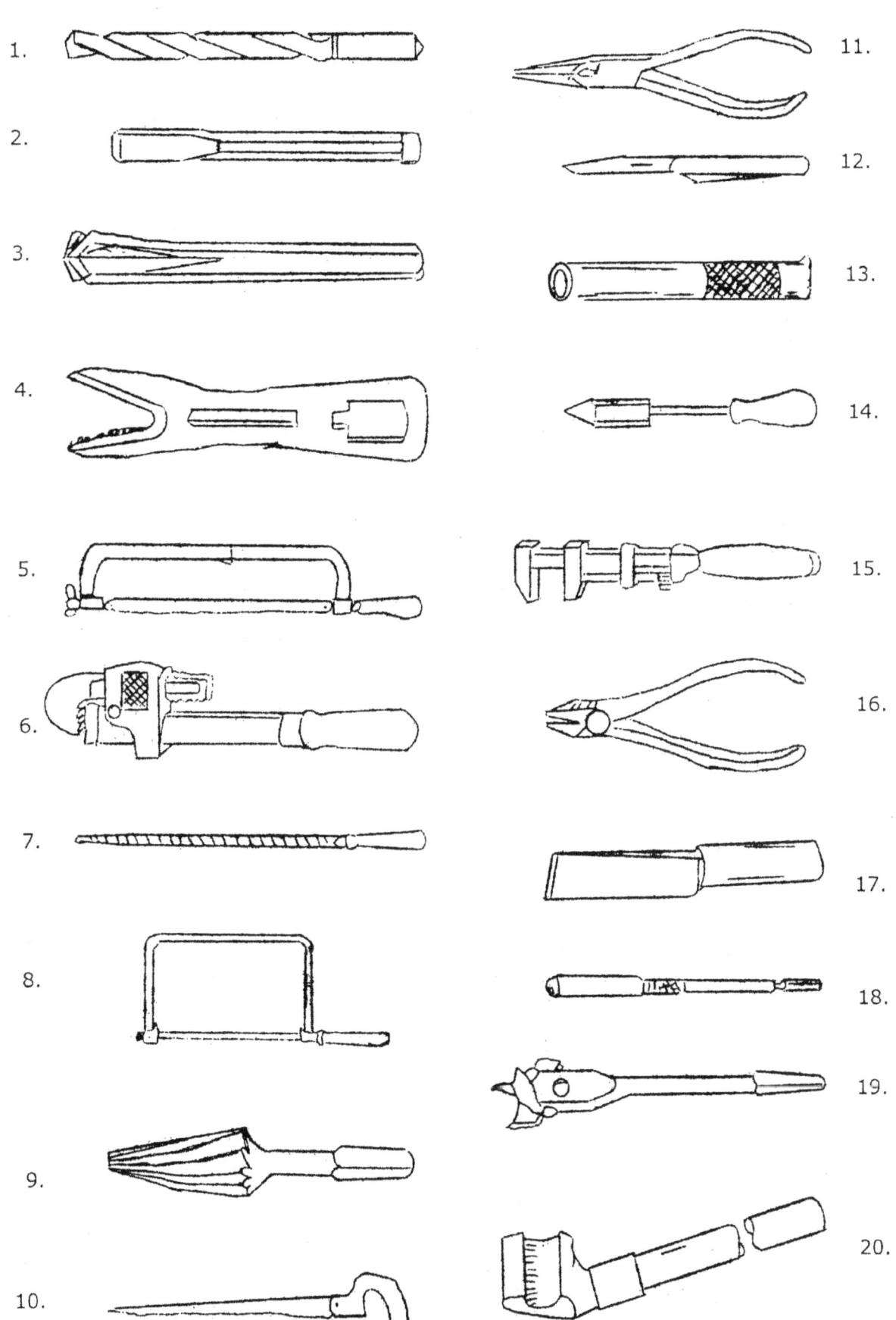

61

16. The tool that should be used for cutting thin wall steel conduit is Number   16.____
    A. 5   B. 8   C. 10   D. 16

17. The tool that should be used for cutting a 1 7/8 inch diameter hole in a wood joist is Number   17.____
    A. 3   B. 9   C. 14   D. 19

18. The tool that should be used for soldering splices in electrical wire is Number   18.____
    A. 3   B. 7   C. 13   D. 14

19. After cutting off a piece of 3/4 inch diameter electrical conduit, the tool that should be used for removing a burr from the inside of the conduit is Number   19.____
    A. 9   B. 11   C. 12   D. 14

20. The tool that should be used for turning a coupling onto a threaded conduit is Number   20.____
    A. 6   B. 11   C. 15   D. 16

21. The tool that should be used for cutting wood lathing in plaster walls is Number   21.____
    A. 5   B. 7   C. 10   D. 12

22. The tool that should be used for drilling a 3/8 inch diameter hole in a steel beam is Number   22.____
    A. 1   B. 2   C. 3   D. 9

23. Of the following, the BEST tool to use for stripping insulation from electrical hook-up wire is Number   23.____
    A. 11   B. 12   C. 15   D. 20

24. The tool that should be used for bending an electrical wire around a terminal post is Number   24.____
    A. 4   B. 11   C. 15   D. 16

25. The tool that should be used for cutting electrical hookup wire is Number   25.____
    A. 5   B. 12   C. 16   D. 17

KEY (CORRECT ANSWERS)

1. B
2. A
3. B
4. C
5. B

6. C
7. D
8. A
9. C
10. C

11. C
12. D
13. C
14. D
15. A

16. A
17. D
18. D
19. A
20. A

21. C
22. A
23. B
24. B
25. C

TEST 3

DIRECTIONS: Each question or incomplete statement is followed by several suggested answers or completions. Select the one that BEST answers the question or completes the statement. *PRINT THE LETTER OF THE CORRECT ANSWER IN THE SPACE AT THE RIGHT.*

1. An electric circuit has current flowing through it. The panel board switch feeding the circuit is opened, causing arcing across the switch contacts.
   Generally, this arcing is caused by

   A. a lack of energy storage in the circuit
   B. electrical energy stored by a capacitor
   C. electrical energy stored by a resistor
   D. magnetic energy induced by an inductance

2. MOST filter capacitors in radios have a capacity rating given in

   A. microvolts   B. milliamps
   C. millihenries   D. microfarads

3. Of the following, the electrical wire size that is COMMONLY used for telephone circuits is _____ A.W.G.

   A. #6   B. #10   C. #12   D. #22

Questions 4-9.

DIRECTIONS: Questions 4 through 9 are to be answered on the basis of the electrical circuit diagram shown below, where letters are used to identify various circuit components.

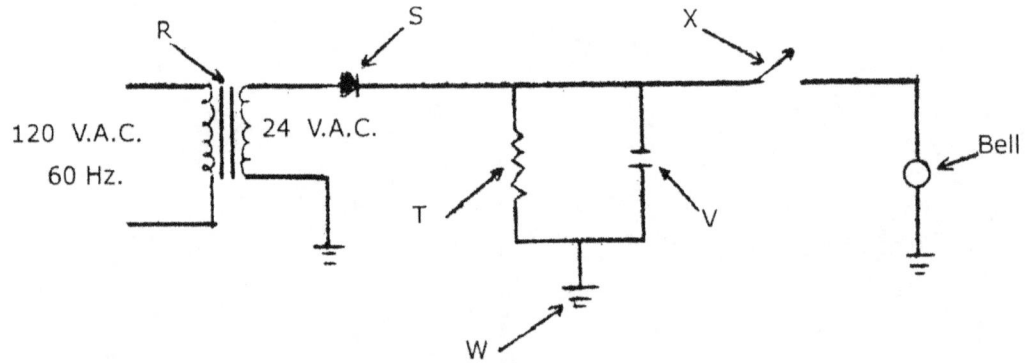

4. The device indicated by the letter R is a

   A. capacitor   B. converter
   C. resistor   D. transformer

5. The device indicated by the letter S is a

   A. transistor   B. diode
   C. thermistor   D. directional relay

64

6. The devices indicated by the letters T and V are used together to _____ components of the secondary current.

    A. reduce the AC
    B. reduce the DC
    C. transform the AC
    D. invert the AC

7. The letter W points to a standard electrical symbol for a

    A. wire
    B. ground
    C. terminal
    D. lightning arrestor

8. Closing switch X will apply the following type of voltage to the bell:

    A. 60 Hz. AC
    B. DC
    C. pulsating AC
    D. 120 Hz. AC

9. The circuit shown contains a _____ rectifier.

    A. mercury-arc
    B. full-wave
    C. bridge
    D. half-wave

10. A bolt specified as 1/4-28 means the following:
    The

    A. bolt is 1/4 inch in diameter and has 28 threads per inch
    B. bolt is 1/4 inch in diameter and is 2.8 inches long
    C. bolt is 1/4 inch long and has 28 threads
    D. threaded portion of the bolt is 1/4 inch long and has 28 threads per inch

11. When cutting 0.045-inch thickness sheet metal, it is BEST to use a hacksaw blade that has _____ teeth per inch.

    A. 7   B. 12   C. 18   D. 32

12. To accurately tighten a bolt to 28 foot-pounds, it is BEST to use a(n) _____ wrench.

    A. pipe   B. open end   C. box   D. torque

13. When bending a 2-inch diameter conduit, the CORRECT tool to use is a

    A. hickey
    B. pipe wrench
    C. hydraulic bender
    D. stock and die

14. When soldering two #20 A.W.G. copper wires together to form a splice, the solder that SHOULD be used is _____ solder.

    A. acid-core
    B. solid-core
    C. rosin-core
    D. liquid

15. A bathroom heating unit draws 10 amperes at 115 volts.
    The hot resistance of the heating unit should be _____ ohms.

    A. .08   B. 8   C. 11.5   D. 1150

16. Of the following materials, the one that is NOT suitable as an electrical insulator is

    A. glass   B. mica   C. rubber   D. platinum

17. An air conditioning unit is rated at 1000 watts. The unit is run for 10 hours per day, five days per week.
    If the cost for electrical energy is 5 cents per kilowatt-hour, the weekly cost for electricity should be

    A. 25¢ B. 50¢ C. $2.50 D. $25.00

18. If a fuse is protecting the circuit of a 15 ohm electric heater and it is designed to blow out at a current exceeding 10 amperes, the MAXIMUM voltage from among the following that should be applied across the terminals of the heater is _____ volts.

    A. 110 B. 120 C. 160 D. 600

19. Before opening a pneumatic hose connection, it is important to remove pressure from the hose line PRIMARILY to avoid

    A. losing air
    B. personal injury
    C. damage to the hose connection
    D. a build-up of pressure in the air compressor

20. If the scale on a shop drawing is 1/4 inch to the foot, then a part which measures 3 3/8 inches long on the drawing has an ACTUAL length of _____ feet _____ inches.

    A. 12; 6 B. 13; 6 C. 13; 9 D. 14; 9

21. The function that is USUALLY performed by a motor controller is to

    A. start and stop a motor
    B. protect a motor from a short circuit
    C. prevent bearing failure of a motor
    D. control the brush wear in a motor

22. Of the following galvanized sheet metal electrical outlet boxes, the one that is NOT a commonly used size is the _____ box.

    A. 4" square   B. 4" octagonal
    C. 4" x 2 1/8"   D. 4" x 1"

23. When soldering a transistor into a circuit, it is MOST important to protect the transistor from

    A. the application of an excess of rosin flux
    B. excessive heat
    C. the application of an excess of solder
    D. too much pressure

24. When installing BX type cable, it is important to protect the wires in the cable from the cut ends of the armored sheath.
    The APPROVED method of providing this protection is to

    A. use a fiber or plastic insulating bushing
    B. file the cut ends of the sheath smooth
    C. use a connector where the cable enters a junction box
    D. tie the wires into an Underwriter's knot

25. While lifting a heavy piece of equipment off the floor, a person should NOT 25._____
    A. twist his body
    B. grasp it firmly
    C. maintain a solid footing on the ground
    D. bend his knees

26. It is important that metal cabinets and panels that house electrical equipment should be grounded PRIMARILY in order to 26._____
    A. prevent short circuits from occurring
    B. keep all circuits at ground potential
    C. minimize shock hazards
    D. reduce the effects of electrolytic corrosion

27. A foreman explains a technical procedure to a new employee. If the employee does not understand the instructions he has received, it would be BEST if he were to 27._____
    A. follow the procedure as best he could
    B. ask the foreman to explain it to him again
    C. avoid following the procedure
    D. ask the foreman to give him other work

28. Of the following, the BEST connectors to use when mounting an electrical panel box directly onto a concrete wall are 28._____
    A. threaded studs   B. machine screws
    C. lag screws   D. expansion bolts

29. Of the following, the BEST instrument to use to measure the small gap between relay contacts is 29._____
    A. a micrometer   B. a feeler gage
    C. inside calipers   D. a plug gage

30. A POSSIBLE result of mounting a 40 ampere fuse in a fuse box for a circuit requiring a 20 ampere fuse is that the 40 ampere fuse may 30._____
    A. provide twice as much protection to the circuit from overloads
    B. blow more easily than the smaller fuse due to an overload
    C. cause serious damage to the circuit from an overload
    D. reduce power consumption in the circuit

KEY (CORRECT ANSWERS)

1.	D	16.	D
2.	D	17.	C
3.	D	18.	B
4.	D	19.	B
5.	B	20.	B
6.	A	21.	A
7.	B	22.	D
8.	B	23.	B
9.	D	24.	A
10.	A	25.	A
11.	D	26.	C
12.	D	27.	B
13.	C	28.	D
14.	C	29.	B
15.	C	30.	C

MECHANICAL APTITUDE
Tools and Their Use

EXAMINATION SECTION
TEST 1

DIRECTIONS: Each question or incomplete statement is followed by several suggested answers or completions. Select the one that BEST answers the question or completes the statement. *PRINT THE LETTER OF THE CORRECT ANSWER IN THE SPACE AT THE RIGHT.*

Questions 1-10.

DIRECTIONS: Questions 1 through 10 refer to the tools shown below. The numbers in the answers refer to the numbers beneath the tools.
NOTE: These tools are NOT shown to scale.

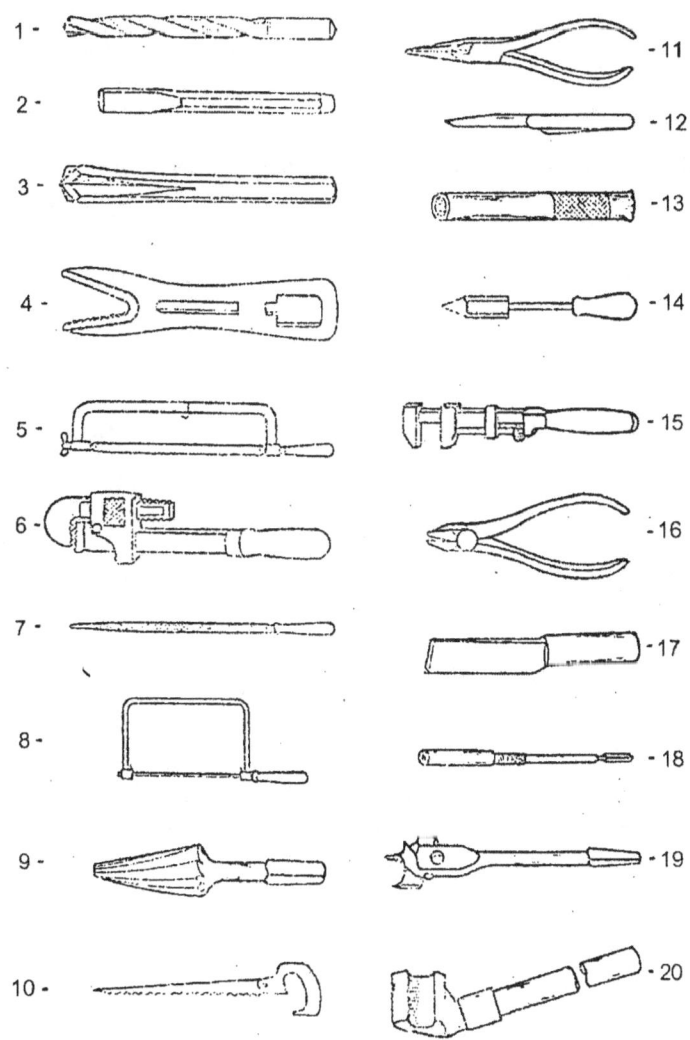

1. The tool that should be used for cutting a 1 7/8" diameter hole in a wood joist is number
   A. 3   B. 9   C. 14   D. 19

2. The tool that should be used for cutting thin-wall steel conduit is number qq
   A. 5   B. 8   C. 10   D. 16

3. The tool that should be used for soldering splices in electrical wire is number
   A. 3   B. 7   C. 13   D. 14

4. After cutting off a piece of a 3/4" diameter electrical conduit, the tool that should be used for removing a burr from the inside of the conduit is number
   A. 9   B. 11   C. 12   D. 14

5. The tool that should be used for turning a coupling onto a threaded conduit is number
   A. 6   B. 11   C. 15   D. 16

6. The tool that should be used for cutting wood lathing in plaster walls is number
   A. 5   B. 7   C. 10   D. 12

7. The tool that should be used for drilling a 3/8" diameter hole in a steel beam is number
   A. 1   B. 2   C. 3   D. 9

8. Of the following, the BEST tool to use for stripping insulation from electrical hook-up wire is number
   A. 11   B. 12   C. 15   D. 20

9. The tool that should be used for bending an electrical wire around a terminal post is number
   A. 4   B. 11   C. 15   D. 16

10. The tool that should be used for cutting electrical hook-up wire is number
    A. 5   B. 12   C. 16   D. 17

KEY (CORRECT ANSWERS)

1. D   6. C
2. A   7. A
3. D   8. B
4. A   9. B
5. A   10. C

TEST 2

DIRECTIONS: Each question or incomplete statement is followed by several suggested answers or completions. Select the one that BEST answers the question or completes the statement. *PRINT THE LETTER OF THE CORRECT ANSWER IN THE SPACE AT THE RIGHT.*

1. Round-nose pliers are *especially* useful for
    A. forming wire loops
    B. tightening small nuts
    C. crimping wires
    D. gripping small screws

2. A slight coating of rust on small tools is BEST removed by
    A. rubbing the tool with a dry cloth
    B. scraping the tool with a sharp knife
    C. scraping the tool with a small file having vaseline on it
    D. rubbing the tool with fine steel wool moistened with kerosene

3. The stake that should be used for hand-forming a small sheet metal cone is a _____ stake.
    A. hatchet   B. bottom   C. solid mandrel   D. blowhorn

4. Of the following types of pliers, the BEST one to use to clamp down sheet metal to the top of a work bench is the
    A. channel-lock   B. vise grip   C. slip-joint   D. duck bill

5. Angle brackets for supporting ductwork are *commonly* anchored to concrete walls by means of _____ bolts.
    A. carriage   B. J-   C. expansion   D. foot

6. Of the following bolts, the *one* that should be used when attaching a hanger to a wooden joist is a _____ bolt.
    A. dead   B. lag   C. dardalet   D. toggle

7. When bending sheet metal by hand, the BEST tool to use is a
    A. hand groover
    B. hand seamer
    C. hand ball tooler
    D. hand plier

8. Of the following types of steel rivets of the same size, the STRONGEST is the _____ rivet.
    A. tinners'   B. flathead   C. roundhead
    D. countersunk

9. Of the following snips, the one that can cut relatively thick sheet metal with the LEAST effort is _____ snips.
    A. straight   B. aviation   C. duck bill   D. hawk bill

10. Of the following, the BEST tool to use to make a hole in a concrete floor for a machine hold-down bolt is a

 A. counterboring tool
 B. cold chisel
 C. drift punch
 D. star drill

11. Of the following, the BEST type of saw to use to cut a 4" diameter hole through a 5/8" wooden partition is a _____ saw.

 A. back B. saber C. circular D. cross-cut

12. While using a hacksaw to cut through a 1" diameter steel bar, a helper should not press down too heavily on the hacksaw because this may

 A. break the blade
 B. overheat the bar
 C. permanently distort the frame
 D. cause the hacksaw to slip

13. A miter box is used

 A. for locating dowel holes in two pieces of wood to be joined together
 B. to hold a saw at a fixed angle while sawing
 C. to hold a saw while sharpening its teeth
 D. to clamp two pieces of wood together at 90 degrees

14. Wing nuts are *especially* useful on equipment where

 A. the nuts must be removed frequently and easily
 B. the nuts are locked in place with a cotter pin
 C. critical adjustments are to be made frequently
 D. a standard hex head wrench cannot be used

15. The BEST device to employ to make certain that two points, separated by an unobstructed vertical distance of 12 feet, are in the best possible vertical alignment is a

 A. carpenter's square
 B. level
 C. folding ruler
 D. plumb bob

16. In a shop, snips should be used to

 A. hold small parts steady while machining them
 B. cut threaded pipe
 C. cut thin gauge sheet metal
 D. remove nuts that are seized on a bolt

17. A clutch is a device that is used

 A. to hold a work piece in a fixture
 B. for retrieving small parts from hard-to-reach areas
 C. to disengage one rotating shaft from another
 D. to level machinery on a floor

18. Of the following, the BEST device to use to determine whether the surface of a work bench is horizontal is a

 A. surface gage
 B. spirit level
 C. dial vernier
 D. profilometer

19. Of the following, the machine screw having the SMALLEST diameter is the 19.____

    A. 10-24 x 3/4"   B. 6-32 x 1 1/4"
    C. 12-24 x 1"   D. 8-32 x 1 1/2"

20. To close off one opening in a pipe tee when the line connecting into it is to be temporarily 20.____
    removed, it is necessary to use a

    A. pipe cap   B. pipe plug   C. nipple   D. bushing

21. The tool that should be used to cut a 1" x 4" plank down to a 3" width is a _____ saw. 21.____

    A. hack   B. crosscut   C. rip   D. back

22. Sharpening a hand saw consists of four major steps, *namely,* 22.____

    A. jointing, shaping, setting and filing
    B. adzing, clinching, forging and machining
    C. brazing, chiseling, grinding and mitering
    D. bushing, dressing, lapping, and machining

23. If it is necessary to shorten the length of a bolt by cutting through the threaded portion, 23.____
    the SIMPLEST procedure to avoid difficulty with the thread is to

    A. cut parallel to the threads in the groove of the thread
    B. run on a die after cutting
    C. turn on a nut past the cutting point prior to cutting
    D. clear the injured thread with a 3-cornered file

24. The wrench that would prove LEAST useful in uncoupling several pieces of pipe is a 24.____
    _____ wrench.

    A. socket   B. chain   C. strap   D. stillson

25. Gaskets are *commonly* used between the flanges of large pipe joints to 25.____

    A. provide space for assembly
    B. take up expansion and contraction
    C. prevent the flanges from rusting together
    D. make a tight connection

KEY (CORRECT ANSWERS)

1. A
2. D
3. D
4. B
5. C

6. B
7. B
8. C
9. B
10. D

11. B
12. A
13. B
14. A
15. D

16. C
17. C
18. B
19. B
20. B

21. C
22. A
23. C
24. A
25. D

MECHANICAL APTITUDE
MECHANICAL COMPREHENSION
EXAMINATION SECTION
TEST 1

DIRECTIONS: Each question or incomplete statement below is followed by several suggested answers or completions. Select the *one* that *BEST* answers the question or completes the statement. *PRINT THE LETTER OF THE CORRECT ANSWER IN THE SPACE AT THE RIGHT.*

Questions 1-3.

DIRECTIONS: Questions 1 to 3 inclusive are based upon the following paragraph.

The only openings permitted in fire partitions except openings for ventilating ducts shall be those required for doors. There shall be but one such door opening unless the provision of additional openings would not exceed, in total width of all doorways, 25 percent of the length of the wall. The minimum distance between openings shall be three feet. The maximum area for such a door opening shall be 80 square feet, except that such openings for the passage of motor trucks may be a maximum of 140 square feet.

1. According to the above paragraph, openings in fire partitions are permitted *only* for   1____

    A. doors
    B. doors and windows
    C. doors and ventilation ducts
    D. doors, windows and ventilation ducts

2. In a fire partition, 22 feet long and 10 feet high, the *MAXIMUM* number of doors, 3 feet wide and 7 feet high, is   2____

    A. 1   B. 2   C. 3   D. 4

3.   3____

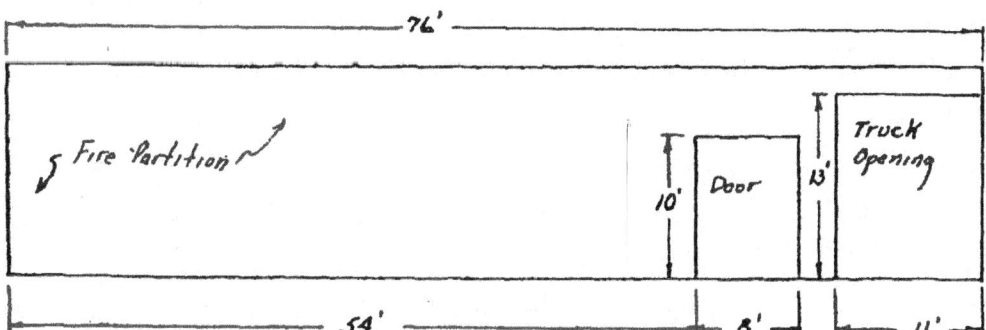

   The *one* of the following statements about the layout shown above that is *MOST* accurate is that the

    A. total width of the openings is too large
    B. truck opening is too large
    C. truck and door openings are too close together
    D. layout is acceptable

75

4. At a given temperature, a wet hand will freeze to a bar of metal, but NOT to a piece of wood, because the

   A. metal expands and contracts more than the wood
   B. wood is softer than the metal
   C. wood will burn at a lower temperature than the metal
   D. metal is a better conductor of heat than the wood

5. Of the following items commonly found in a household, the one that uses the MOST electric current is a(n)

   A. 150-watt light bulb
   B. toaster
   C. door buzzer
   D. 8" electric fan

6. Sand and ashes are frequently placed on icy pavements to prevent skidding. The effect of the sand and ashes is to increase

   A. inertia   B. gravity   C. momentum   D. friction

7. The air near the ceiling of a room usually is warmer than the air near the floor because

   A. there is better air circulation at the floor level
   B. warm air is lighter than cold air
   C. windows usually are nearer the floor than the ceiling
   D. heating pipes usually run along the ceiling

8.

   DIA. 1   DIA. 2

   It is safer to use the ladder positioned as shown in diagram 1 than as shown in diagram 2 because, in diagram 1,

   A. less strain is placed upon the center rungs of the ladder
   B. it is easier to grip and stand on the ladder
   C. the ladder reaches a lower height
   D. the ladder is less likely to tip over backwards

9.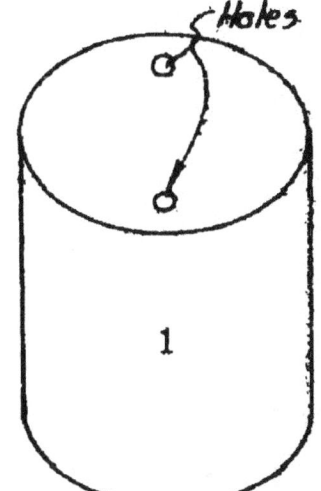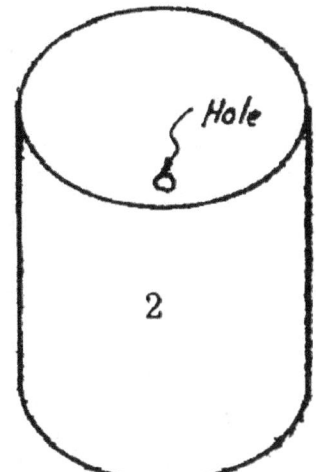

It is *easier* to pour a liquid from:

- A. Can 1 because there are two holes from which the liquid can flow
- B. Can 1 because air can enter through one hole while the liquid comes out the other hole
- C. Can 2 because the liquid comes out under greater pressure
- D. Can 2 because it is easier to direct the flow of the liquid when there is only one hole

10. A substance which is subject to "spontaneous combustion" is one that

- A. is explosive when heated
- B. is capable of catching fire without an external source of heat
- C. acts to speed up the burning of material
- D. liberates oxygen when heated

11. The sudden shutting down of a nozzle on a hose discharging water under high pressure is a *bad* practice CHIEFLY because the

- A. hose is likely to whip about violently
- B. hose is likely to burst
- C. valve handle is likely to snap
- D. valve handle is likely to jam

12. Fire can continue where there are present fuel, oxygen from the air or other source, and a sufficiently high temperature to maintain combustion. The method of extinguishment of fire MOST commonly used is to

- A. remove the fuel
- B. exclude the oxygen from the burning material
- C. reduce the temperature of the burning material
- D. smother the flames of the burning material

13.

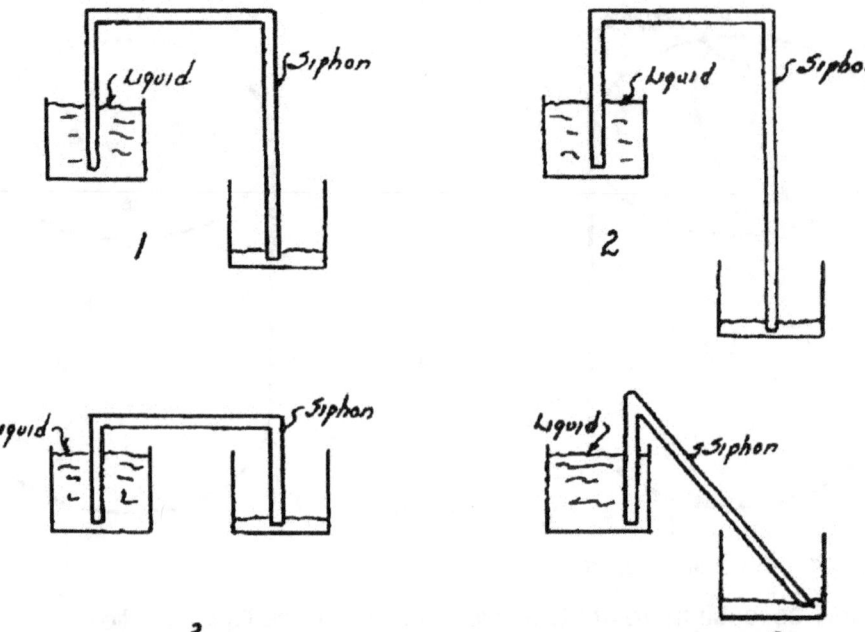

The *one* of the siphon arrangements shown above which would *MOST* quickly transfer a solution from the container on the left side to the one on the right side is numbered

A. 1   B. 2   C. 3   D. 4

14. Static electricity is a hazard in industry CHIEFLY because it may cause

   A. dangerous or painful burns
   B. chemical decomposition of toxic elements
   C. sparks which can start an explosion
   D. overheating of electrical equipment

15.

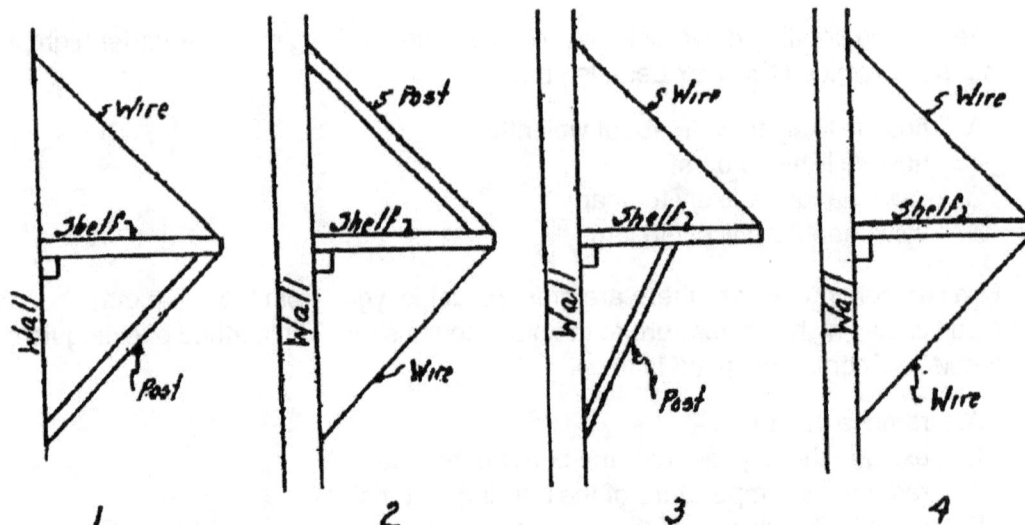

The *STRONGEST* method of supporting the shelf is shown in diagram

A. 1   B. 2   C. 3   D. 4

16. A row boat will float *deeper* in fresh water than in salt water *because*

    A. in the salt water the salt will occupy part of the space
    B. fresh water is heavier than salt water
    C. salt water is heavier than fresh water
    D. salt water offers less resistance than fresh water

17.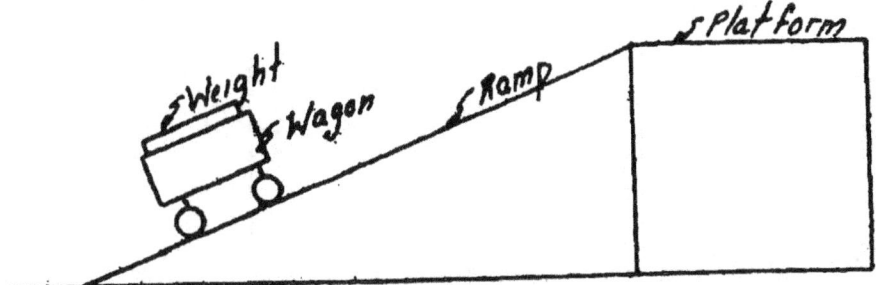

    It is easier to get the load onto the platform by using the ramp than it is to lift it directly onto the platform. This is *true* because the effect of the ramp is to

    A. reduce the amount of friction so that less force is required
    B. distribute the weight over a larger area
    C. support part of the load so that less force is needed to move the wagon
    D. increase the effect of the moving weight

18.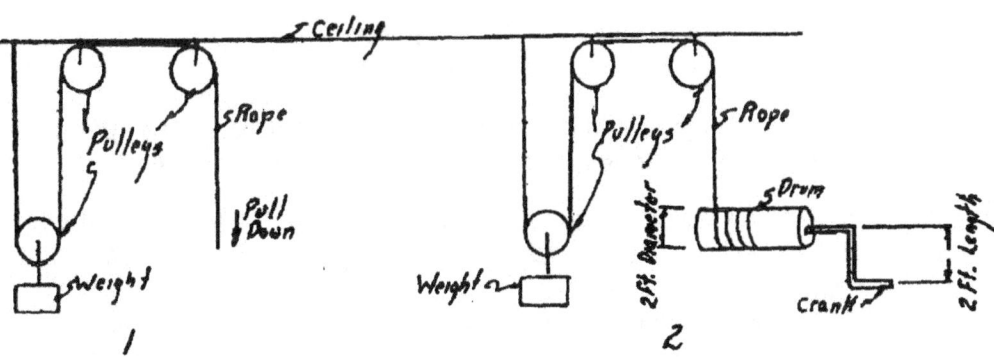

    More weight can be lifted by the method shown in diagram 2 than as shown in diagram 1 because

    A. it takes less force to turn a crank than it does to pull in a straight line
    B. the drum will prevent the weight from falling by itself
    C. the length of the crank is larger than the radius of the drum
    D. the drum has more rope on it easing the pull

19.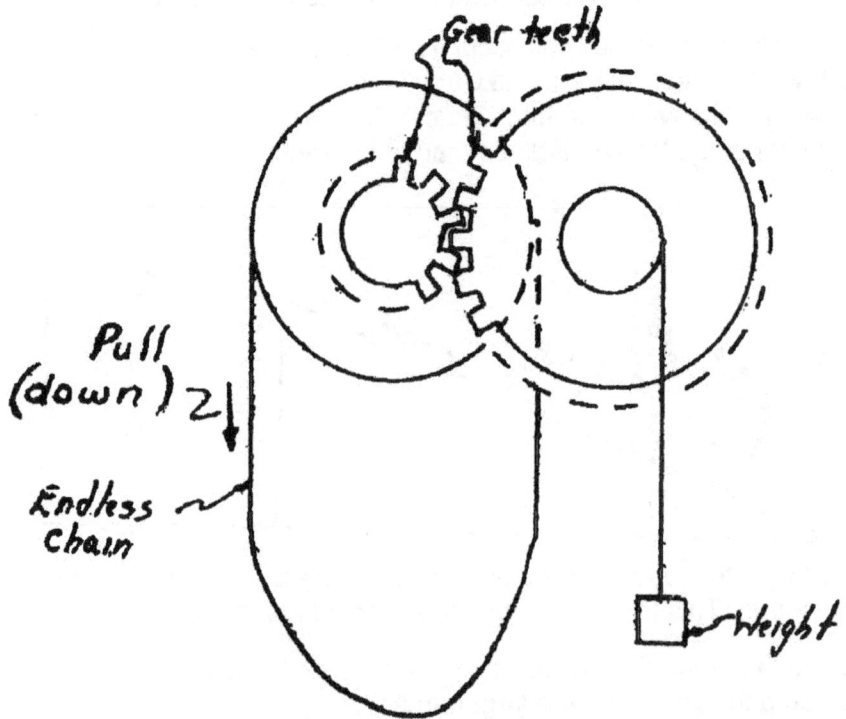

As the endless chain is pulled down in the direction shown, the weight will move

- A. *up* faster than the endless chain is pulled down
- B. *up* slower than the endless chain is pulled down
- C. *down* faster than the endless chain is pulled down
- D. *down* slower than the endless chain is pulled down

20. Two balls of the same size, but different weights, are both dropped from a 10-ft. height. The one of the following statements that is MOST accurate is that

- A. both balls will reach the ground at the same time because they are the same size
- B. both balls will reach the ground at the same time because the effect of gravity is the same on both balls
- C. the heavier ball will reach the ground first because it weighs more
- D. the lighter ball will reach the ground first because air resistance is greater on the heavier ball

21. It is considered poor practice to increase the leverage of a wrench by placing a pipe over the handle of the wrench. This is true PRINCIPALLY because

- A. the wrench may break
- B. the wrench may slip off the nut
- C. it is harder to place the wrench on the nut
- D. the wrench is more difficult to handle

22.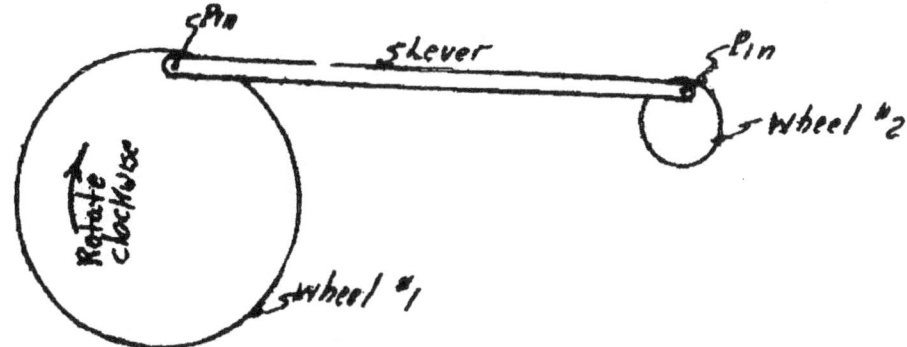

If wheel #1 is turned in the direction shown, wheel #2 will

- A. turn continously in a clockwise direction
- B. turn continously in a counterclockwise direction
- C. move back and fourth
- D. became jammed and both wheels will shop

23. ALL SOLID AREAS REPRESENT EQUAL WEIGHTS ATTACHED TO THE FLYWHEEL

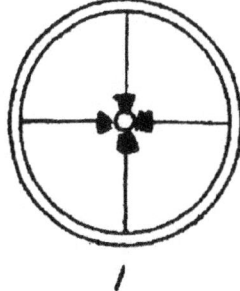 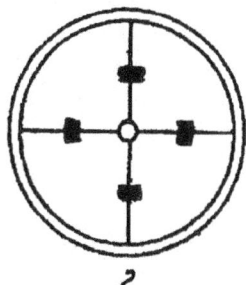 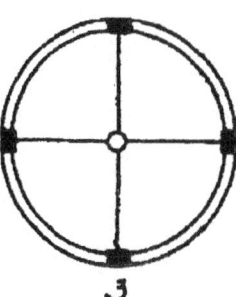

1   2   3

The above diagrams are of flywheels made of the same material with the same dimensions and attached to similar engines. The solid areas represent equal weights attached to the fly wheel. If all three engines are running at the same speed for the same length of time and the power to the engines is shut of simultaneously,

- A. wheel 1 will continue turning longest
- B. wheel 2 will continue turning longest
- C. wheel 3 will continue turning longest
- D. all three wheels will continue turning for the same time

24. The one of the following substance which expands when freezing is

    A. alcohol   B. ammonia   C. mercury   D. water

25. A piece of copper wire 30 feet long is cut into two pieces, 20 feet and 10 feet. The resistance of the *longer* piece, compared to the shorter, is

    A. one-half as much   B. two-thirds as much
    C. one and one-half as much   D. twice as much

KEY (CORRECT ANSWERS)

1.	C	11.	B
2.	A	12.	C
3.	B	13.	B
4.	D	14.	C
5.	B	15.	A
6.	D	16.	C
7.	B	17.	C
8.	D	18.	C
9.	B	19.	D
10.	B	20.	B

21. A
22. D
23. C
24. D
25. D

TEST 2

DIRECTIONS: Each question or incomplete statement below is followed by several suggested answers or completions. Select the one that BEST answers the question or completes the statement. *PRINT THE LETTER OF THE CORRECT ANSWER IN THE SPACE AT THE RIGHT.*

Questions 1-2.

DIRECTIONS: Questions 1 and 2 are to be answered in accordance with the information in the following statement:

The electrical resistance of copper wires varies directly with their lengths and inversely with their cross section areas.

1. A piece of copper wire 30 feet long is cut into two pieces, 20 feet and 10 feet. The resistance of the *longer* piece, compared to the shorter, is

    A. one-half as much
    B. two-thirds as much
    C. one and one-half as much
    D. twice as much

2. Two pieces of copper wire are each 10 feet long but the cross section area of one is 2/3 that of the other. The resistance of the piece with the *larger* cross-section area is

    A. one-half the resistance of the smaller
    B. two-thirds the resistance of the smaller
    C. one and one-half times the resistance of the smaller
    D. twice the resistance of the smaller

3.

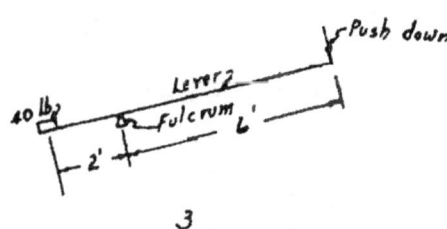

The arrangement of the lever which would require the LEAST amount of force to move the weight is shown in the diagram numbered

    A. 1   B. 2   C. 3   D. 4

4. Steel supporting beams in buildings often are surrounded by a thin layer of concrete to keep the beams from becoming hot and collapsing during a fire.
The *one* of the following statements which BEST explains how collapse is prevented by this arrangement is that concrete

    A. becomes stronger as its temperature is increased

B. acts as an insulating material
C. protects the beam from rust and corrosion
D. reacts chemically with steel at high temperatures

5. If boiling water is poured into a drinking glass, the glass is likely to crack. If, however, a metal spoon first is placed in the glass, it is much less likely to crack. The reason that the glass with the spoon is *less likely* to crack is that the spoon

   A. distributes the water over a larger surface of the glass
   B. quickly absorbs heat from the water
   C. reinforces the glass
   D. reduces the amount of water which can be poured into the glass

6. It takes *more* energy to force water through a *long* pipe than through a *short* pipe of the same diameter. The PRINCIPAL reason for this is

   A. gravity
   B. friction
   C. inertia
   D. cohesion

7. A pump, discharging at 300 lbs.-per-sq.-inch pressure, delivers water through 100 feet of pipe laid horizontally. If the valve at the end of the pipe is shut so that no water can flow, then the pressure at the valve is, for practical purposes,

   A. *greater* than the pressure at the pump
   B. *equal to* the pressure at the pump
   C. *less* than the pressure at the pump
   D. *greater or less* than the pressure at the pump, depending on the type of pump used

8. The explosive force of a gas when stored under various pressures is given in the following table:

Storage Pressure	Explosive Force
10	1
20	8
30	27
40	64
50	125

   The *one* of the following statements which BEST expresses the relationship between the storage pressure and explosive force is that
   A. there is no systematic relationship between an increase in storage pressure and an increase in explosive force
   B. the explosive force varies as the square of the pressure
   C. the explosive force varies as the cube of the pressure
   D. the explosive force varies as the fourth power of the pressure

9.

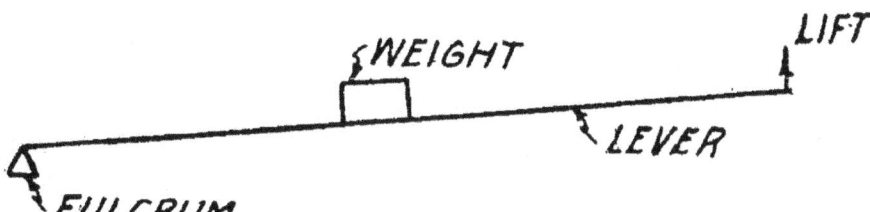

The leverage system in the sketch above is used to raise a weight. In order to *reduce* the amount of force required to raise the weight, it is necessary to

A. decrease the length of the lever
B. place the weight closer to the fulcrum
C. move the weight closer to the person applying the force
D. move the fulcrum further from the weight

10. In the accompanying sketch of a block and fall, if the end of the rope P is pulled so that it moves one foot, the distance the weight will be *raised* is
A. 1/2 ft.
B. 1 ft.
C. 1 1/2 ft.
D. 2 ft.

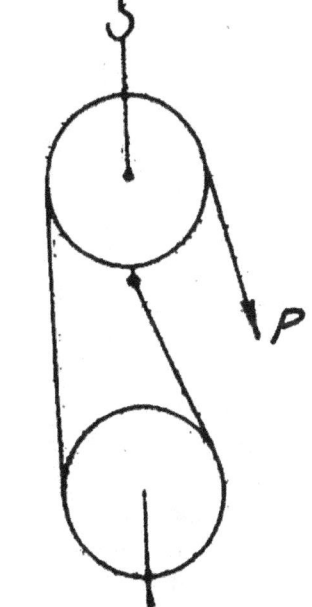

11.

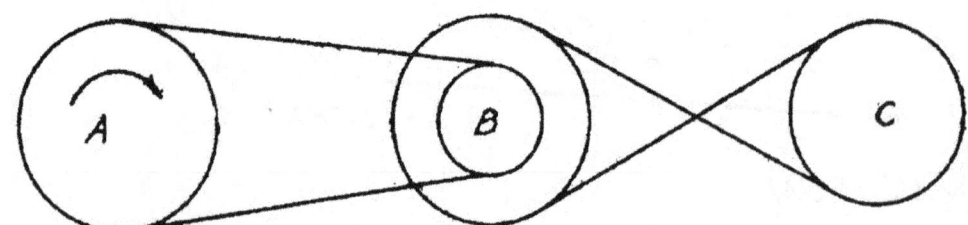

The above sketch diagrammatically shows a pulley and belt system. If pulley A is made to rotate in a clockwise direction, *then* pulley C will rotate

A. faster than pulley A and in a clockwise direction
B. slower than pulley A and in a clockwise direction
C. faster than pulley A and in a counter-clockwise direction
D. slower than pulley A and in a counter-clockwise direction

12.

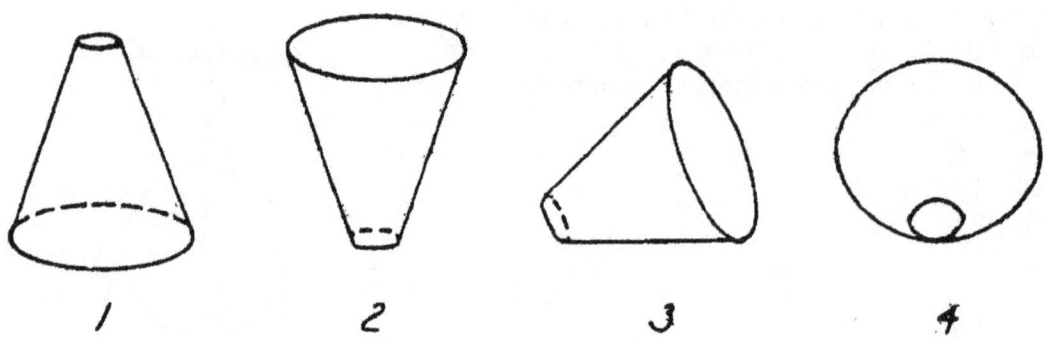

The above diagrams show four positions of the same object. The position in which this object is *MOST* stable is

A. 1 B. 2 C. 3 D. 4

13. The accompanying sketch diagrammatically shows a system of meshing gears with relative diameters as drawn. If gear 1 is made to rotate in the direction of the arrow, *then* the gear that will turn *FASTEST* is numbered

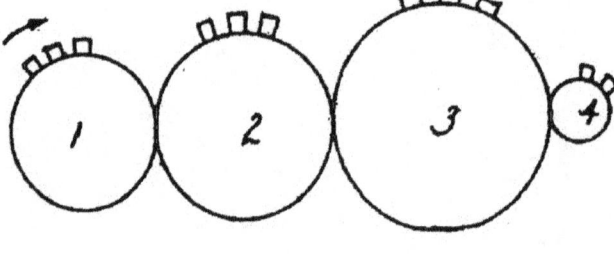

A. 1 B. 2 C. 3 D. 4

14.

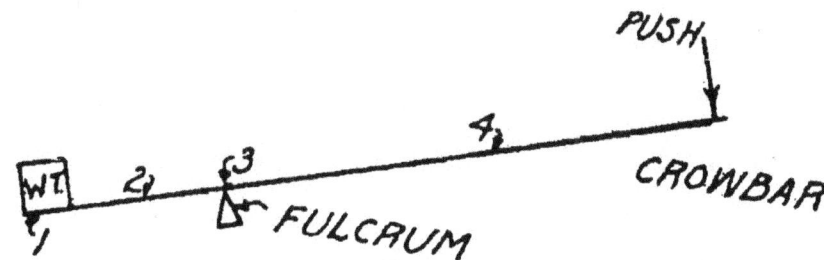

The above sketch shows a weight being lifted by means of a crowbar.
The point at which the tendency for the bar to break is GREATEST is

A. 1   B. 2   C. 3   D. 4

15.

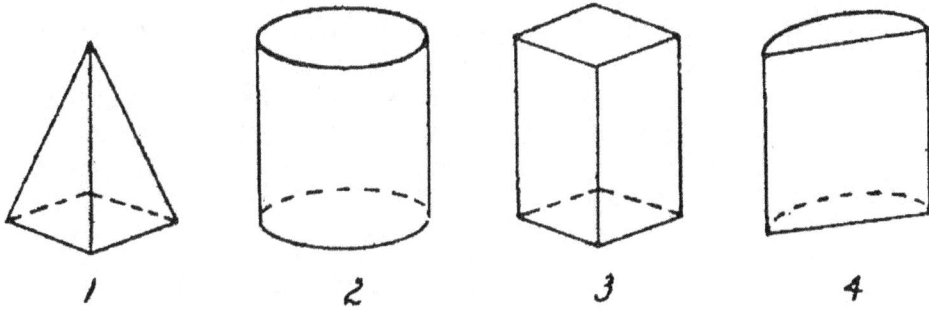

The above sketches show four objects which weigh the same but have different shapes.
The object which is MOST difficult to tip over is numbered

A. 1   B. 2   C. 3   D. 4

16.

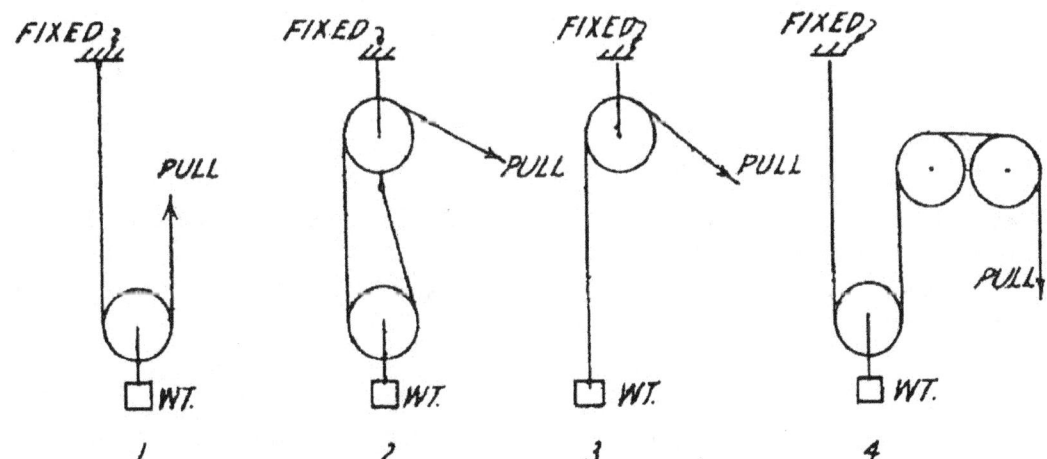

An object is to be lifted by means of a system of lines and pulleys. Of the systems shown above, the *one* which would require the GREATEST force to be used in lifting the weight is the one numbered

A. 1   B. 2   C. 3   D. 4

17. An intense fire develops in a room in which carbon dioxide cylinders are stored. The
PRINCIPAL hazard in this situation is that

    A. the CO_2 may catch fire
    B. toxic fumes may be released
    C. the cylinders may explode
    D. released CO_2 may intensify the fire

18. At a fire involving the roof of a 5-story building, the firemen trained their hose stream on the fire from a vacant lot across the street, aiming the stream at a point about 15 feet above the roof.
In this situation, water in the stream would be traveling at the GREATEST speed

    A. as it leaves the hose nozzle
    B. at a point midway between the ground and the roof
    C. at the maximum height of the stream
    D. as it drops on the roof

19. A principle of lighting is that the intensity of illumination at a point is inversely proportional to the square of the distance from the source of illumination.
Assume that a pulley lamp is lowered from a position of 6 feet to one of three feet above a desk. According to the above principle, we would expect that the amount of illumination reaching the desk from the lamp in the lower position, as compared to the higher position, will be

    A. half as much   B. twice as much
    C. four times as much   D. nine times as much

20.

[Diagram: Four figures labeled 1, 2, 3, 4 — (1) circle with diameter 120', (2) square with diagonal 120', (3) circle with diameter 240', (4) square with diagonal 240']

When standpipes are required in a structure, sufficient risers must be installed so that no point on the floor is more than 120 feet from a riser.
The one of the above diagrams which gives the MAXIMUM area which can be covered by one riser is

    A. 1   B. 2   C. 3   D. 4

21. Spontaneous combustion may be the reason for a pile of oily rags catching fire.
In general, spontaneous combustion is the DIRECT result of

    A. application of flame   B. falling sparks
    C. intense sunlight   D. chemical action
    E. radioactivity

22. In general, firemen are advised not to direct a solid stream of water on fires burning in electrical equipment. Of the following, the MOST logical reason for this instruction is that 22____

    A. water is a conductor of electricity
    B. water will do more damage to the electrical equipment than the fire
    C. hydrogen in water may explode when it comes in contact with electric current
    D. water will not effectively extinguish fires in electrical equipment
    E. water may spread the fire to other circuits

23. The height at which a fireboat will float in still water is determined CHIEFLY by the 23____

    A. weight of the water displaced by the boat
    B. horsepower of the boat's engines
    C. number of propellers on the boat
    D. curve the bow has above the water line
    E. skill with which the boat is maneuvered

24. When firemen are working at the nozzle of a hose they usually lean forward on the hose. The *most likely* reason for taking this position is that 24____

    A. the surrounding air is cooled, making the firemen more comfortable
    B. a backward force is developed which must be counteracted
    C. the firemen can better see where the stream strikes
    D. the fireman are better protected from injury by falling debris
    E. the stream is projected further

25. In general, the color and odor of smoke will BEST indicate 25____

    A. the cause of the fire
    B. the extent of the fire
    C. how long the fire has been burning
    D. the kind of material on fire
    E. the exact seat of the fire

KEY (CORRECT ANSWERS)

1.	D	11.	C
2.	B	12.	A
3.	A	13.	D
4.	B	14.	C
5.	B	15.	A
6.	B	16.	C
7.	B	17.	C
8.	C	18.	A
9.	B	19.	C
10.	A	20.	C

21. D
22. A
23. A
24. B
25. D

TEST 3

DIRECTIONS: Each question or incomplete statement below is followed by several suggested answers or completions. Select the *one* that *BEST* answers the question or completes the statement. *PRINT THE LETTER OF THE CORRECT ANSWER IN THE SPACE AT THE RIGHT.*

1. As a demonstration, firemen set up two hose lines identical in every respect except that one was longer than the other. Water was then delivered through these lines from one pump and it was seen that the stream from the longer hose line had a shorter "throw," Of the following, the *MOST* valid explanation of this difference in "throw" is that the

    A. air resistance to the water stream is proportional to the length of hose
    B. time required for water to travel through the longer hose is greater than for the shorter one
    C. loss due to friction is greater in the longer hose than in the shorter one
    D. rise of temperature is greater in the longer hose than in the shorter one
    E. longer hose line probably developed a leak at one of the coupling joints

2. Of the following toxic gases, the *one* which is *MOST* dangerous because it cannot be seen and has no odor, is

    A. ether B. carbon monoxide C. chlorine
    D. ammonia E. cooking gas

3. You are visiting with some friends when their young son rushes into the room with his clothes on fire. You immediately wrap him in a rug and roll him on the floor. The *MOST* important reason for your action is that the

    A. flames are confined within the rug
    B. air supply to the fire is reduced
    C. burns sustained will be third degree, rather than first degree
    D. whirling action will put out the fire
    E. boy will not suffer from shock

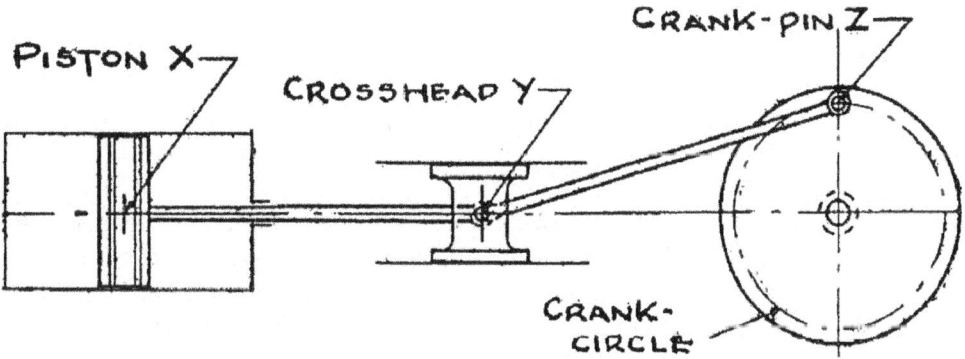

FIGURE I

91

Questions 4-6,

DIRECTIONS: The device shown in Figure I above represents schematically a mechanism commonly used to change reciprocating (back and forth) motion to rotation (circular) motion.
The following questions, numbered 4 to 6 inclusive, are to be answered with reference to this device.

4. Assume that piston X is placed in its extreme left position so that X, Y and Z are in a horizontal line. If a horizontal force to the right is applied to the piston X, we may then expect that

    A. the crank-pin Z will revolve clockwise
    B. the crosshead Y will move in a direction opposite to that of X
    C. the crank-pin Z will revolve counterclockwise
    D. no movement will take place
    E. the crank-pin Z will oscillate back and forth

5. If we start from the position shown in the above diagram, and move piston X to the right, the result will be that

    A. the crank-pin Z will revolve counterclockwise and cross-head Y will move to the left
    B. the crank-pin Z will revolve clockwise and crosshead Y will move to the left
    C. the crank-pin Z will revolve clockwise and crosshead Y will move to the right
    D. the crank-pin Z will revolve clockwise and crosshead Y will move to the right
    E. crosshead Y will move to the left as piston X moves to the right

6. If crank-pin Z is moved closer to the center of the crank circle, then the length of the

    A. stroke of piston X is increased
    B. stroke of piston X is decreased
    C. stroke of piston X is unchanged
    D. rod between the piston X and crosshead Y is increased
    E. rod between the piston X and crosshead Y is decreased

Questions 7-8.

DIRECTIONS: Figure II represents schematically a block-and-fall tackle. The advantage derived from this machine is that the effect of the applied force is multiplied by the number of lines of rope directly supporting the load. The following two questions, numbered 7 and 8, are to be answered with reference to this figure.

7. Pull P is exerted on line T to raise the load L. The line in which the *LARGEST* strain is finally induced is line

    A. T   B. U   C. V   D. X   E. Y

8. If the largest pull P that two men can apply to line T is 280 lbs., the MAXIMUM load L that they can raise without regard to frictional losses is, *most nearly*, _____ lbs.
   A. 1960
   B. 1680
   C. 1400
   D. 1260
   E. 1120

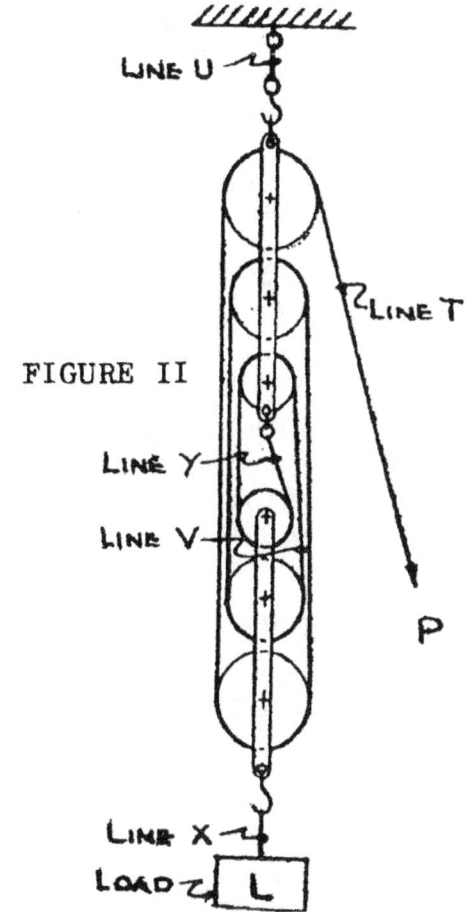

FIGURE II

Questions 9-13.

DIRECTIONS: Answer Questions 9 to 13 on the basis of Figure III. The diagram schematically illustrates part of a water tank. 1 and 5 are outlet and inlet pipes, respectively. 2 is a valve which can be used to open and close the outlet pipe by hand. 3 is a float which is rigidly connected to valve 4 by an iron bar, thus causing that valve to open or shut as the float rises or falls 4 is a hinged valve which controls the flow of water into the tank.

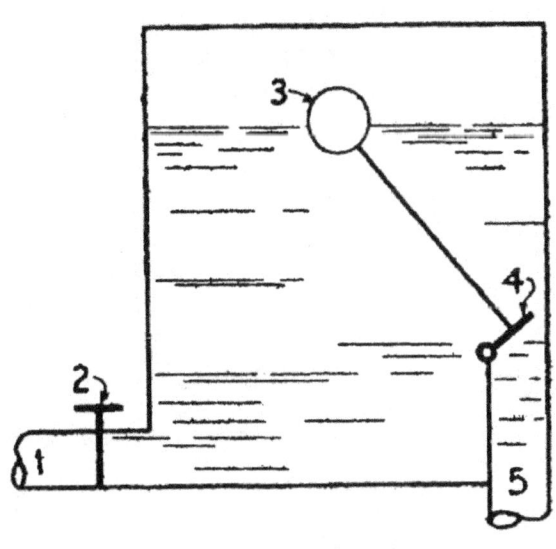

FIGURE III

9. If the tank is half filled and water is going out of pipe 1 more rapidly than it is coming in through pipe 5, *then*

    A. valve 2 is closed
    B. float 3 is rising in the tank
    C. valve 4 is opening wider
    D. valve 4 is closed
    E. float 3 is stationary

10. If the tank is half filled with water and water is coming in through inlet pipe 5 more rapidly than it is going out through outlet pipe 1, *then*

    A. valve 2 is closed
    B. float 3 is rising in the tank
    C. valve 4 is opening wider
    D. valve 4 is closed
    E. float 3 is stationary

11. If the tank is empty, then it can *normally* be expected that

    A. float 3 is at its highest position
    B. float 3 is at its lowest position
    C. valve 2 is closed
    D. valve 4 is closed
    E. water will not come into the tank

12. If float 3 develops a leak, *then*

    A. the tank will tend to empty
    B. water will tend to stop coming into the tank
    C. valve 4 will tend to close
    D. valve 2 will tend to close
    E. valve 4 will tend to remain open

13. Without any other changes being made, if the bar joining the float to valve 4 is removed and a slightly shorter bar substituted, *then*

    A. a smaller quantity of water in the tank will be required before the float closes valve 4
    B. valve 4 will not open
    C. valve 4 will not close
    D. it is not possible to determine what will happen
    E. a greater quantity of water in the tank will be required before the float closes valve 4

Questions 14-18.

DIRECTIONS: Answer Questions 14 to 18 on the basis of Figure IV. A, B, C and D are four meshed gears forming a gear train. Gear A is the driver. Gears A and D each have twice as many teeth as gear B, and gear C has four times as many teeth as gear B. The diagram is schematic: the teeth go all around each gear.

14. *Two* gears which turn in the *same* direction are:

    A. A and B
    B. B and C
    C. C and D
    D. D and A
    E. B and D

15. The *two* gears which revolve at the *same* speed are gears

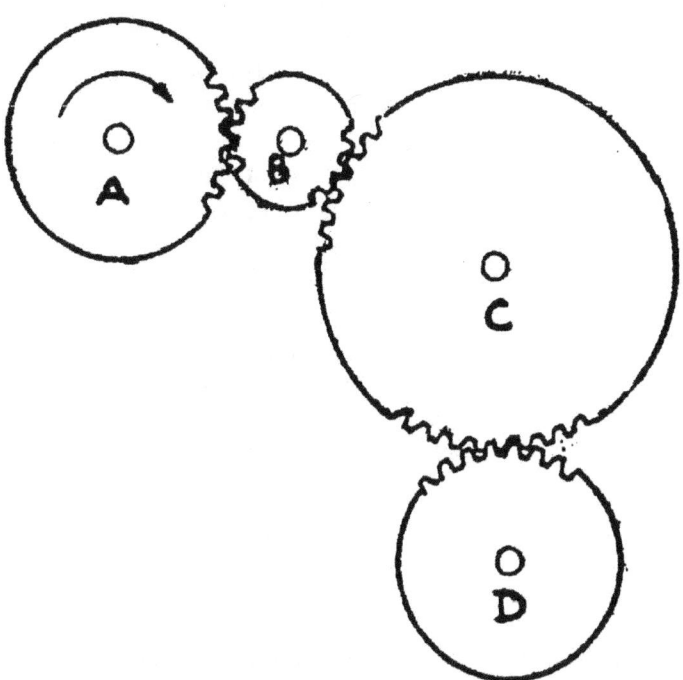

FIGURE IV

   A. A and C   B. A and D   C. B and C
   D. B and D   E. D and C

16. If all the teeth on gear C are stripped without affecting the teeth on gears A, B, and D, then rotation would occur *only* in gear(s)

   A. C   B. D   C. A and B
   D. A, B, and D   E. B and D

17. If gear D is rotating at the rate of 100 RPM, then gear B is rotating at the rate of _____ RPM.

   A. 25   B. 50   C. 100   D. 200   E. 400

18. If gear A turns at the rate of two revolutions per second, then the number of revolutions per second that gear C turns is

   A. 1   B. 2   C. 3   D. 4   E. 8

Questions 19-23.

DIRECTIONS: Answer Questions 19 to 23 on the basis of Figure V. The diagram shows a water pump in cross section: 1 is a check valve, 2 and 3 are the spring and diaphragm, respectively, of the discharge valve, 4 is the pump piston; 5 is the inlet valve, and 6 is the pump cylinder. All valves permit the flow of water in one direction only.

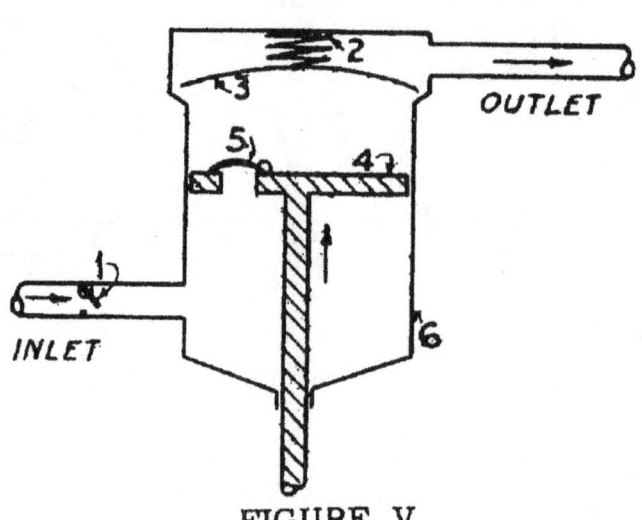

FIGURE V

19. When water is flowing through the outlet pipe,

    A. check valve 1 is closed
    B. diaphragm 3 is closed
    C. valve 5 is closed
    D. spring 2 is fully extended
    E. the piston is on the downstroke

20. If valve 5 does not work properly and stays closed, *then*

    A. the piston cannot move down
    B. the piston cannot move up
    C. diaphragm 3 cannot open
    D. check valve 1 cannot close
    E. the flow of water will be reversed

21. If diaphragm 3 does not work properly and stays in the open position, *then*

    A. check valve 1 will not open
    B. valve 5 will not open
    C. spring 2 will be compressed
    D. spring 2 will be extended
    E. water will not flow through the inlet pipe

22. When valve 5 is open during normal operation of the pump, *then*

    A. spring 2 is fully compressed
    B. the piston is on the upstroke
    C. water is flowing through check valve 1
    D. a vacuum is formed between the piston and the bottom of the cylinder
    E. diaphragm 3 is closed

23. If check valve 1 jams and stays closed, *then*

    A. valve 5 will be open on both the upstroke and down stroke of the piston
    B. a vacuum will tend to form in the inlet pipe between the source of the water supply and check valve 1
    C. pressure on the cylinder side of check valve 1 will increase

D. less force will be required to move the piston down
E. more force will be required to move the piston down

24. The one of the following which *BEST* explains why smoke usually rises from a fire is that   24____

    A. cooler, heavier air displaces lighter, warm air
    B. heat energy of the fire propels the smoke upward
    C. suction from the upper air pulls the smoke upward
    D. burning matter is chemically changed into heat energy

25. The practice of racing a car engine to warm it up in cold weather, generally, is   25____

    A. *good, MAINLY* because repeated stalling of the engine and drain on the battery is avoided
    B. *bad, MAINLY* because too much gas is used to get the engine heated
    C. *good, MAINLY* because the engine becomes operational in the shortest period of time
    D. *bad, MAINLY* because proper lubrication is not established rapidly enough

KEY (CORRECT ANSWERS)

1.	C	11.	B
2.	B	12.	E
3.	B	13.	A
4.	D	14.	E
5.	D	15.	B
6.	B	16.	C
7.	B	17.	D
8.	B	18.	A
9.	C	19.	C
10.	B	20.	A

21. C
22. E
23. D
24. A
25. D

READING COMPREHENSION
UNDERSTANDING AND INTERPRETING WRITTEN MATERIAL
EXAMINATION SECTION
TEST 1

DIRECTIONS: Each question or incomplete statement is followed by several suggested answers or completions. Select the one that BEST answers the question or completes the statement. *PRINT THE LETTER OF THE CORRECT ANSWER IN THE SPACE AT THE RIGHT.*

Questions 1-3.

DIRECTIONS: Questions 1 through 3, inclusive, are to be answered in accordance with the following paragraph.

All cement work contracts, more or less, in setting. The contraction in concrete walls and other structures causes fine cracks to develop at regular intervals. The tendency to contract increases in direct proportion to the quantity of cement in the concrete. A rich mixture will contract more than a lean mixture. A concrete wall which has been made of a very lean mixture and which has been built by filling only about one foot in depth of concrete in the form each day will frequently require close inspection to reveal the cracks.

1. According to the above paragraph,

    A. shrinkage seldom occurs in concrete
    B. shrinkage occurs only in certain types of concrete
    C. by placing concrete at regular intervals, shrinkage may be avoided
    D. it is impossible to prevent shrinkage

1.____

2. According to the above paragraph, the one of the factors which reduces shrinkage in concrete is the

    A. volume of concrete in wall
    B. height of each day's pour
    C. length of wall
    D. length and height of wall

2.____

3. According to the above paragraph, a rich mixture

    A. pours the easiest
    B. shows the largest amount of cracks
    C. is low in cement content
    D. need not be inspected since cracks are few

3.____

Questions 4-6.

DIRECTIONS: Questions 4 through 6, inclusive, are to be answered SOLELY on the basis of the following paragraph.

It is best to avoid surface water on freshly poured concrete in the first place. However, when there is a very small amount present, the recommended procedure is to allow it to evaporate before finishing. If there is considerable water, it is removed with a broom, belt, float, or by other convenient means. It is never good practice to sprinkle dry cement, or a mixture of cement and fine aggregate, on concrete to take up surface water. Such fine materials form a layer on the surface that is likely to dust or hair check when the concrete hardens.

4. The MAIN subject of the above passage is

    A. surface cracking of concrete
    B. evaporation of water from freshly poured concrete
    C. removing surface water from concrete
    D. final adjustments of ingredients in the concrete mix

5. According to the above passage, the sprinkling of dry cement on the surface of a concrete mix would MOST LIKELY

    A. prevent the mix from setting
    B. cause discoloration on the surface of the concrete
    C. cause the coarse aggregate to settle out too quickly
    D. cause powdering and small cracks on the surface of the concrete

6. According to the above passage, the thing to do when considerable surface water is present on the freshly poured concrete is to

    A. dump the concrete back into the mixer and drain the water
    B. allow the water to evaporate before finishing
    C. remove the water with a broom, belt, or float
    D. add more fine aggregate but not cement

Questions 7-9.

DIRECTIONS: Questions 7 through 9, inclusive, are to be answered ONLY in accordance with the information given in the paragraph below.

Before placing the concrete, check that the forms are rigid and well braced and place the concrete within 45 minutes after mixing it. Fill the forms to the top with the wearing-course concrete. Level off the surfaces with a strieboard. When the concrete becomes stiff but still workable (in a few hours), finish the surface with a wood float. This fills the hollows and compacts the concrete and produces a smooth but gritty finish. For a non-gritty and smoother surface (but one that is more slippery when wet), follow up with a steel trowel after the water sheen from the wood-troweling starts to disappear. If you wish, slant the tread forward a fraction of an inch so that it will shed rain water.

7. Slanting the tread a fraction of an inch gives a surface that will

    A. have added strength
    B. not be slippery when wet
    C. shed rain water
    D. not have hollows

8. In addition to giving a smooth but gritty finish, the use of a wood float will tend to 8._____

   A. give a finish that is slippery when wet
   B. compact the concrete
   C. give a better wearing course
   D. provide hollows to retain rain water

9. Which one of the following statements is most nearly correct? 9._____

   A. Having checked the forms, one may place the concrete immediately after mixing same.
   B. One must wait at least 15 minutes after mixing the concrete before it may be placed in the forms.
   C. A gritty compact finish and one which is more slippery when wet will result with the use of a wood float.
   D. A steel trowel used promptly after a wood float will tend to give a non-gritty smooth finish.

Questions 10-11.

DIRECTIONS: Questions 10 and 11 are to be answered SOLELY on the basis of information contained in the following paragraph.

Tools and plastering methods have changed very little over the years. Most of the changes are mere improvements of the basic tools. The tools formerly made by hand are now machine-made and are *rigidly* constructed of light, but strong, materials in contrast to the clumsy constructions of the early types. The power-driven mixers and hoisting equipment used on large plastering jobs today produce better mortars and lighten the tasks involved.

10. According to the above paragraph, present day tools used for plastering 10._____

    A. have made plastering much more complicated than it used to be
    B. are heavier than the old-fashioned tools they replaced
    C. produce poorer results but speed up the job
    D. are lighter and stronger than the hand-made tools of the past

11. As used in the above paragraph, the word *rigidly* means MOST NEARLY 11._____

    A. feeble   B. weakly   C. firmly   D. flexibly

Questions 12-18.

DIRECTIONS: Questions 12 through 18 are to be answered in accordance with the following paragraphs.

SURFACE RENEWING OVERLAYS

A surface renewing overlay should consist of material which can be constructed in very thin layers. The material must fill surface voids and provide an impervious skid-resistant surface. It must also be sufficiently resistant to traffic abrasion to provide an economical service life.

Materials meeting these requirements are:
- a. Asphalt concrete having small particle size
- b. Hot sand asphalts
- c. Surface seal coats

Fine-graded asphalt concrete or hot sand asphalt can be constructed in layers as thin as one-half inch and fulfill all requirements for surface renewing overlays. They are recommended for thin resurfacing of pavements having high traffic volumes, as their service lives are relatively long when constructed properly. They can be used for minor leveling, they are quiet riding, and their appearance is exceptionally pleasing. Seal coats or slurry seals may fulfill surface requirements for low traffic pavements.

12. A surface renewing overlay must fill surface voids, provide an impervious skid-resistant surface, and

    A. be resistant to traffic abrasion
    B. have small particle size
    C. be exceptionally pleasing in appearance
    D. be constructed in half-inch layers

13. An *impervious skid-resistant surface* means a surface that is

    A. rough to the touch and fixed firmly in place
    B. waterproof and provides good gripping for tires
    C. not damaged by skidding vehicles
    D. smooth to the touch and quiet riding

14. The number of types of materials that can be constructed in very thin layers and are also suitable for surface renewing overlays is

    A. 1   B. 2   C. 3   D. 4

15. The SMALLEST thickness of asphalt concrete or hot sand asphalt that can fulfill all requirements for surface renewing overlays is _____ inch(es).

    A. ¼   B. ½   C. 1   D. 2

16. The materials that are recommended for thin resurfacing of pavements having high traffic volumes are

    A. those that have relatively long service lives
    B. asphalt concretes with maximum particle size
    C. surface seal coats
    D. slurry seals with voids

17. Fine-graded asphalt concrete and hot sand asphalt are quiet riding and are also

    A. recommended for low traffic pavements
    B. used as slurry seal coats
    C. suitable for major leveling
    D. exceptionally pleasing in appearance

18. The materials that may fulfill surface requirements for low traffic pavements are 18.____

    A. fine-graded asphalt concretes
    B. hot sand asphalts
    C. seal coats or slurry seals
    D. those that can be used for minor leveling

Questions 19-25.

DIRECTIONS: Questions 19 through 25 are to be answered SOLELY on the basis of the paragraphs below.

OPEN-END WRENCHES

Solid, non-adjustable wrenches with openings in one or both ends are called open-end wrenches. Wrenches with small openings are usually shorter than wrenches with large openings. This proportions the lever advantage of the wrench to the bolt or stud and helps prevent wrench breakage or damage to the bolt or stud.

Open-end wrenches may have their jaws parallel to the handle or at angles anywhere up to 90 degrees. The average angle is 15 degrees. This angular displacement variation permits selection of a wrench suited for places where there is room to make only a part of a complete turn of a nut or bolt. Handles are usually straight, but may be curved. Those with curved handles are called S-wrenches. Other open-end wrenches may have offset handles. This allows the head to reach nut or bolt heads that are sunk below the surface.

There are a few basic rules that you should keep in mind when using wrenches. They are:

    I. ALWAYS use a wrench that fits the nut properly. Otherwise, the wrench may slip, or the nut may be damaged.
    II. Keep wrenches clean and free from oil. Otherwise, they may slip, resulting in possible serious injury to you or damage to the work.
    III. Do NOT increase the leverage of a wrench by placing a pipe over the handle. Increased leverage may damage the wrench or the work.

19. Open-end wrenches 19.____

    A. are adjustable
    B. are solid
    C. always have openings at both ends
    D. are always S-shaped

20. Wrench proportions are such that wrenches with _____ openings have _____ handles. 20.____

    A. larger; shorter   B. smaller; longer
    C. larger; longer   D. smaller; thicker

21. The average angle between the jaws and the handle of a wrench is _____ degrees. 21.____

    A. 0   B. 15   C. 22   D. 90

22. Offset handles are intended for use MAINLY with

    A. offset nuts
    B. bolts having fine threads
    C. nuts sunk below the surface
    D. bolts that permit limited swing

23. The wrench which is selected should fit the nut properly because this

    A. prevents distorting the wrench
    B. insures use of all wrench sizes
    C. avoids damaging the nut
    D. overstresses the bolt

24. Oil on wrenches is

    A. *good* because it prevents rust
    B. *good* because it permits easier turning
    C. *bad* because the wrench may slip off the nut
    D. *bad* because the oil may spoil the work

25. Extending the handle of a wrench by slipping a piece of pipe over it is considered

    A. *good* because it insures a tight nut
    B. *good* because less effort is needed to loosen a nut
    C. *bad* because the wrench may be damaged
    D. *bad* because the amount of tightening can not be controlled

---

KEY (CORRECT ANSWERS)

1.	D	11.	C
2.	B	12.	A
3.	B	13.	B
4.	C	14.	C
5.	D	15.	B
6.	C	16.	A
7.	C	17.	D
8.	B	18.	C
9.	A	19.	B
10.	D	20.	C

21. B
22. C
23. C
24. C
25. C

TEST 2

DIRECTIONS: Each question or incomplete statement is followed by several suggested answers or completions. Select the one that BEST answers the question or completes the statement. *PRINT THE LETTER OF THE CORRECT ANSWER IN THE SPACE AT THE RIGHT.*

Questions 1-3.

DIRECTIONS: Questions 1 through 3 are to be answered SOLELY on the basis of the following passage.

    A utility plan is a floor plan which shows the layout of a heating, electrical, plumbing, or other utility system. Utility plans are used primarily by the persons reponsible for the utilities, but they are important to the craftsman as well. Most utility installations require the leaving of openings in walls, floors, and roofs for the admission or installation of utility features. The craftsman who is, for example, pouring a concrete foundation wall must study the utility plans to determine the number, sizes, and locations of the openings he must leave for piping, electric lines, and the like.

1. The one of the following items of information which is LEAST likely to be provided by a utility plan is the

    A. location of the joists and frame members around stairwells
    B. location of the hot water supply and return piping
    C. location of light fixtures
    D. number of openings in the floor for radiators

1.____

2. According to the passage, the persons who will *most likely* have the GREATEST need for the information included in a utility plan of a building are those who

    A. maintain and repair the heating system
    B. clean the premises
    C. paint housing exteriors
    D. advertise property for sale

2.____

3. According to the passage, a repair crew member should find it MOST helpful to consult a utility plan when information is needed about the

    A. thickness of all doors in the structure
    B. number of electrical outlets located throughout the structure
    C. dimensions of each window in the structure
    D. length of a roof rafter

3.____

Questions 4-9.

DIRECTIONS: Questions 4 through 9 are to be answered SOLELY on the basis of the following passage.

    The basic hand-operated hoisting device is the tackle or purchase, consisting of a line called a fall, reeved through one or more blocks. To hoist a load of given size, you must set up a rig with a safe working load equal to or in excess of the load to be hoisted. In order to do this, you must be able to calculate the safe working load of a single part of line of given size, the safe working load of a given purchase which contains a line of given size, and the minimum size of hooks or shackles which you must use in a given type of purchase to hoist a given load. You must also be able to calculate the thrust which a given load will exert on a gin pole or a set of shears inclined at a given angle, the safe working load which a spar of a given size used as a gin pole or as one of a set of shears will sustain, and the stress which a given load will set up in the back guy of a gin pole or in the back guy of a set of shears inclined at a given angle.

4. The above passage refers to the lifting of loads by means of

   A. erected scaffolds
   B. manual rigging devices
   C. power-driven equipment
   D. conveyor belts

5. It can be concluded from the above passage that a set of shears serves to

   A. absorb the force and stress of the working load
   B. operate the tackle
   C. contain the working load
   D. compute the safe working load

6. According to the above passage, a spar can be used for a

   A. back guy   B. block   C. fall   D. gin pole

7. According to the above passage, the rule that a user of hand-operated tackle MUST follow is to make sure that the safe working load is AT LEAST

   A. equal to the weight of the given load
   B. twice the combined weight of the block and falls
   C. one-half the weight of the given load
   D. twice the weight of the given load

8. According to the above passage, the two parts that make up a tackle are

   A. back guys and gin poles
   B. blocks and falls
   C. rigs and shears
   D. spars and shackles

9. According to the above passage, in order to determine whether it is safe to hoist a particular load, you MUST

   A. use the maximum size hooks
   B. time the speed to bring a given load to a desired place
   C. calculate the forces exerted on various types of rigs
   D. repeatedly lift and lower various loads

Questions 10-15.

DIRECTIONS: Questions 10 through 15 are to be answered SOLELY on the basis of the following set of instructions.

PATCHING SIMPLE CRACKS IN A BUILT-UP ROOF

If there is a visible crack in built-up roofing, the repair is simple and straightforward:

1. With a brush, clean all loose gravel and dust out of the crack, and clean three or four inches around all sides of it.
2. With a trowel or putty knife, fill the crack with asphalt cement and then spread a layer of asphalt cement about 1/8 inch thick over the cleaned area.
3. Place a strip of roofing felt big enough to cover the crack into the wet cement and press it down firmly.
4. Spread a second layer of cement over the strip of felt and well past its edges.
5. Brush gravel back over the patch.

10. According to the above passage, in order to patch simple cracks in a built-up roof, it is necessary to use a

    A. putty knife and a drill
    B. knife and pliers
    C. tack hammer and a punch
    D. brush and a trowel

11. According to the above passage, the size of the area that should be clear of loose gravel and dust before the asphalt cement is first applied should

    A. be the exact size of the crack itself
    B. extend three or four inches on all sides of the crack
    C. be 1/8 inch greater than the size of the crack itself
    D. extend the length of the roofing strip

12. According to the above passage, loose gravel and dust in the crack should be removed with a

    A. brush   B. felt pad   C. trowel   D. dust mop

13. Assume that both layers of asphalt cement needed to patch the crack are of the same thickness.
    The total thickness of asphalt cement used in the patch should be MOST NEARLY _____ inch.

    A. 1/2   B. 1/3   C. 1/4   D. 1/8

14. According to the instructions in the above passage, how large should the strip of roofing felt be cut?

    A. Three of four inches square
    B. Smaller than the crack and small enough to be surrounded by cement on all sides of the strip
    C. Exactly the same size and shape of the area covered by the wet cement
    D. Large enough to completely cover the crack

15. The final or finishing action to be taken in patching a simple crack in a built-up roof is to

    A. clean out the inside of the crack
    B. spread a layer of asphalt a second time
    C. cover the crack with roofing felt
    D. cover the patch of roofing felt and cement with gravel

Questions 16-17.

DIRECTIONS: Questions 16 and 17 are to be answered SOLELY on the basis of the information given in the following paragraph.

Supplies are to be ordered from the stockroom once a week. The standard requisition form, Form SP21, is to be used for ordering all supplies. The form is prepared in triplicate, one white original and two green copies. The white and one green copy are sent to the stockroom, and the remaining green copy is to be kept by the orderer until the supplies are received.

16. According to the above paragraph, there is a limit on the 16.___

    A. amount of supplies that may be ordered
    B. day on which supplies may be ordered
    C. different kinds of supplies that may be ordered
    D. number of times supplies may be ordered in one year

17. According to the above paragraph, when the standard requisition form for supplies is prepared, 17.___

    A. a total of four requisition blanks is used
    B. a white form is the original
    C. each copy is printed in two colors
    D. one copy is kept by the stock clerk

Questions 18-21.

DIRECTION: Questions 18 through 21 are to be answered SOLELY on the basis of the following passage.

The Oil Pollution Act for U. S. waters defines an *oily mixture* as 100 parts or more of oil in one million parts of mixture. This mixture is not allowed to be discharged into the prohibited zone. The prohibited zone may, in special cases, be extended 100 miles out to sea but, in general, remains at 50 miles offshore. The United States Coast Guard must be contacted to report all *oily mixture* spills. The Federal Water Pollution Control Act provides for a fine of $10,000 for failure to notify the United States Coast Guard. An employer may take action against an employee if the employee causes an *oily mixture* spill. The law holds your employer responsible for either cleaning up or paying for the removal of the oil spillage.

18. According to the Oil Pollution Act, an *oily mixture* is defined as one in which there are _____ parts or more of oil in _____ parts of mixture. 18.___

    A. 50; 10,000   B. 100; 10,000
    C. 100; 1,000,000   D. 10,000; 1,000,000

19. Failure to notify the proper authorities of an *oily mixture* spill is punishable by a fine. Such fine is provided for by the 19.___

    A. United States Coast Guard
    B. Federal Water Pollution Control Act
    C. Oil Pollution Act
    D. United States Department of Environmental Protection

20. According to the law, the one responsible for the removal of an *oily mixture* spilled into U.S. waters is the

   A. employer
   B. employee
   C. U.S. Coast Guard
   D. U.S. Pollution Control Board

21. The *prohibited zone,* in general, is the body of water

   A. within 50 miles offshore
   B. beyond 100 miles offshore
   C. within 10,000 yards of the coastline
   D. beyond 10,000 yards from the coastline

Questions 22-25.

DIRECTIONS: Questions 22 through 25 are to be answered SOLELY on the basis of the following paragraph.

Synthetic detergents are materials produced from petroleum products or from animal or vegetable oils and fats. One of their advantages is the fact that they can be made to meet a particular cleaning problem by altering the foaming, wetting, and emulsifying properties of a cleaner. They are added to commonly used cleaning materials such as solvents, water, and alkalies to improve their cleaning performance. The adequate wetting of the surface to be cleaned is paramount in good cleaning performance. Because of the relatively high surface tension of water, it has poor wetting ability, unless its surface tension is decreased by addition of a detergent or soap. This allows water to flow into crevices and around small particles of soil, thus loosening them.

22. According to the above paragraph, synthetic detergents are made from all of the following EXCEPT

   A. petroleum products   B. vegetable oils
   C. surface tension oils   D. animal fats

23. According to the above paragraph, water's poor wetting ability is related to

   A. its low surface tension
   B. its high surface tension
   C. its vegetable oil content
   D. the amount of dirt on the surface to be cleaned

24. According to the above paragraph, synthetic detergents are added to all of the following EXCEPT

   A. alkalines   B. water   C. acids   D. solvents

25. According to the above paragraph, altering a property of a cleaner can give an advantage in meeting a certain cleaning problem.
The one of the following that is NOT a property altered by synthetic detergents is the cleaner's

    A. flow ability
    B. foaming property
    C. emulsifying property
    D. wetting ability

25.___

KEY (CORRECT ANSWERS)

1. A
2. A
3. B
4. B
5. A

6. D
7. A
8. B
9. C
10. D

11. B
12. A
13. C
14. D
15. D

16. D
17. B
18. C
19. B
20. A

21. A
22. C
23. B
24. C
25. A

EXAMINATION SECTION

TEST 1

DIRECTIONS: Each question or incomplete statement is followed by several suggested answers or completions. Select the one that BEST answers the question or completes the statement. *PRINT THE LETTER OF THE CORRECT ANSWER IN THE SPACE AT THE RIGHT.*

1. Which of the following fractions is the SMALLEST?
   A. 2/3   B. 4/5   C. 5/7   D. 5/11

2. 40% is equivalent to which of the following?
   A. 4/5   B. 4/6   C. 2/5   D. 4/100

3. How many 100's are in 10,000?
   A. 10   B. 100   C. 10,000   D. 100,000

4. $\frac{6}{7} + \frac{11}{12}$ is approximately
   A. 1   B. 2   C. 17   D. 19

5. The time required to heat water to a certain temperature is directly proportional to the volume of water being heated.
   If it takes 12 minutes to heat 1 ½ gallons of water, how many minutes will it take to heat 2 gallons of water?
   A. 12   B. 16   C. 18   D. 24

6. The cost of an item increased by 25%.
   If the original cost was C dollars, identify the expression which gives the new cost of that item.
   A. C + 0.25   B. 1/4 C   C. 25C   D. 1.25C

7. Given the formula PV = nRT, all of the following are true EXCEPT
   A. T = PV/nR   B. P = nRTN   C. V = P/nRT   D. n = PV/RT

8. If a Fahrenheit (F) temperature reading is 104, find its Celsius (C) equivalent, given that C = i(F-32).
   A. 36   B. 40   C. 72   D. 76

9. If 40% of a graduating class plans to go directly to work after graduation, which of the following must be TRUE?
   A. Less than half of the class plans to go directly to work.
   B. Forty members of the class plan to enter the job market.
   C. Most of the class plans to go directly to work.
   D. Six in ten members of the class are expected not to graduate.

10. Given a multiple-choice test item which has 5 choices, what is the probability of guessing the correct answer if you know nothing about the item content?
   A. 5%   B. 10%   C. 20%   D. 25%

11.
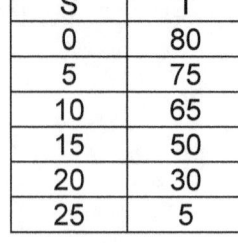

S	T
0	80
5	75
10	65
15	50
20	30
25	5

Which graph BEST represents the data shown in the above table?

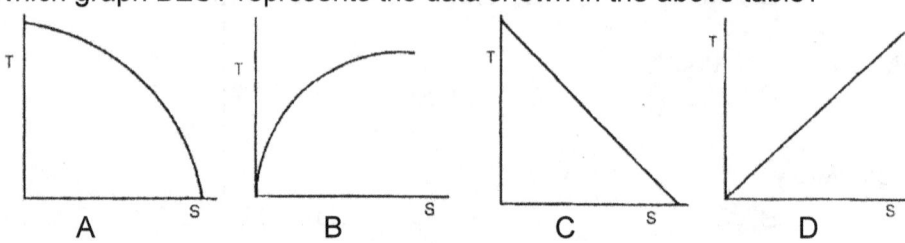

A   B   C   D

12. If 3(x+5y) = 24, find y when x = 3.
   A. 1   B. 3   C. 33/5   D. 7

13. The payroll of a grocery store for its 23 clerks is $395,421. Which expression below shows the average salary of a clerk?
   A. 395,421 × 23
   B. 23 ÷ 395,421
   C. (395,421 × 23
   D. 395,421 ÷ 23

14. If 12.8 pounds of coffee cost $50.80, what is the APPROXIMATE price per pound?
   A. $2.00   B. $3.00   C. $4.00   D. $5.00

15. A road map has a scale where 1 inch corresponds to 150 miles. A distance of 3 3/4 inches on the map corresponds to what actual distance? _____ miles.
   A. 153.75   B. 375   C. 525   D. 562.5

16. How many square feet of plywood are needed to construct the back and 4 adjacent sides of the box shown at the right?
   A. 63
   B. 90
   C. 96
   D. 126

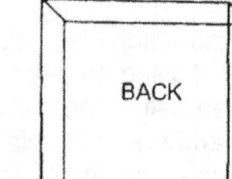

17. One thirty-pound bag of lawn fertilizer costs $20.00 and will cover 600 square feet of lawn. Terry's lawn is a 96 foot by 75 foot rectangle. How much will it cost Terry to buy enough bags of fertilizer for her lawn?
Which of the following do you NOT need in order to solve this problem? The
    A. product of 96 and 75
    B. fact that one bag weighs 30 pounds
    C. fact that one bag covers 600 square feet
    D. fact that one bag costs $20.00

17._____

18. On the graph shown at the right, between which hours was the drop in temperature GREATEST?
    A. 11:00 – Noon
    B. Noon – 1:00
    C. 1:00 – 2:00
    D. 2:00 – 3:00

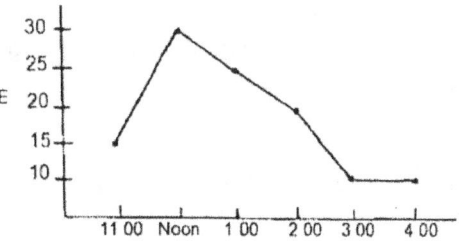

18._____

19. If on a typical railroad track the distance from the center of one railroad tie to the next is 30 inches, approximately how many ties would be needed for one mile of track?
    A. 180   B. 2,110   C. 6,340   D. 63,360

19._____

20. Which of the following is MOST likely to be the volume of a wine bottle?
    A. 750 milliliters   B. 7 kilograms
    C. 7 milligrams   D. 7 liters

20._____

21. What is the reading on the gauge shown at the right?
    A. -7
    B. -3
    C. 1
    D. 3

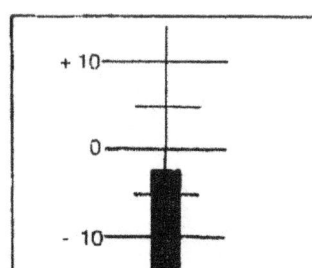

21._____

22. Which statement below disproves the assertion, *All students in Mrs. Marino's 10th grade geometry class are planning to go to college?*
    A. Albert is in Mrs. Marino's class, but he is not planning to take mathematics next year.
    B. Jorge is not in Mrs. Marino's class, but he is still planning to go to college.
    C. Pierre is in Mrs. Marino's class but says he will not be attending school anymore after this year.
    D. Crystal is in Mrs. Marino's class and plans to attend Yale University when she graduates.

22._____

23. A store advertisement reads, *Buy not while our prices are low. There will never be a better time to buy.*
    The customer reading this advertisement should assume that
    A. the prices at the store will probably never be lower
    B. right now, this store has the best prices in town
    C. prices are higher at other stores
    D. prices are always lowest at this store

24. *Given any positive integer, there is always a positive number B such that A × B is less than 1.*
    Which statement below supports this generalization?
    A. 8 × 1/16 = 1/2
    B. 8 × 1/2 = 4
    C. 5/2 × 1/10 = 1/4
    D. 1/2 × 1/2 = 1/2

25. Of the following expressions, which is equivalent to 4C + D = 12E?
    A. C = 4(12E-D)
    B. 4 + D = 12E − C
    C. 4C + 12E = -D
    D. $C = \frac{12E-D}{4}$

KEY (CORRECT ANSWERS)

1.	D		11.	A
2.	C		12.	A
3.	B		13.	D
4.	B		14.	C
5.	B		15.	D
6.	D		16.	C
7.	C		17.	B
8.	B		18.	D
9.	A		19.	B
10.	C		20.	A

21.	B
22.	C
23.	A
24.	A
25.	D

SOLUTIONS TO PROBLEMS

1. Converting to decimals, we get $.\overline{6}$, $.8$, $.714$ (approx..), $\overline{.45}$. The smallest is $\overline{.45}$ corresponding to 5/11.

2. 40% = 40/100 = 2/5

3. 10,000 ÷ 100 = 100

4. $\frac{6}{7} + \frac{11}{12}$ = (72+77) ÷ 84 = $\frac{149}{84}$ ≈ 1.77 ≈ 2

5. Let x = required minutes. Then, 12/1 ½ = x². This reduces to 1 1/2x = 24. Solving, x = 16.

6. New cost is C + .25C = 1.25C

7. For PV = nRT, V = nRT/P

8. C = 5/9 (104-32) = 5/9(72) = 40

9. Since 40% is less than 50% (or half), we conclude that less than half of the class plans to go to work directly after graduation.

10. The probability of guessing right is 1/5 or 20%

11. Curve A is most accurate since as S increases, we see that T decreases. Note, however, that the relationship is NOT linear. Although S increases in equal amounts, the decrease in T is NOT in equal amounts.

12. 3(3+5y) = 24. This simplifies to 9 + 15y = 24. Solving, y = 1

13. The average salary is $395,421 ÷ 23

14. The price per pound is $50.80 ÷ 12.8 = $3,96875 or approximately $4.

15. Actual distance is (3 3/4)(150) = 562.5 miles.

16. The area of the back = (6)(5) = 30 sq. ft. The combined area of the two vertical sides is (2)(6)(3) = 36 sq. ft. The combined area of the horizontal sides is (2)(5)(3) = 30 sq. ft. Total area = 30 + 36 30 = 96 square feet.

17. Choice B is not relevant to solving the problem since the cost will be [(96)(75)/600][$20] = $240. So, the weight per bag is not needed.

18. For the graph, the largest temperature drop was from 2:00 P.M. to 3:00 P.M. The temperature dropped 20 – 10 = 10 degrees.

19. 1 mile = 5280 feet = 63,360 inches. Then, 63,360 ÷ 30 = 2112 or about 2110 ties are needed.

20. Since 1 liter = 1.06 quarts, 750 milliliters = (750/1000)(1.06) = .795 quarts. This is a reasonable volume for a wine bottle.

21. The reading is -3.

22. Statement C contradicts the given information, since Pierre is in Mrs. Marino's class. Then he should plan to go to college.

23. Since there will never be a better time to buy at this particular store, the customer can assume the current prices will probably never be lower.

24. Statement A illustrates this concept. Note that in general, if n is a positive integer. then
$(n)(\frac{1}{n-1}) < 1$

25.

TEST 2

DIRECTIONS: Each question or incomplete statement is followed by several suggested answers or completions. Select the one that BEST answers the question or completes the statement. *PRINT THE LETTER OF THE CORRECT ANSWER IN THE SPACE AT THE RIGHT.*

1. Which of the following lists numbers in INCREASING order?
   A. 0.4, 0.04, 0.004
   B. 2.71, 3.15, 2.996
   C. 0.7, 0.77, 0.777
   D. 0.06, 0.5, 0.073

   1.____

2. $\frac{4}{10}+\frac{7}{100}+\frac{5}{1000} =$
   A. 4.75 B. 0.475 C. 0.0475 D. 0.00475

   2.____

3. 700 times what number equals 7?
   A. 10 B. 0.1 C. 0.01 D. 0.001

   3.____

4. 943-251 is approximately
   A. 600 B. 650 C. 700 D. 1200

   4.____

5. The time needed to set up a complicated piece of machinery is inversely proportional to the number of years' experience of the worker.
   If a worker with 10 years' experience needs 6 hours to do the job, how long will it take a worker with 15 years' experience?
   A. 4 B. 5 C. 9 D. 25

   5.____

6. Let W represent the number of waiters and D, the number of diners in a particular restaurant.
   Identify the expression which represents the statement: There are 10 times as many diners as waiters.
   A. 10W = D B. 10D = W C. 10D + 10W D. 10 = D + W

   6.____

7. Which of the following is equivalent to the formula F = XC + Y?
   A. F – C = X + Y
   B. Y = F + XC
   C. $C = \frac{FY}{X}$
   D. $C = \frac{FX}{Y}$

   7.____

8. Given the formula A = BC/D, if A = 12, B = 6, and D = 3, what is the value of C?
   A. 2/3 B. 6 C. 18 D. 24

   8.____

9. 5 is to 7 as X is to 35. X =
   A. 7 B. 12 C. 24 D. 49

   9.____

10. Kramer Middle School has 5 seventh grade mathematics teachers: two of the math teachers are women and three are men.
    If you are assigned a teacher at random, what is the probability of getting a female teacher?
    A. 0.2 B. 0.4 C. 0.6 D. 0.8

    10.____

11. Which statement BEST describes the graph shown at the right?
    Temperature
    A. and time decrease at the same rate
    B. and time increase at the same rate
    C. increases over time
    D. decreases over time

    11.____

12. If $3x + 4 = 22y$, find y when $x = 2$.
    A. 0   B. 3   C. 4 1/2   D. 5

    12.____

13. A car goes 243 miles on 8.7 gallons of gas.
    Which numeric expression should be used to determine the car's miles per gallon?
    A. 243×87 B. $8.7 \div 243$ C. $243 \div 8.7$ D. $243 - 8.7$

    13.____

14. What is the average cost per book if you buy six books at $4.00 each and four books at $5.00 each?
    A. $4.40   B. $4.50   C. $4.60   D. $5.40

    14.____

15. A publisher's sale offers a 15% discount to anyone buying more than 100 workbooks.
    What will be the discount on 200 workbooks selling at $2.25 each?
    A. $15.00   B. $30.00   C. $33.75   D. $67.50

    15.____

16. A road crew erects 125 meters of fencing in one workday.
    How many workdays are required to erect a kilometer of fencing?
    A. 0.8   B. 8   C. 80   D. 800

    16.____

17. Last month Kim made several telephone calls to New York City totaling 45 minutes in all.
    What does Kim need in order to calculate the average duration of her New York City calls?
    The
    A. total number of calls she made to New York City
    B. cost per minute of a call to New York City
    C. total cost of her telephone bill last month
    D. days of the week on which the calls are made

    17.____

18.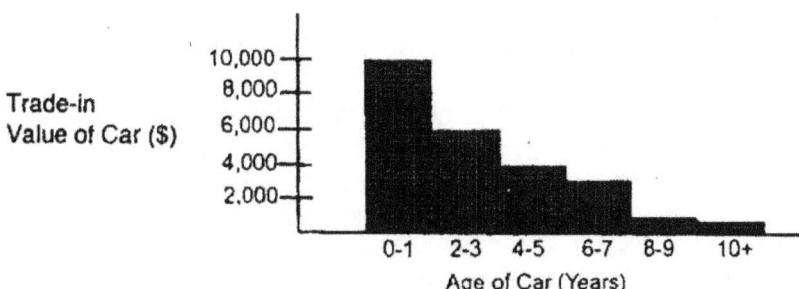

The above chart relates a car's age to its trade-in value.
Based on the chart, which of the following is TRUE?
   A. A 4- to 5-year old car has a trade-in value of about $2,000
   B. The trade-in vale of an 8- to 9-year old car is about 1/3 that of a 2- to 3-year old car.
   C. A 6- to 7-year old car has no trade-in value.
   D. A 4- to 5-year old car's trade-in value is about $2,000 less than that of a 2- to 3-year old car.

19. Which of the following expressions could be used to determine how many seconds are in a 24-hour day?
   A. 60 × 60 × 24
   B. 60 × 12 × 24
   C. 60 × 2 × 24
   D. 60 × 24

20. For measuring milk, we could use each of the following EXCEPT
   A. liters
   B. kilograms
   C. millimeters
   D. cubic centimeters

21. What is the reading on the gauge shown at the right?
   A. 51
   B. 60
   C. 62.5
   D. 70

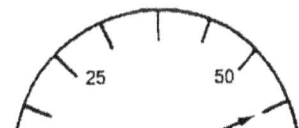

22. Bill is taller than Yvonne. Yvonne is shorter than Sue. Sue is 5' tall.
Which of the following conclusions must be TRUE?
   A. Bill is taller than Sue.
   B. Yvonne is taller than 5'4".
   C. Sue is taller than Bill.
   D. Yvonne is the shortest.

23. The Bass family traveled 268 miles during the first day of their vacation and another 300 miles on the next day. Maria Bass said they were 568 miles from home.
Which of the following facts did Maria assume?
   A. They traveled faster on the first day and slower on the second.
   B. If she plotted the vacation route on a map, it would be a straight line.
   C. Their car used more gasoline on the second day.
   D. They traveled faster on the second day than they did on the first day.

4 (#2)

24. The word LEFT in a mathematics problem indicate that it is a subtraction problem.
Which of the following mathematics problems prove this statement FALSE?
    A. I want to put 150 bottles into cartons which hold 8 bottles each. After I completely fill as many cartons as I can, how many bottles will be left?
    B. Sarah has 5 books but gave one to John. How many books did Sarah have left?
    C. Carlos had $4.25 but spent $3.75. How much did he have left?
    D. We had 38 models in stock but after yesterday's sale, only 12 are left. How many did we sell?

24.____

25. Let Q represent the number of miles Dave can jog in 15 minutes.
Identify the expression which represents the number of miles Dave can jog between 3:00 P.M. and 4:45 P.M.
    A. 1 3/4 Q   B. 7Q   C. 15 × 1 3/4xQ   D. Q/7

25.____

KEY (CORRECT ANSWERS)

1.	C		11.	D
2.	B		12.	D
3.	C		13.	C
4.	C		14.	A
5.	A		15.	D
6.	A		16.	B
7.	C		17.	A
8.	B		18.	D
9.	C		19.	A
10.	B		20.	C

21. C
22. D
23. B
24. A
25. B

SOLUTIONS TO PROBLEMS

1. Choice C is in ascending order since $.y < .77 < .777$

2. Rewrite in decimal form: $.4 + .07 + .005 = .475$

3. Let x = missing number. Then, $700x = 7$. Solving, $x = 7/700 = .01$

4. $943 - 251 = 692 \approx 700$

5. Let x = hours needed. Then, $10/15 = x/6$. Solving, $x = 4$

6. The number of diners (D) is 10 times as many waiters (10W). So, $D = 10W$, or $10W = D$

7. Given $F = XC + Y$, subtract Y from each side to get $F - Y = XC$. Finally, dividing by X, we get $(F-Y)/X = C$

8. $12 = 6C/3$. Then, $12 = 2C$, so $C = 6$

9. $5/7 = x/35$. Then, $7x = 175$, so $x = 25$

10. Probability of a female teacher = $2/5 = .4$

11. Statement D is best, since as time increases, the temperature decreases.

12. $(3)(2) + 4 = 2y$. Then, $10 = 2y$, so $y = 5$.

13. Miles per gallon = $243/8.7$

14. Total purchase is $(6)(\$4) + (4)(\$5) = \$44$. The average cost per book is $\$44 \div 10 = \$4.40$

15. $(220)(\$2.25) = \$450$. The discount is $(.15)(\$450) = \$67.50$

16. The number of workdays is $1000 \div 125 = 8$

17. Choice A is correct because the average duration of the phone calls = total time ÷ total number of calls.

18. Statement D is correct since a 4-5 year old car's value is $4,000, whereas a 2-3 year-old car's value is $6000.

19. 60 seconds = 1 minute and 60 minutes = 1 hour. Thus, 24 hours = $(24)(60)(60)$ or $(60)(60)(24)$ seconds.

20. We can't use millimeters in measuring milk since millimeters is a linear measurement.

21. The reading shows the average of 50 and 75 = 62.5

6 (#2)

22. Since Yvonne is shorter than both Bill and Sue, Yvonne is the shortest.

23. Statement B is assumed correct since 568 = 269 + 300 could only be true if the mileage traveled represents a straight line.

24. To find the number of bottles left, we look only for the remainder when 150 is divided b 8 (which happens to be 6).

25. 3:00 P.M. to 4:45 P.M. = 1 hour and 45 minutes = 105 minutes
Let Q = 15 minutes
105 / 15 = 7
7(15) = 105 = 7Q

ARITHMETICAL REASONING

EXAMINATION SECTION
TEST 1

DIRECTIONS: Each question or incomplete statement is followed by several suggested answers or completions. Select the one that BEST answers the question or completes the statement. *PRINT THE LETTER OF THE CORRECT ANSWER IN THE SPACE AT THE RIGHT.*

1. A canvas tarpaulin measures 6 feet by 9 feet.
   The LARGEST circular area that can be covered completely by this tarpaulin is a circle with a diameter of _____ feet.

   A. 9   B. 8   C. 7   D. 6

   1.____

2. The population of Maple Grove was 1,000 in 2006. In 2007, the population increased 40 percent, but in 2008, 2009, and 2010, the population decreased 20 percent, 10 percent, and 25 percent, respectively. (For each year, the percentage change in population is based upon a comparison with the preceding year.)
   At the end of this period, the population was MOST NEARLY

   A. 900   B. 850   C. 800   D. 750

   2.____

3. The ratio of boys to girls in one school is 6 to 4. A second school contains half as many boys and twice as many girls as the first.
   The one of the following statements that is MOST accurate is that

   A. both schools have the same number of pupils
   B. the first school has 10 percent more pupils than the second
   C. the second school has 10 percent more pupils than the first
   D. there is not sufficient information to reach any conclusion about which school has more pupils

   3.____

4. In a certain city, X number of cases of malaria have occurred over a 10-year period, resulting in Y number of deaths.
   The AVERAGE annual death rate from malaria in this city is

   A. Y/10   B. 10/X   C. 10·X/Y   D. $\dfrac{Y(10X)}{X+Y}$

   4.____

5. A firemen's softball team wins 6 games out of the first 9 played. They go on to win all their remaining games and finish the season with a final average of games won of .750.
   The TOTAL number of games they played that season was

   A. 10   B. 12   C. 15   D. 18

   5.____

6. While inspecting a cylindrical gravity tank for an automatic sprinkler system, a chief observes that the water in the tank is 10 feet deep and that the tank has a diameter of 9 feet. He asks the building manager how many gallons are in the tank and receives the reply, *About 10,000.* (Cubic foot of water contains 7 1/2 gallons.) Based on his own observation and calculations, the chief should

   6.____

123

A. agree that the manager's answer is probably correct
B. disagree with the manager's answer; the answer is more nearly 20,000 gallons
C. disagree with the manager's answer; the answer is more nearly 15,000 gallons
D. disagree with the manager's answer; the answer is more nearly 5,000 gallons

7. The diagram at the right represents the storage space of a fire engine. The amount of space available for the storage of hose in the fire engine is MOST NEARLY _____ cubic feet.
   A. 40
   B. 75
   C. 540
   D. 600

8. If a piece of rope 100 feet long is cut so that one piece is 2/3 as long as the other piece, the length of the longer piece must be _____ feet.

   A. 60
   B. 66 2/3
   C. 70
   D. 75

9. A water tank has a discharge valve which is capable of emptying the tank when full in two hours. It also has an inlet valve which can fill the tank, when empty, in four hours and a second inlet valve which can fill the tank, when empty, in six hours.
   If the tank is full and all three valves are opened fully, with water flowing through each valve to capacity, the tank will be emptied in _____ hours.

   A. 2
   B. 6
   C. 12
   D. a period of time which cannot be determined from the information given

10. Final grades in a history course are determined as follows:
    Class recitations - weight 50
    Weekly quizzes - weight 25
    Final examination - weight 25
    A student has an average of 60 on a class recitation and 80 on weekly quizzes.
    In order to receive a final grade of 75, he must obtain on his final examination a grade of

    A. 75
    B. 80
    C. 90
    D. 100

11. Suppose that 8 inches of snow contribute as much water to the reservoir system as one inch of rain.
    If, during a snowstorm, an average of 12 inches of snow fell during a six-hour period, with drifts as high as three feet, the addition to the water supply as a result of this snowfall ultimately will be the equivalent of _____ inches of rain.

    A. 1 1/2
    B. 3
    C. 4 1/2
    D. an amount of rain which cannot be determined from the information given

12. A fire engine carries 900 feet of 2 1/2" hose, 500 feet of 2" hose, and 350 feet of 1 1/2" hose.
    Of the total hose carried, the percentage of 1 1/2" hose is MOST NEARLY

    A. 35 B. 30 C. 25 D. 20

13. An engine company made 96 runs in the month of April, which was a decrease of 20% from the number of runs made in March.
    The number of runs made in March was MOST NEARLY

    A. 136 B. 128 C. 120 D. 110

14. A water tank has a capacity of 6,000 gallons. Connected to the tank is a pump capable of supplying water at the rate of 25 gallons per minute, which goes into operation automatically when the water in the tank falls to the one-half mark.
    If we start with a full tank and drain the water from the tank at the rate of 50 gallons a minute, the tank can continue supplying water at the required rate for_____ hours.

    A. 2 1/2 B. 3 C. 3 1/2 D. 4

15. Three firemen are assigned the task of cleaning fire apparatus which usually takes three men five hours to complete. After they have been working three hours, three additional firemen are assigned to help them. Assuming that they all work at the normal rate, the assignment of the additional men will reduce the time required to complete the task by _____ minutes.

    A. 20 B. 30 C. 50 D. 60

16. Assume that at the beginning of the calendar year, an employee was earning $48,000 per year. On July 1st, he received an increase of $2,400 per year. On November 1st, he was promoted to a position paying $60,000 per year. The total earnings for the year were MOST NEARLY

    A. $51,000 B. $49,000 C. $50,000 D. $53,000

17. Engine A leaves its firehouse at 1:48 P.M. and travels 3 miles to a fire at an average speed of 30 miles per hour. Engine B leaves its firehouse at 1:51 P.M. and travels 6 miles to the same fire at an average speed of 40 miles per hour.
    From the above facts, we may conclude that Engine A arrives _____ minutes _____ Engine B.

    A. 3; before B. 6; before
    C. 3; after   D. 6; after

18. A widely used formula for calculating the quantity of water discharged from a hose is $GPM = 29.7d^2/P$, where GPM = gallons per minute, d = diameter of the nozzle in inches, and P = pressure at the nozzle in pounds per square inch.
    If it takes 1 minute to extinguish a fire using a 1 1/2" nozzle at 100 pounds pressure per square inch, the number of gallons discharged is, according to the above formula, MOST NEARLY

    A. 730 B. 650 C. 690 D. 670

19. The spring of a spring balance will stretch in proportion to the amount of weight placed on the balance.
    If a 2-pound weight placed on a certain balance stretches the spring 1/4", then a stretch in the spring of 1 3/4" will be caused by a weight of _____ lbs.

    A. 10   B. 12   C. 14   D. 16

20. In a yard 100 feet by 60 feet, a dog is tied by a leash to a stake driven into the ground in the center of the yard.
    If the dog is to be kept from going off the property, the MAXIMUM acceptable length of the leash is _____ feet.

    A. 60   B. 50   C. 30   D. 28

21. From a length of pipe 10 feet long, a 3 1/3 foot piece is to be cut.
    If the diameter of the 10-foot length is 5 inches, the diameter of the piece to be cut will be

    A. 5"   B. 2 1/3"   C. 2"   D. 1 2/3"

22. A certain crew consists of one foreman who is paid $15.00 per hour, 2 carpenters who are paid $12.60 per hour, 4 helpers who are paid $10.50 per hour, and 10 laborers who are paid $7.50 per hour.
    The average hourly earnings of the members of the crew is MOST NEARLY

    A. $11.40   B. $10.50   C. $10.05   D. $9.30

23. The fraction which is equivalent to the sum of .125, .25, .375, and .0625 is

    A. 5/8   B. 13/16   C. 7/8   D. 15/16

24. If the pay period of an employee is changed from every two weeks to twice a month, his gross pay (before deductions) from each pay period will

    A. increase by one-tenth
    B. increase by one-twelfth
    C. decrease by one-thirteenth
    D. decrease by one-fifteenth

25. In a certain state, the automobile license tags consist of two letters followed by three digits, e.g., AA-122. The MAXIMUM number of different combinations of numbers and letters which can be obtained under this system is MOST NEARLY

    A. 13,500   B. 75,000   C. 325,000   D. 675,000

KEY (CORRECT ANSWERS)

1.	D	11.	A
2.	D	12.	D
3.	C	13.	C
4.	A	14.	B
5.	B	15.	D
6.	D	16.	A
7.	C	17.	B
8.	A	18.	D
9.	C	19.	C
10.	D	20.	C

21. A
22. D
23. B
24. B
25. D

SOLUTIONS TO PROBLEMS

1. The largest circular area completely covered by the tarpaulin would have a diameter of the lesser of 6 ft. and 9 ft.

2. At the end of 2010, the population was $(1000)(1.40)(.80)(.90)(.75) = 756 \approx 750$.

3. Let 6x and 4x represent the number of boys and girls, respectively, at the first school. Then, 3x and 8x will represent the number of boys and girls, respectively, at the second school. The enrollment of the second school, 11x, is 10% higher than the enrollment at the first school, 10x.

4. Since Y deaths have occurred over a 10-year period due to malaria, the annual death rate caused by malaria is Y/10. X, the number of cases of malaria, has no effect on the annual death rate.

5. Let x = number of games played, after the first 9 games. Then, $(6+x)/(9+x) = .750$. Solving, x = 3. The total number of games played = 9 + 3 = 12.

6. Volume = $(\pi)(4.5)^2(10) \approx 636$ cu.ft. Then, $(636)(7\ 1/2) = 4770 \approx 5000$

7. 15x8x3 = 360; 15x6x2 = 180; 360 + 180 = 540 cu.ft.

8. Let 2x and 3x represent the two pieces. Then, 2x + 3x = 100. Solving, x = 20. The longer piece = (3)(20) = 60 ft.

9. Let x = number of hours required. Then, $\frac{x}{2} - \frac{x}{4} - \frac{x}{6} = 1$ Simplifying, x/12 = 1. Thus, x = 12

10. Let x = final exam grade. Then, $(60)(.50) + (80)(.25) + (x)(.25) = 75$. Simplifying, 50 + ,25x = 75. Solving, x = 100

11. If 8 in. of snow contribute 1 in. of rain, then 12 in. of snow contribute (1)(12/8) = 1 1/2 in. of rain.

12. $350 \div (900+500+350) = .20 = 20\%$

13. The number of runs in March was $96 \div .80 = 120$

14. The time required to extract 3000 gallons at 50 gallons per minute = $3000 \div 50 = 60$ min. = 1 hour. At this point, the tank is half full. Also, a pump begins replenishing the tank at 25 gallons per minute. Thus, the effect on draining has been slowed to 50 - 25 = 25 gallons per minute. To drain the remaining 3000 gallons will require $3000 \div 25 = 120$ minutes = 2 hours. Total draining time = 3 hours.

15. (3)(5) = 15 man-hours. After 3 hours, 9 man-hours have been used. At this point, 6 men are working, and since only 6 man-hours remaining, the time needed is 1 hour = 60 minutes.

16. ($48,000)(1/2) + ($50,400)(1/3) + ($60,000)(1/6) = $50,800 ≈ $51,000

17. Engine A requires (3)(60/30) = 6 minutes to get to the fire.
So, Engine A arrives at 1:54 PM. Engine B requires (6)(60/40) = 9 minutes to get to the fire. So, Engine B arrives at 2:00 PM. Thus, Engine A arrives 6 minutes before Engine B.

18. GPM = $(29.7)(1.5)^2(\sqrt{100})$ = 668.25 ≈ 670

19. Let x = required number of pounds. Then, 2/x = 1/4/1 3/4.
So, 1/4x = 3 1/2. Solving, x = 14

20. The shorter of the two dimensions is 60 ft. If the dog is in the center of the yard, the maximum length allowed for the leash is 60/2 = 30 ft.

21. The diameter of the cut piece = diameter of entire pipe = 5"

22. [($15.00)(1)+($12.60)(2)+($10.50)(4)+($7.50)(10)]/17 = $157.20/17 9.25 (closest answer in answer key is $9.30).

23. .125 + .25 + .375 + .0625 = .8125 = 13/16

24. Let x = annual pay. Then, x/26 = pay every two weeks, whereas pay every half month. His increase is $\frac{x}{24} - \frac{x}{26} = \frac{x}{312}$, which represents a fractional increase of $\frac{x}{312} / \frac{x}{26} = \frac{1}{12}$

25. The number of different license tags = (26)(26)(10)(10)(10) = 676,000 (closest answer in answer key is 675,000).

TEST 2

DIRECTIONS: Each question or incomplete statement is followed by several suggested answers or completions. Select the one that BEST answers the question or completes the statement. *PRINT THE LETTER OF THE CORRECT ANSWER IN THE SPACE AT THE RIGHT.*

1. If cast iron weighs 450 pounds per cubic foot, the weight of a solid cast iron manhole cover 2 feet in diameter and 1 inch thick is MOST NEARLY _____ pounds. 1._____

   A. 94   B. 118   C. 136   D. 164

2. The sum of 2 5/8, 3 3/16, 1 1/2, and 4 1/4 is 2._____

   A. 9 13/16   B. 10 7/16   C. 11 9/16   D. 13 3/16

3. A pump is able to fill a tank holding 15,000 gallons in 2 hours and 30 minutes. Pumping at the same rate, an empty 60,000 gallon tank can be filled in 3._____

   A. 10 hours   B. 10 hours, 30 minutes
   C. 11 hours   D. 11 hours, 30 minutes

4. Assume you want to add 10,000 gallons of water to a tank. If you pump water into the tank at the rate of 100 gallons per minute for one hour and 50 gallons per minute after the first hour, the total time required to add the 10,000 gallons is MOST NEARLY 4._____

   A. 1 hour, 20 minutes   B. 2 hours
   C. 2 hours, 20 minutes   D. 3 hours

5. A tank 25 feet long, 15 feet wide, and 10 feet deep is enlarged by extending the length another 25 feet. 5._____
   The enlarged tank will be able to hold _____ more than the original tank.

   A. 50%   B. 100%   C. 150%   D. 200%

6. If cast iron weighs 450 pounds per cubic foot, the weight of a solid cast iron manhole cover 4 feet in diameter and 1 inch thick is MOST NEARLY _____ pounds. 6._____

   A. 188   B. 236   C. 328   D. 471

7. If four men work seven hours during the day, the number of man-hours of work done is 7._____

   A. 4   B. 7   C. 11   D. 28

8. If it takes four men fourteen days to do a certain job, seven men working at the same rate should be able to do the same job in _____ days. 8._____

   A. 8   B. 7   C. 6   D. 5

9. A truck leaves the garage at 9:26 A.M. and returns the same day at 3:43 P.M. The period of time that the truck was away from the garage is MOST NEARLY _____ hours, _____ minutes. 9._____

   A. 5; 17   B. 5; 43   C. 6; 17   D. 6; 26

10. Assume that it takes 6 men 8 days to do a certain job. Working at the same speed, the number of days that it will take 4 men to do this job is

    A. 9 B. 10 C. 12 D. 14

11. The sum of 3 5/8 + 4 1/4 + 6 1/2 + 7 1/8 is

    A. 20 7/8 B. 21 1/4 C. 21 1/2 D. 22 1/8

12. The fraction which is equal to .0625 is

    A. 1/64 B. 3/64 C. 1/16 D. 5/8

13. The volume, in cubic feet, of a rectangular coal bin 8 feet long by 5 feet wide by 7 feet high is MOST NEARLY

    A. 40 B. 56 C. 186 D. 280

14. Assume that a car travels at a constant speed of 36 miles per hour.
    The speed of this car, in feet per second, is MOST NEARLY (one mile equals 5,280 ft.)

    A. 3 B. 24.6 C. 52.8 D. 879.8

15. If one-third of a 19-foot length of lumber is cut off, the length of the remaining piece will measure APPROXIMATELY

    A. 8'8" B. 9'8" C. 12'8" D. 13'8"

16. The circumference of a circle having a diameter of 10" is MOST NEARLY _____ inches.

    A. 3.14 B. 18.72 C. 24.96 D. 31.4

17. Assume that in the purchase of paint, the seller quotes a discount of 10%.
    If the price per gallon is $19.05, the actual payment, in dollars per gallon, is MOST NEARLY

    A. $17.15 B. $17.85 C. $18.75 D. $19.50

18. Assume that a cubic foot of water contains 7 1/2 gallons. The number of gallons of water which could be contained in a rectangular tank 3 feet long, 2 feet wide, and 2 feet deep is MOST NEARLY

    A. 12 B. 45 C. 90 D. 120

19. The volume, in cubic feet, of a slab of concrete that is 5'0" wide, 6'0" long, and 0'6" in depth is MOST NEARLY

    A. 15.0 B. 13.5 C. 12.0 D. 10.5

20. The sum of the following pipe lengths, 22 1/8", 7 3/4", 19 7/16", and 43 5/8", is

    A. 91 7/8" B. 92 1/16" C. 92 1/2" D. 92 15/16"

21. The area, in square feet, of a plant floor that is 42 feet wide and 75 feet long is

    A. 3,150 B. 3,100 C. 3.075 D. 2,760

22. The sum of the following dimensions, 1 5/8, 2 1/4, 4 1/16, and 3 3/16, is

    A. 10 15/16 B. 11 C. 11 1/8 D. 11 1/4

23. Assume that six men, working together at the same rate of speed, can complete a certain job in 3 hours.
If, however, there were only four men available to do this job, and they all worked at the same rate of speed, to complete this job would take MOST NEARLY _____ hours.

   A. 4 1/4   B. 4 1/2   C. 4 3/4   D. 5

24. Due to unforeseen difficulties, a job which would normally take 17 hours to complete was actually completed in 21 hours.
This represents a percent increase over the normal time of MOST NEARLY

   A. 19%   B. 2.4%   C. 24%   D. 124%

25. Truck A costs $30,000 and gets 12 mpg and truck B costs $35,000 and gets 15 mpg. After 1 year driving 12,000 miles, how much would be saved by purchasing truck A if gasoline costs $1.50 per gallon?

   A. $1,000   B. $3,000   C. $4,700   D. $6,000

KEY (CORRECT ANSWERS)

1. B
2. C
3. A
4. C
5. B
6. D
7. D
8. A
9. C
10. C

11. C
12. C
13. D
14. C
15. C
16. D
17. A
18. C
19. A
20. D

21. A
22. C
23. B
24. C
25. C

4 (#2)

SOLUTIONS TO PROBLEMS

1. $(450)(\pi)(1)^2(1/12) \approx 118$ pounds. (Note: $V = \pi R^2 H$)

2. 2 5/8 + 3 3/16 + 1 1/2 + 4 1/4 = 10 25/16 = 11 9/16

3. To fill a 60,000 gallon tank would require (4)(2 1/2 hrs.) = 10 hrs.

4. After 1 hour, (100)(60) = 6000 gallons have been added. To add the remaining 4000 gallons will require 4000 ÷ 50 = 80 minutes = 1 hour 20 minutes. Thus, total time needed is 2 hrs. 20 min.

5. The original volume = (25)(15)(10) = 3750 cu.ft., and the new volume = (50)(15)(10) = 7500 cu.ft. The increased volume of 3750 represents an increase of (3750/3750)(100) = 100%.

6. $(450)(\pi)(2)^2(1/12) \approx 471$ pounds

7. (4)(7) = 28 man-hours

8. (4)(14) = 56 man-days. Then, 56 ÷ 7 = 8 days

9. From 9:26 A.M. to 3:43 P.M. = 6 hrs. 17 min.

10. (6)(8) = 48 man-days. Then, 48 ÷ 4 = 12 days

11. 3 5/8 + 4 1/4 + 6 1/2 + 7 1/8 = 20 12/8 = 21 1/2

12. .0625 = 625/10,000 = 1/16

13. (8)(5)(7) = 280 cu.ft.

14. (36)(5280) = 190,080 ft. per hour. Since there are 3600 seconds in 1 hour, the speed = 190,080 ÷ 3600 = 52.8 ft. per second.

15. 19' - 1/3(19') = 12 2/3, = 12'8"

16. Circumference = $(\pi)(10")$ 31.4"

17. ($19.05)(.90) ≈ $17.15

18. (7 1/2)(3)(2)(2) = 90 gallons

19. (5)(6)(1/2) = 15 cu.ft.

20. 22 1/8" + 7 3/4" + 19 7/16" + 43 5/8" = 9l 31/16" = 92 15/16"

21. Area = (42)(75) = 3150 sq.ft.

22. 1 5/8 + 2 1/4 + 4 1/16 + 3 3/16 = 10 18/16 = 11 1/8

23. (6) (3) = 18 man-hours. Then, 18 / 4 = 4 1/2 hours

24. 21 - 17 = 4. Then, 4/17 ≈ 24%

25. For Truck A, the expenses are $30,000 + (1000)($1.50) = $31,500 For Truck B, the expenses are $35,000 + (800)($1.50) = $36,200. $36,200 - $31,500 = $4,700

TEST 3

DIRECTIONS: Each question or incomplete statement is followed by several suggested answers or completions. Select the one that BEST answers the question or completes the statement. *PRINT THE LETTER OF THE CORRECT ANSWER IN THE SPACE AT THE RIGHT.*

1. Assume that a light maintainer and his helper replaced 25 lamps on one round of their assigned territory.
   If it took two hours to complete this round, and the maintainer's pay rate was $9.60 per hour and the helper's rate was $8.40 per hour, the labor cost of replacing each burned out lamp averaged _____ cents.

   A. 18   B. 36   C. 72   D. 144

   1._____

2. A certain power distribution job will require two main-tainers at $16.00 per hour and two helpers at $13.20 per hour. The job will take three 8-hour days to complete and will require 6 hours of planning and supervision by a foreman at $19.60 per hour.
   The TOTAL labor cost for this job is

   A. $264.80   B. $501.60   C. $818.40   D. $1,519.20

   2._____

3. Two identical containers are partly filled with bolts and weigh 40 lbs. and 75 lbs., respectively. To save storage space, all the bolts are put in one of the containers. The two containers now weigh 5 lbs. and 110 lbs., respectively.
   If three bolts weigh 1/2 lb., the TOTAL number of bolts is

   A. 210   B. 450   C. 630   D. 660

   3._____

4. The sum of the following dimensions, 2'7 1/2", 1'8 1/2", 2'1 1/16", and 3/4", is

   A. 5'15 9/16"   B. 5'15 11/16"
   C. 5'7/16"   D. 6'4 9/16"

   4._____

5. If a 3-foot length of contact rail weighs 150 pounds, then 39 feet of contact rail weighs _____ pounds.

   A. 1,850   B. 1,900   C. 1,950   D. 2,000

   5._____

6. The sum of the following dimensions, 3'2 1/2", 8 7/8", 2'6 3/8", 2'9 3/4", and 1'0", is

   A. 9'3 1/4"   B. 10'3 1/4"   C. 10'7 1/4"   D. 16'7 1/4"

   6._____

7. If a drawing for a contact rail installation is made to a scale of 1 1/2" to the foot, the drawing is said to be one _____ size.

   A. sixteenth   B. eight   C. quarter   D. half

   7._____

8. If a drawing has a scale of 1/4" = 1', a dimension of 1 3/4" on the drawing would be equal to

   A. 4'   B. 5'   C. 6'   D. 7'

   8._____

9. A reel weighs 600 lbs. when fully loaded with cable and 200 lbs. when empty.
   If the cable weighs 2.5 lbs. per foot, the number of reels a foreman should order for a job requiring 700 feet of this cable is _____ reels.

   A. 2   B. 3   C. 4   D. 5

   9._____

10. If the scale on a working drawing is shown as 1/4" = 1', a scaled measurement of 4 1/2 inches represents an actual length of _____ feet.

    A. 8   B. 9   C. 16   D. 18

11. A gap on the third rail starts at a subway column marked 217+79. The gap extends 68 feet to another column marked 217+11.
    A column midway between these columns would be marked 217+_____

    A. 34   B. 39   C. 45   D. 68

12. Assume a foreman decided that 100 contact rail ties need replacing. Each tie measures 9' x 6" x 8".
    In providing room for storing these ties at the job site, the MINIMUM storage volume required is APPROXIMATELY _____ cubic feet.

    A. 300   B. 360   C. 432   D. 576

13. Assume a certain job was done a year ago and took 8 men a total of 5 days to complete. The records show that each day involved 5 hours of overtime for half the men. Your assistant supervisor now assigns you the identical job to be done using 6 men and no overtime.
    The MINIMUM number of regular work days that should be scheduled for this job is _____ days.

    A. 13   B. 11   C. 9   D. 6

14. The sum of the following dimensions, 12'11 3/16", 9'8 5/8", 7'3 3/4", 5'2 1/2", and 3'1 1/4", is

    A. 39'5 9/16"   B. 38'3 5/16"
    C. 36'2 3/8"   D. 35'1 7/8"

15. If the scale on a drawing is 1/4" to the foot, then a 5/8" measurement would represent an actual length of

    A. 5'4"   B. 4'8"   C. 2'6"   D. 1'3"

16. The sum of 1 9/16", 3 1/2", 7 3/8", 10 3/4", and 12 5/8" is

    A. 33 11/16"   B. 34 13/16"   C. 35 11/16"   D. 35 13/16"

17. A reel containing an unknown length of cable weighs 340 pounds.
    If the empty reel weighs 119 lbs. and the cable weighs 0.85 lb. per foot, the number of feet of cable on the reel is

    A. 140   B. 260   C. 400   D. 540

18. If the scale on a shop drawing is 1/4" to the foot, then a part which measures 3 3/8 inches long on the drawing has an actual length of_____ feet _____ inches.

    A. 12; 6   B. 13; 6   C. 13; 9   D. 14; 9

19. Taking into account time and one-half payment for time over 40 hours of work, the gross pay of an employee who works 43 hours in a week at a rate of pay of $5.34 per hour is

    A. $213.60   B. $229.62   C. $237.63   D. $245.64

20. The sum of 0.365 + 3.941 + 10.676 + 0.784 is   20.____

    A. 13.766   B. 15.666   C. 15.756   D. 15.766

21. An air conditioning unit is rated at 1000 watts. The unit is run for 10 hours per day, five   21.____
    days per week. If the cost for electrical energy is 50 cents per kilowatt-hour, the weekly
    cost for electricity should be

    A. $2.50   B. $5.00   C. $25.00   D. $250.00

22. Assume that the cost of a certain wiring installation is broken down as follows: Materials   22.____
    $1,200, Labor $800, and Rental of equipment $400.
    The percentage of the total cost of the job that can be charged to Labor is MOST
    NEARLY

    A. 12.3   B. 33.3   C. 40.0   D. 66.6

23. Assume that it takes 4 electrician's helpers 6 days to do a certain job.   23.____
    Working at the same rate of speed, the number of days it will take 3 electrician's help-
    ers to do the same job is

    A. 6   B. 7   C. 8   D. 9

24. Assume that a 120-volt, 25-cycle magnetic coil is to be rewound to operate properly on   24.____
    60-cycles at the same voltage.
    If the coil at 25-cycles has 1,000 turns, at 60-cycles the number of turns should be
    MOST NEARLY

    A. 2,400   B. 1,200   C. 416   D. 208

25. A light maintainer whose rate is $14.40 per hour is assigned to replace burned-out sta-   25.____
    tion and tunnel lamps. During 4 hours, he replaces 28 lamps.
    The average labor cost for replacing each of these burned-out lamps was NEAREST
    to

    A. 56¢   B. $1.04   C. $2.00   D. $3.60

KEY (CORRECT ANSWERS)

1. D
2. D
3. C
4. D
5. C

6. B
7. B
8. D
9. D
10. D

11. C
12. A
13. C
14. B
15. C

16. D
17. B
18. B
19. C
20. D

21. C
22. B
23. C
24. C
25. C

SOLUTIONS TO PROBLEMS

1. (2)($9.60+$8.40) = $36.00. Then, $36.00 ÷ 25 = $1.44 or 144 cents.

2. (2)($16.00)(24) + (2)($13.20)(24) + (6)($19.60) = $1519.20

3. An empty container weighs 5 lbs., so the container which contains bolts and weighs 110 lbs. actually has 105 lbs. of bolts. Since 3 bolts weigh 1/2 lb., 105 lbs. would contain (105/1/2)(3) = 630 bolts.

4. 2'7 1/4" + 1'8 1/2" + 2'1/16" + 3/4" = 5'15 25/16" = 6 '4 9/16"

5. 39 feet of rail weighs (13)(150) = 1950 pounds

6. 3'2 1/4" + 8 7/8" + 2'6 3/8" + 2'9 3/4" + 1'0" = 8'25 18/8" = 10'3 1/4"

7. 1 1/2"/1" = 3/2.1/12=1/8

8. I 3/4" ÷ 1/4" = 7 Then, (7)(1') = 7'

9. 600 - 200 = 400. Then, 400 ÷ 2.5 = 160 ft. of cable per reel. Since 700 ft. of cable is needed, 700/160 = 4.375, which means 5 reels will be required (must round up).

10. 4 1/2" ÷ 1/4" = 9/2 4/1 = 18 Then, (18)(1') = 18'

11. Half of 68 = 34; 11 + 34 = 45; 79 - 34 = 45

12. (100)(9')(1/2')(2/3') = 300 cu.ft.

13. Number of man-days = (4)(5) + (4)(5)(1 5/8) =52.5
    For 6 men working only 8-hour days, 52.5 ÷ 6 = 8.75 = 9 days needed.

14. 12'11 3/16" + 9'8 5/8" + 7'3 3/4" + 5'2 1/2" + 3'1 1/4" = 36'25 37/16" = 38'3 5/16"

15. 5/8" ÷ 1/4" = 5/8 . 4/1 = 2 1/2. Then, (2 1/2)(1') = 2'6"

16. 1 9/16" + 3 1/2" + 7 3/8" + 10 3/4" + 12 5/8" = 33 45/16" = 35 13/36"

17. 340 - 119 = 221 lbs. Then, 221 ÷ .85 = 260 ft.

18. 3 3/8" ÷ 1/4" = 27/8 . 4/1 = 13/ 1/2. Then, (13 1/2) (1') = 13 ft. 6 in.

19. (40)($5.34) + (3)($5.34)(1.5) = $237.63

20. 0.365 +3.941 + 10.676 + 0.784 = 15.766

21. (1000)(10)(5) = 50,000 watt-hours = 50 kilowatt-hours. Then, (50)($.50) = $25.00

22. $800 / ($1200+$800+$400) =1/3 ≈ 33.3%

23. (4)(6) = 24. Then, 24/ 3 = 8 days

24. Let x = number of required turns. Since the number of cycles varies inversely as the number of turns, 25/60 = x/1000.
    Solving, x 416 (actually 416 2/3)

25. ($14.40)(4) = $57.60. Then, $57.60 ÷ 28 ≈ $2.06

EXAMINATION SECTION
TEST 1

DIRECTIONS: Each question or incomplete statement is followed by several suggested answers or completions. Select the one that BEST answers the question or completes the statement. *PRINT THE LETTER OF THE CORRECT ANSWER IN THE SPACE AT THE RIGHT.*

Questions 1-9.

DIRECTIONS: Questions 1 through 9 each consists of a series of numbers which follow in sequence according to a certain rule. Determine the rule and use it to select the next number from among the four choices given on the right side of each row.

SAMPLE X:

						(A)	(B)	(C)	(D)
3	6	9	12	15	18	19	20	21	22

In Sample X above, the rule is to add 3 to each successive number in the series in order to get the next number. Therefore, since 18 plus 3 is 21, the CORRECT choice is C.

SAMPLE Y:

						(A)	(B)	(C)	(D)
4	6	9	13	18	24	27	28	29	31

In Sample Y above, the rule is to add 2, then add 3, then add 4, etc., to each successive number in the series to get the next number. Therefore, the CORRECT choice is D.

1. 3 9 4 12 7 21
   - A. 25
   - B. 18
   - C. 16
   - D. 8

2. 5 3 6 3 9 5
   - A. 20
   - B. 18
   - C. 10
   - D. 3

3. 10 8 12 4 20 -12
   - A. 52
   - B. 48
   - C. 0
   - D. -26

4. 3 10 9 15 13 18
   - A. 12
   - B. 15
   - C. 20
   - D. 36

5. 1   1   3   9   13   65
   A. 15
   B. 26
   C. 71
   D. 102

6. 2   6   5   15   13   39
   A. 4
   B. 18
   C. 36
   D. 39

7. 48   8   40   10   30   15
   A. 15
   B. 20
   C. 25
   D. 42

8. 20   5   30   10   50   25
   A. 110
   B. 100
   C. 75
   D. 40

9. 4   24   12   60   20   80
   A. 40
   B. 36
   C. 20
   D. 8

10. Below is a series of numbers. In this series, the numbers follow some definite order. Look at the numbers in the series and determine what the order is; then, from the suggested answers, consisting of two numbers each and lettered A, B, C, and D, choose the one that gives the next two numbers in the series.
    9 9 2 11 11 4 13

    A. 14 14   B. 13 6   C. 13 5   D. 14 6

11. In the letter series A, C, F, J, _____, the letter which logically belongs in the blank space is

    A. L   B. M   C. N   D. 0

Questions 12-16.

DIRECTIONS: Each series of numbers is made up according to a certain rule or order. Indicate the NEXT number in the series.

12. 7, 21, 42, 126, 252, _____
    A. 275   B. 294   C. 378   D. 756

13. 4, 10, 7, 13, 10, 16, _____
    A. 13   B. 12   C. 14   D. 18

14. 9, 27, 25, 75, 73, 219, _____
    A. 217   B. 216   C. 222   D. 637

15. 3, 9, 10, 30, 31, 93, _____

   A. 91   B. 92   C. 94   D. 83

16. 12, 6, 24, 12, 48, 24, _____

   A. 72   B. 96
   C. 144   D. none of the above

Questions 17-20.

DIRECTIONS: Each question or incomplete statement is followed by several suggested answers or completions. Select the one that BEST answers the question or completes the statement.

17. The number which logically belongs in the blank box is

6		3		9
12		18		7
4		1		

   A. 6   B. 7   C. 8   D. 9

18. The number which logically belongs in the blank space is
    3, 5, 9, 17, _____

    A. 25   B. 33   C. 39   D. 41

19. The number which logically belongs in the blank box is

3		4		2
6		12		
2		3		6

   A. 11   B. 12   C. 15   D. 16

20. The number which logically belongs in the blank space is

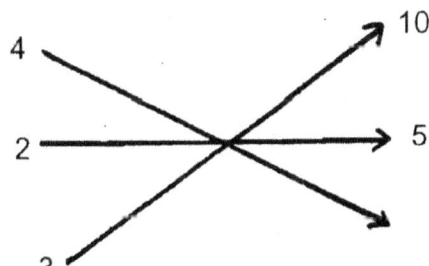

   A. 11   B. 13   C. 16   D. 17

KEY (CORRECT ANSWERS)

1.	C	11.	D
2.	A	12.	D
3.	A	13.	A
4.	B	14.	A
5.	C	15.	C
6.	C	16.	B
7.	A	17.	A
8.	B	18.	B
9.	C	19.	B
10.	B	20.	D

TEST 2

DIRECTIONS: The following consists of a series of numbers which follow in sequence according to a certain rule. Determine the rule and use it to select the next number from among the four choices given on the right side of each row.

1. 16 13 10 7
    A. 3
    B. 5
    C. 19
    D. None of these

    1._____

2. 15 12 13 10 11 8 9
    A. 6
    B. 7
    C. 14
    D. None of these

    2._____

3. 33 36 31 34 29 32
    A. 28
    B. 30
    C. 35
    D. None of these

    3._____

4. 10 15 21 28 36
    A. 41
    B. 42
    C. 44
    D. None of these

    4._____

5. 9 7.2 5.4 3.6 1.8
    A. 0
    B. .8
    C. .9
    D. None of these

    5._____

6. 8 11 22 25 50 53 106
    A. 109
    B. 159
    C. 212
    D. None of these

    6._____

7. 8 1/3 7 5 2/3 4 1/3
    A. 2
    B. 2 2/3
    C. 3
    D. None of these

    7._____

8. 77 78 79 83 87 94 101
    A. 102
    B. 108
    C. 111
    D. None of these

    8._____

9. 40 42 47 44 46 51 48
    A. 46
    B. 50
    C. 53
    D. None of these

    9._____

145

2 (#2)

10. 21 24 32 36 44 49 57
    A. 60
    B. 63
    C. 65
    D. None of these

10.____

11. 4 11 14 20 22 27
    A. 28
    B. 31
    C. 32
    D. None of these

11.____

12. 2 1/6 3 1/3 4 1/2 5 2/3 6 5/6
    A. 7 1/2
    B. 8
    C. 9
    D. None of these

12.____

13. 9 14 21 25 32 35 42
    A. 40
    B. 44
    C. 45
    D. None of these

13.____

14. 99 91 87 78 73 63 57
    A. 46
    B. 49
    C. 68
    D. None of these

14.____

15. 40 35 30 24 18 13
    A. 7
    B. 8
    C. 9
    D. None of these

15.____

KEY (CORRECT ANSWERS)

1. D   6. A
2. A   7. C
3. D   8. C
4. D   9. B
5. A   10. B

11. A
12. B
13. B
14. A
15. B

TEST 3

DIRECTIONS: Each of the following series is made up according to some rule. Addition, subtraction, multiplication, division, or various combinations of these operations are used in forming each series. Discover the rule for each series and decide which of the four suggested answers is CORRECT as the next term. *PRINT THE LETTER OF THE CORRECT ANSWER IN THE SPACE AT THE RIGHT.*

Sample: 1   3   5   7
       A. 7   B. 8   C. 9   D. 10

The correct answer is C, since 9 is the next term in the series.

1. 12   0   10   0   8   0 _____
   A. 0   B. 6   C. 7   D. 10

2. 42   37   32   27 _____
   A. 22   B. 23   C. 24   D. 25

3. r^6 $6r$ r^5 $5r$ r^4 _____
   A. r^3 B. $3r$ C. $4r^3$ D. $4r$

4. 2   4   8   16   3   2 _____
   A. 46   B. 48   C. 54   D. 64

5. 8   11   14   17 _____
   A. 18   B. 19   C. 20   D. 21

6. 1   4   7   10   13 _____
   A. 17   B. 16   C. 15   D. 14

7. 4   5   7   8   10 _____
   A. 14   B. 13   C. 12   D. 11

8. 17   17   13   9   9 _____
   A. 4   B. 5   C. 6   D. 7

9. ab   4589   2ab   458   3ab _____
   A. 45   B. 58   C. 48   D. 4ab

10. $\dfrac{a+4}{2a}$ $\dfrac{a+10}{5a}$ $\dfrac{a+16}{8a}$
   A. $\dfrac{a+18}{9a}$ B. $\dfrac{a+20}{11a}$ C. $\dfrac{a+22}{11a}$ D. $\dfrac{a+22}{12a}$

2 (#3)

11. 64   32   16   8 _____   11.____
    A. 0   B. 2   C. 4   D. 6

12. 56342   xy²   5634   x2y³   563   x³y⁴ _____   12.____
    A. x^4y^5 B. y^4y^5 C. 63   D. 56

13. 48.08   24.04   12.02 _____   13.____
    A. 6.06   B. 6.02   C. 6.01   D. 6.1

14. 2   6   10   11   15   19 _____   14.____
    A. 20   B. 21   C. 22   D. 23

15. $2y^3$-10 $6y^8$-16 $10y^{13}$-22 _____   15.____
    A. $16y^{18}$-28   B. $16y^{16}$-24   C. $14y^{16}$-24   D. $14y^{18}$-28

16. $4y^8$ $5y^7$ $4y^6$ $7y^5$ $4y^4$ _____   16.____
    A. $5y^7$ B. $9y^3$ C. $4y^2$ D. $5y^3$

17. 2   5   9   14   20 _____   17.____
    A. 27   B. 26   C. 25   D. 24

18. 3   2   4   3   5   4 _____   18.____
    A. 6   B. 5   C. 4   D. 3

19. 2   4   6   7   9   11 _____   19.____
    A. 15   B. 14   C. 12   D. 11

20. 3   8   13   18   23 _____   20.____
    A. 31   B. 29   C. 28   D. 27

21. 1   3   6   10   15 _____   21.____
    A. 17   B. 19   C. 20   D. 21

22. 3/5   1 1/5   1 4/5   2 2/5 _____   22.____
    A. 2 1/2   B. 2 4/5   C. 3   D. 3 1/5

23. 2   4   8   14   22 _____   23.____
    A. 30   B. 32   C. 34   D. 36

24. 4   5   10   11   22   23 _____   24.____
    A. 24   B. 44   C. 45   D. 46

25. 1   3   7   15 _____   25.____
    A. 31   B. 29   C. 27   D. 22

26. 24 23 22 20 19 18 _____   26._____
    A. 13   B. 14   C. 15   D. 16

27. 5/32   5/16   5/8   1 1/4   2 1/2 _____   27._____
    A. 5   B. 3 3/4   C. 3 1/2   D. 3 1/4

28. 5/108   5/36   5/12   5/4   3 3/4 _____   28._____
    A. 11 1/4   B. 7 1/4   C. 6 3/4   D. 6 1/4

29. 1   1   2   6   24 _____   29._____
    A. 124   B. 120   C. 96   D. 42

30. 1   4   9   16 _____   30._____
    A. 23   B. 24   C. 25   D. 27

KEY (CORRECT ANSWERS)

1.	B	16.	D
2.	A	17.	A
3.	D	18.	A
4.	D	19.	C
5.	D	20.	C
6.	B	21.	D
7.	D	22.	C
8.	B	23.	B
9.	A	24.	D
10.	C	25.	A
11.	C	26.	D
12.	D	27.	A
13.	C	28.	A
14.	A	29.	B
15.	D	30.	C

TEST 4

DIRECTIONS: Each question or incomplete statement is followed by several suggested answers or completions. Select the one that BEST answers the question or completes the statement. *PRINT THE LETTER OF THE CORRECT ANSWER IN THE SPACE AT THE RIGHT.*

1. 1, 2, 3, 4, _____
   A. 8   B. 7   C. 6   D. 5   1.____

2. 1, 5, 9, 13, _____
   A. 15   B. 17   C. 22   D. 19   2.____

3. A B D E G H _____
   A. K   B. I   C. F   D. J   3.____

4. C, E, G, K, M, _____
   A. V   B. S   C. Q   D. R   4.____

5. A, D, G, J, _____
   A. L   B. M   C. N   D. K   5.____

6. b, c, d, f, g, h, _____
   A. i   B. j   C. k   D. l   6.____

7. f, e, d, c, _____
   A. 3, 4, 5, 6   B. 6, 5, 4, 3
   C. z, y, x, w   D. 2, 4, 6, 8   7.____

8. A, 1, D, 4, J, 10, M, _____
   A. 13   B. 14   C. 16   D. 18   8.____

9. 1, 3, 9, 27, _____
   A. 36   B. 69   C. 45   D. 81   9.____

10. 1203004000500 _____
    A. 600   B. 0   C. 006   D. 00   10.____

11. 1, 2, 4, 7, 11, _____
    A. 16   B. 14   C. 18   D. 15   11.____

12. 4, 9, 16, _____
    A. 23   B. 25   C. 27   D. 24   12.____

13. If A = B, then X = 101
    If A is greater than B, X = 102
    If A is less than B, X = 103
    If A = 0, X = 104.
    Now, if A - B = 3 and B is greater than O, then x =

    A. 101   B. 102   C. 103   D. 104

14. 2000, 1999, 1996, 1991, _____

    A. 1986   B. 1899   C. 1984   D. 1987

15. a = b, b ≠ c
    Which is NOT true?

    A. a + b ≠ c   B. a - 1 = c
    C. b + 1 = c   D. c - 1 = a

16. 1, 8, 22, 50, _____

    A. 64   B. 106   C. 134   D. 100

17. 3, 8, 15, 26, 39, _____

    A. 51   B. 45   C. 56   D. 47

18. XooXXoXo _____

    A. oo   B. oX   C. Xo   D. XX

19. XXoooo _____

    A. one o   B. 6 X's
    C. 5 X's   D. one o, three X's

20. 4, 6, 8, 10, 14, _____

    A. 18   B. 20   C. 24   D. 16

21. 2, 2, 4, 12, 48, _____

    A. 60   B. 96   C. 144   D. 240

22. XoooXXXXX

    A. 3 X's, 2 o's   B. 5 o's
    C. 7 X's   D. 7 o's

23. 2, 5, 13, 36, _____

    A. 72   B. 49   C. 68   D. 104

24. XooXXXoo _____

    A. oX   B. Xo   C. XX   D. oo

25. a   cd   ghi   mnop _____

    A. uvwx   B. vwxyz   C. wxyz   D. uvwxy

KEY (CORRECT ANSWERS)

1. D
2. B
3. D
4. C
5. B

6. B
7. B
8. A
9. D
10. C

11. A
12. B
13. B
14. C
15. B

16. B
17. C
18. B
19. B
20. D

21. D
22. D
23. D
24. D
25. D

ABSTRACT REASONING

COMMENTARY

The mathematical or quantitative ability of the candidate is generally measured through the form of questions and/or problems involving arithmetical reasoning, algebraic problem solving, and the interpretation of visual materials graphs, charts, tables, diagrams, maps, cartoons, and pictures.

A more recent development, which attempts to assay facets of quantitative ability not ordinarily discernible or measurable, is the nonverbal test of reasoning of the type commonly designated as the figure analogy. Figure analogies are novel and differentiated measures of non-numerical mathematics reasoning.

Since intelligence exists in many forms or phases and the theory of differential aptitudes is now firmly established in testing, other manifestations and measurements of intelligence than verbal or purely arithmetical must be identified and measured.

Classification inventory, or figure classification, involves the aptitude of form perception, i.e., the ability to perceive pertinent detail in objects or in pictorial or graphic material. It involves making visual comparisons and discriminations and discerning slight differences in shapes and shading figures and widths and lengths of lines.

One aspect of this type of nonverbal question takes the form of a *positive* requirement to find the COMPATIBLE PATTERN (i.e., the one that *does* belong) from among two (2) sets of figure groups. The prescription for this question-type is as follows:

A group of three drawings lettered A, B, and C, respectively, is presented, followed on the same line by five (5) numbered alternative drawings labeled 1, 2, 3, 4, and 5, respectively.

The first two (2) drawings (A, B) in each question are related in some way.

The candidate is then to decide what characteristic *each* of the figures labeled A and B has that causes them to be related, and is then to select the one alternative from the five (5) numbered figures that is related to figure C in the same way that drawing B is related to drawing A.

Leading examples of presentation are the figure analogy and the figure classification. The section that follows presents progressive and varied samplings of this type of question.

2 (#1)

FIGURE ANALOGIES

Figure analogies are a novel and differentiated measure of non-numerical mathematics reasoning.

This question takes the form of, and, indeed, is similar to, the one-blank verbal analogy. However, pictures or drawings are used instead of words.

SAMPLE QUESTIONS AND EXPLANATIONS

DIRECTIONS: Each question in this part consists of 3 drawings lettered A,B,C, followed by 5 alternative drawings, numbered 1 to 5. The first 2 drawings in each question are related in some way. Choose the number of the alternative that is related to the third drawing in the same way that the second drawing is related to the first, and mark the appropriate space on your answer sheet.

1. 1.____

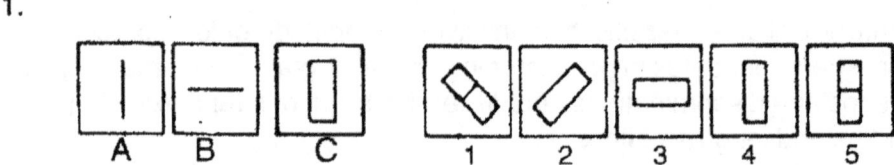

The CORRECT answer is 3. A vertical line has the same relationship to a horizontal line that a rectangle standing on its end has to a rectangle lying on its side.

2. 2.____

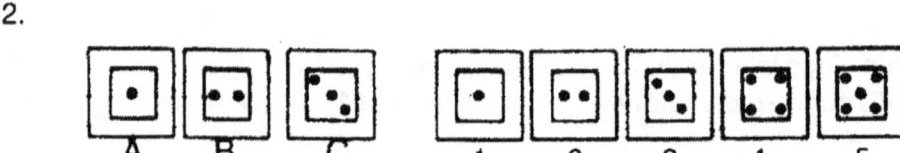

The second square has one more dot than the first square. Therefore the CORRECT answer is alternative 4, which has one more dot than the third square.

3. 3.____

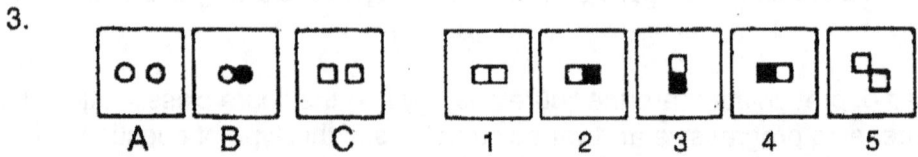

In the second drawing the circles are moved together and the circle on the right darkened. Therefore the CORRECT answer is 2, in which the squares are moved together and the right-hand square darkened.

4. 4.____

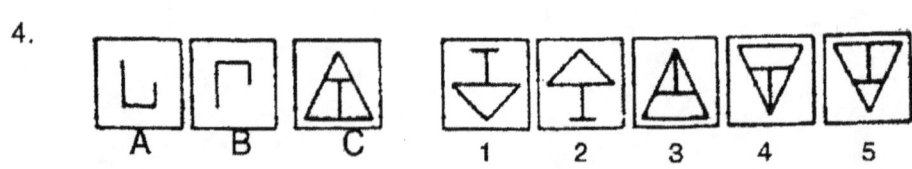

The CORRECT answer is 5. The second drawing is the inverted version of the first; alternative 5 is the inverted version of the third drawing.

5.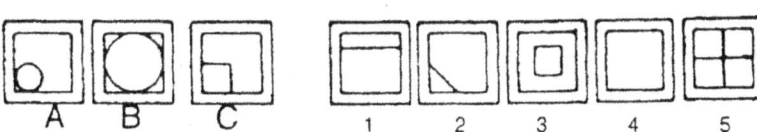

The CORRECT answer is 4. Drawing A has a small circle within a square; drawing B contains a circle completely filling the square. Drawing C has a small square within a square; in alternative 4, this small square has been magnified to its complete size within the square so that this magnified square coincides with the enclosing square, leaving the outline of only one square.

6.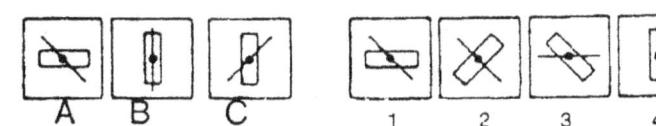

The CORRECT answer is 5. Drawing A appears in a horizontal position, with a diagonal line drawn through the center dot; drawing B appears in a vertical position, with a straight line drawn through the center dot. Drawing C is similar to drawing A, except that it appears in a vertical position; drawing 5 is similar to drawing B, except that it appears in a horizontal position. Our analogy may, therefore, be verbally expressed as
A:B:C:5.

SUGGESTIONS FOR ANSWERING THE FIGURE ANALOGY QUESTION

1. In doing the actual questions, there can be little practical gain in rationalizing each answer that you attempt. What is needed is a quick and ready perceptive sense in this matter.

2. The BEST way to prepare for this type of question is to do the "Tests" in figure analogies that follow. By this method, you will gain enough functional skill to enable you to cope successfully with this type of question on the Examination.

PLEASE NOTE -- In the tests which begin on page 5, after the sample questions, the three (3) drawings are unlabeled and the answers have four (4) choices instead of five (5) labeled A, B, C and D. They are to be answered in the same way.

SAMPLE TEST

1.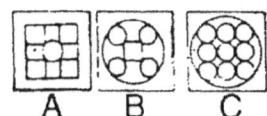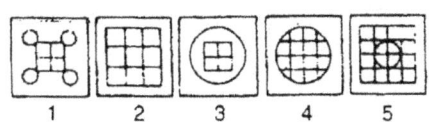

4 (#1)

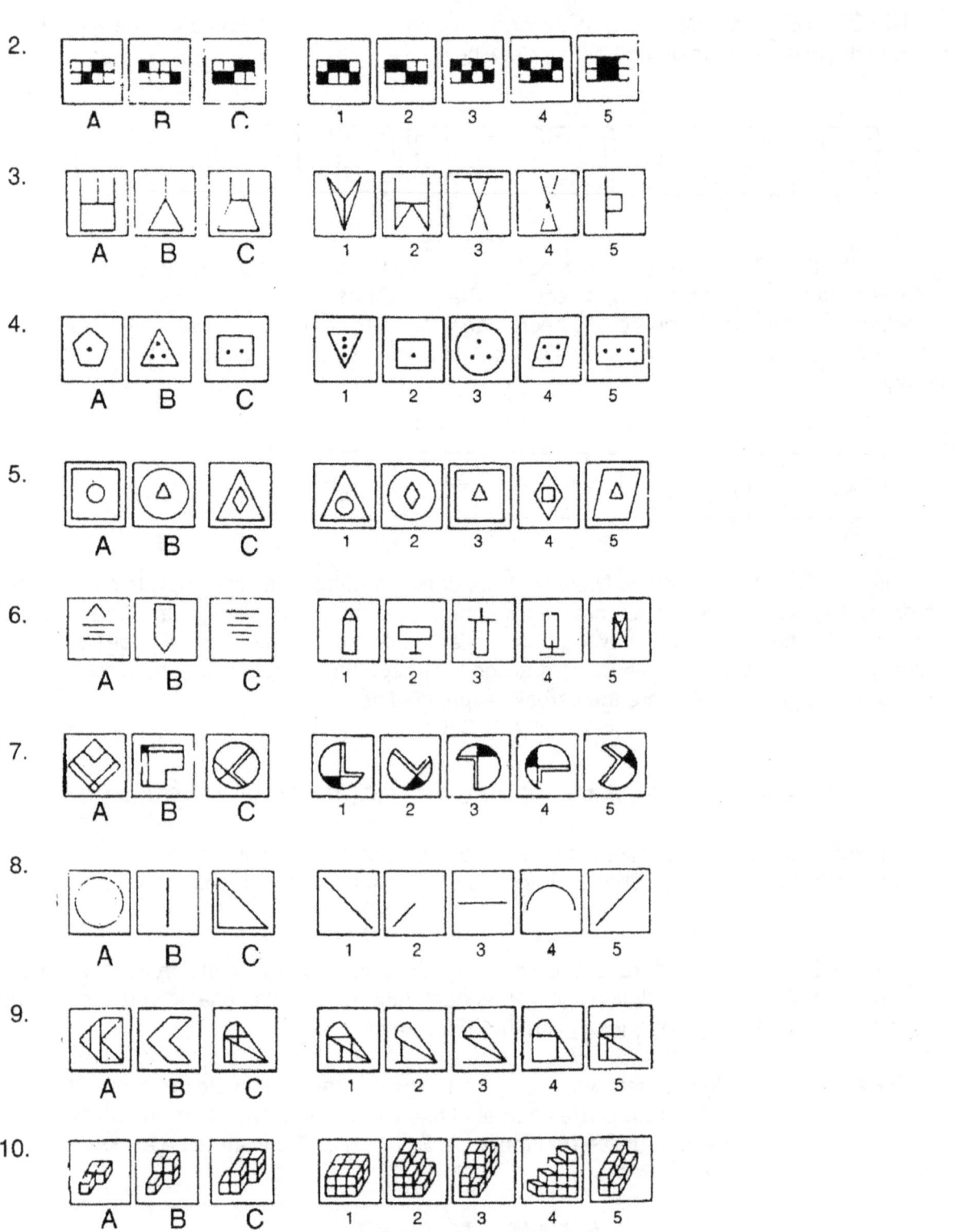

KEY (CORRECT ANSWERS)

1. 2
2. 2
3. 4
4. 1

5. 4
6. 3
7. 3
8. 2

6 (#1)

EXPLANATION OF ANSWERS

1. In the second figure, the squares are changed to circles and the circles to squares.

2. In the second figure, the upper darkened area has moved two squares to left; the lower, two squares to right.

3. The second figure has a flat base, like the first.

4. The sum of sides and dots in the second figure equals that of the first.

5. The outside part of the second figure is the inside part of the first.

6. The second figure is constructed from the lines given in the first.

7. The second figure is obtained from the first by rotating it 135 clockwise, darkening the smaller area and deleting the larger.

8. The second figure is the bisector of the area of the first.

9. The second figure is obtained from the first by deleting all the vertical lines.

10. The second figure contains two blocks more than the first.

EXAMINATION SECTION

PROBLEM FIGURES   ANSWER FIGURES

1.
2.
3.
4.
5.
6.
7.
8.

159

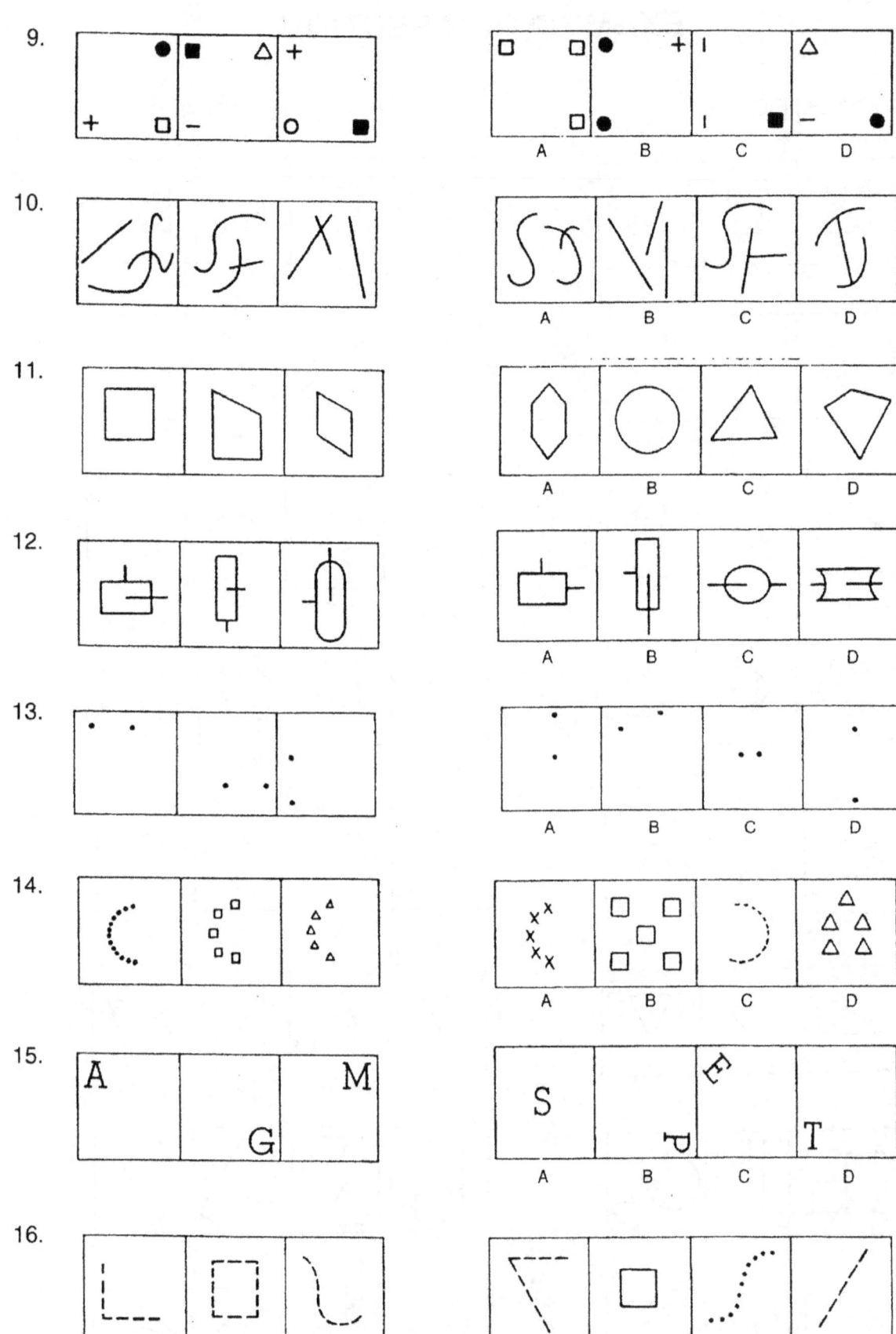

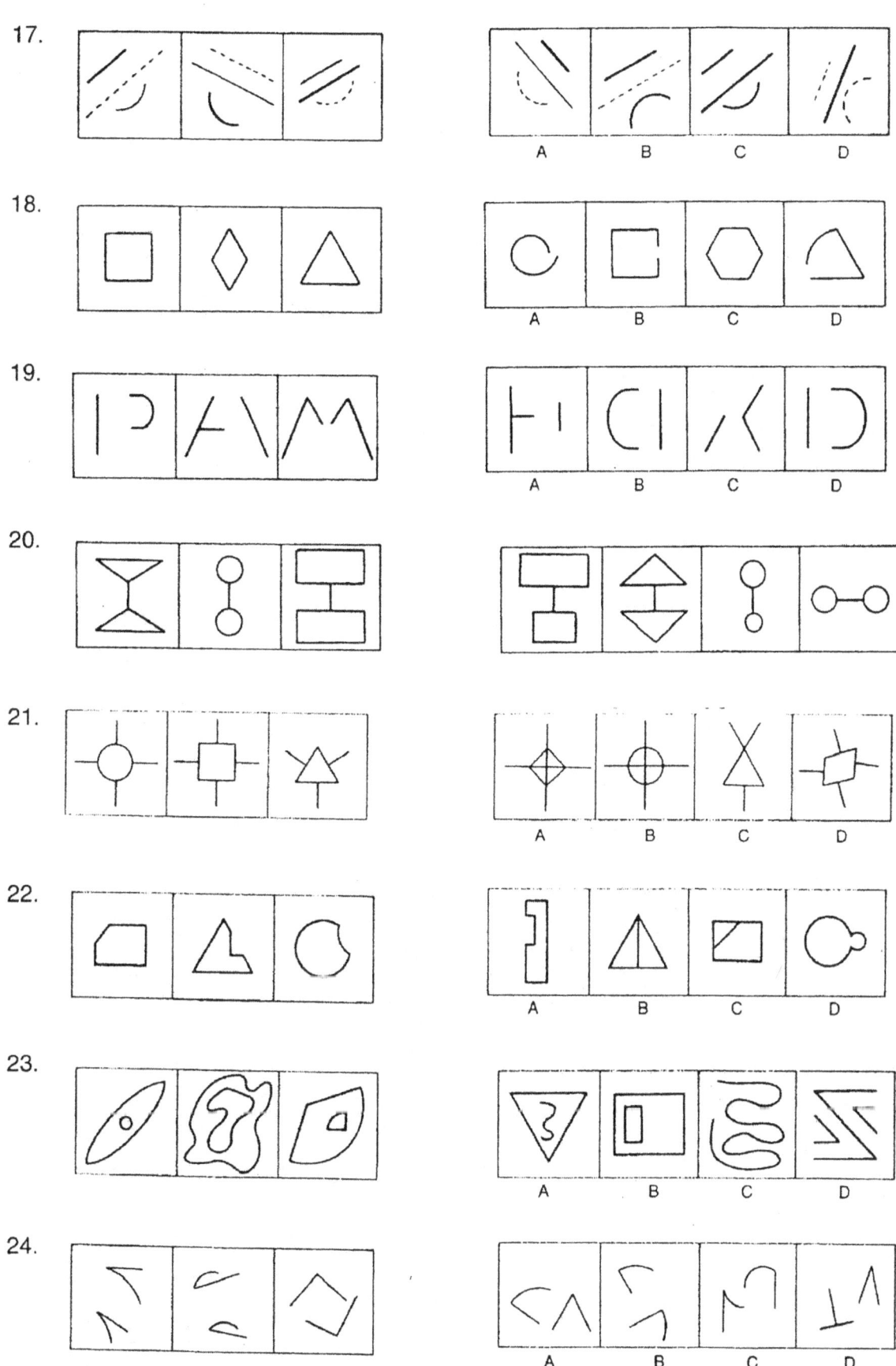

10 (#1)

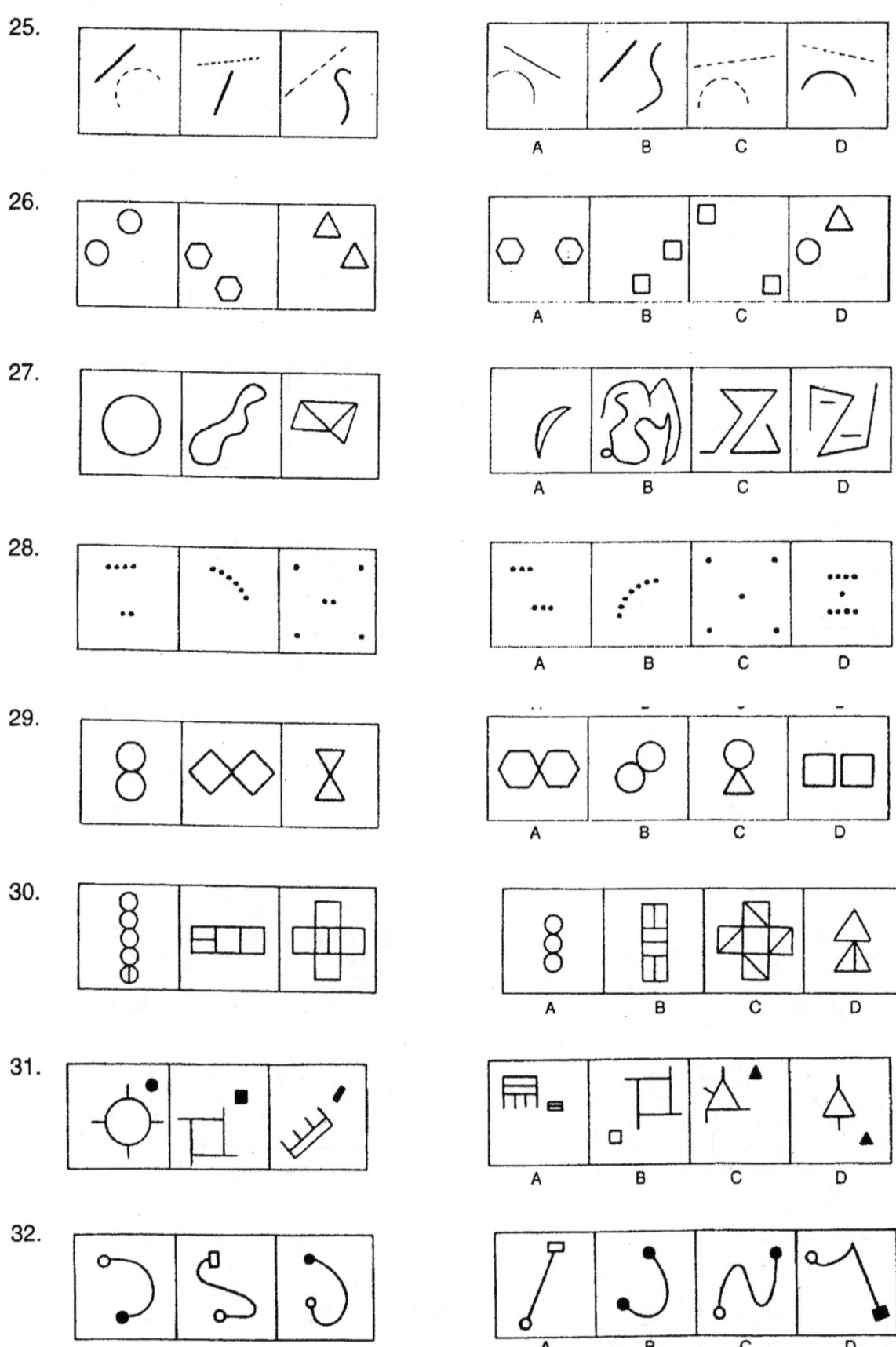

162

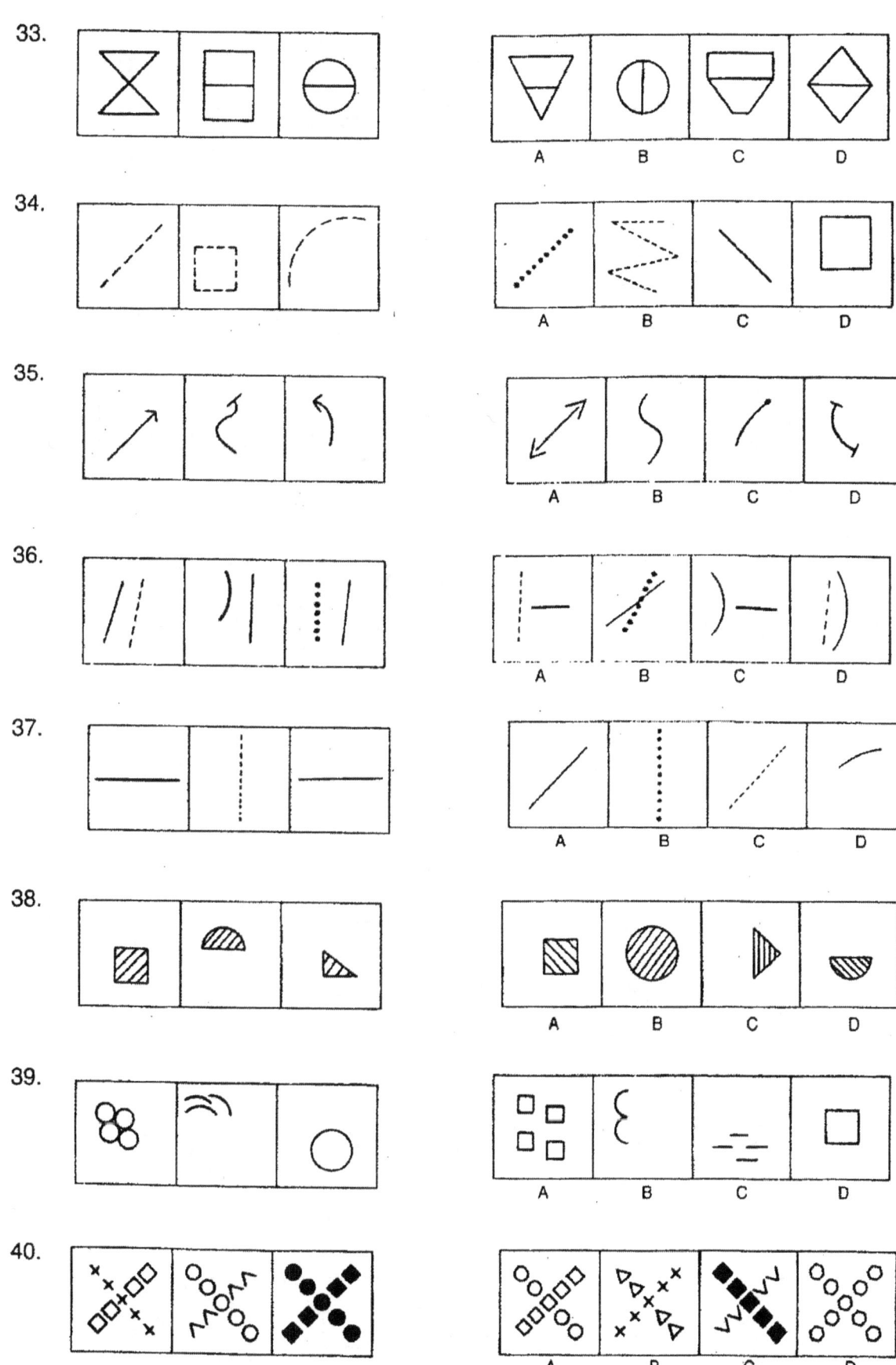

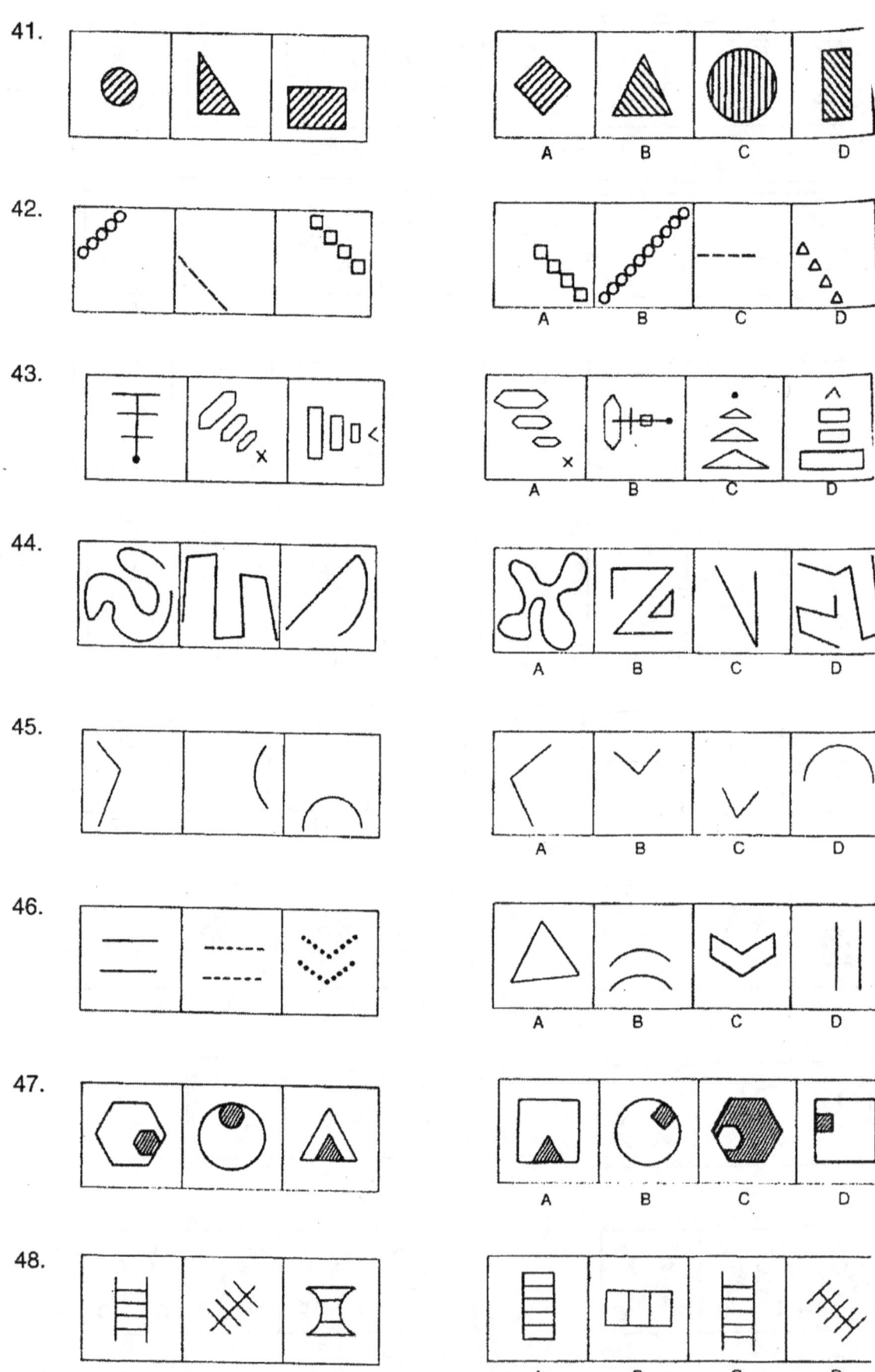

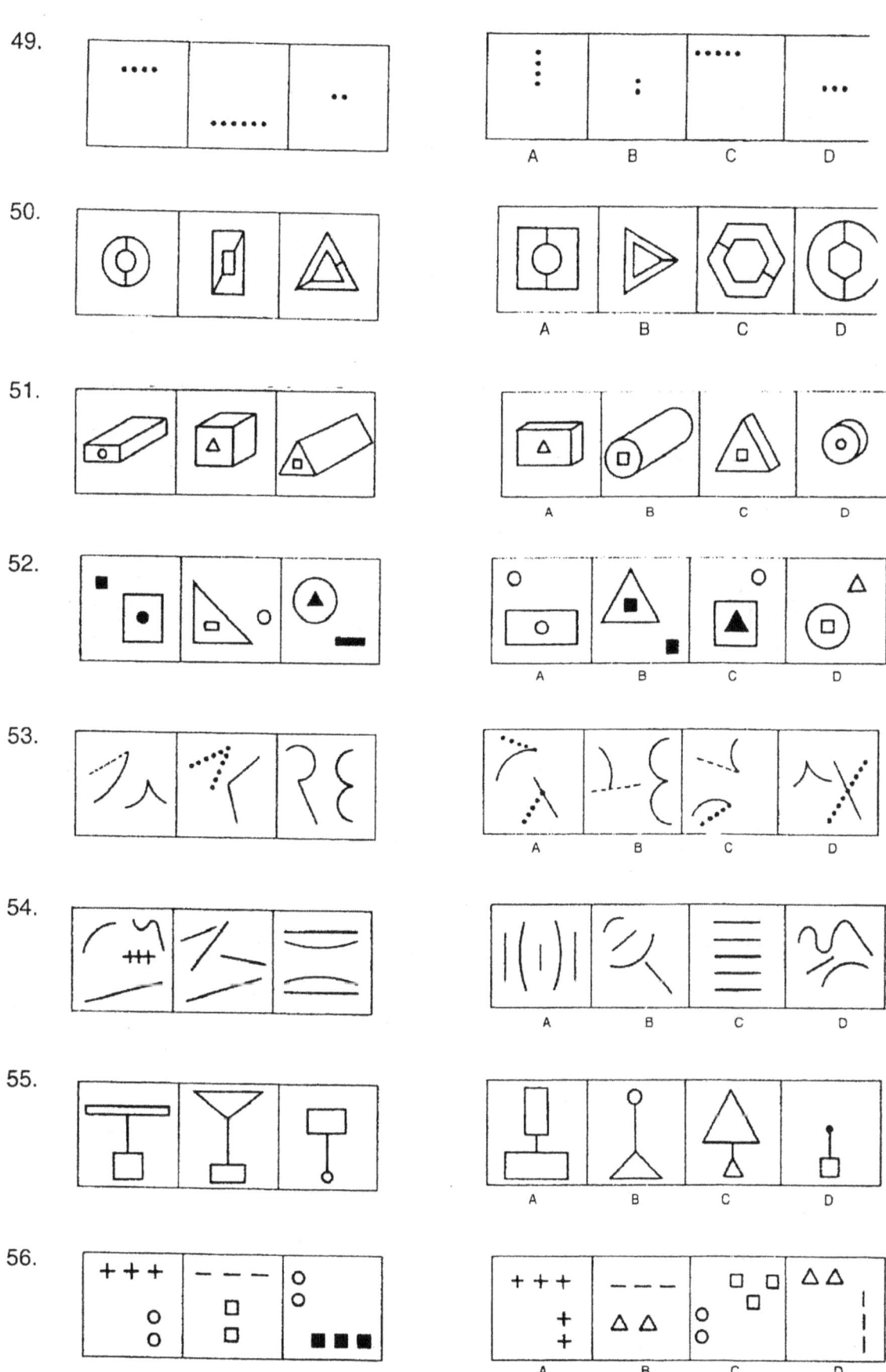

14 (#1)

57.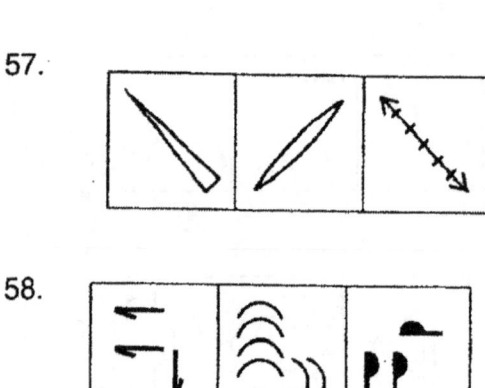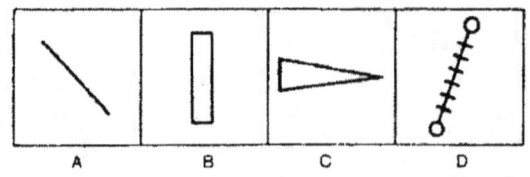

58.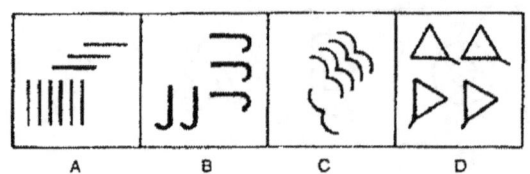

59.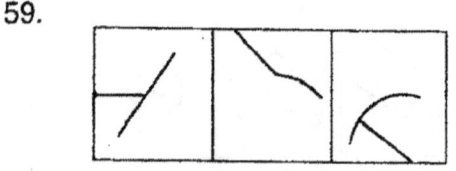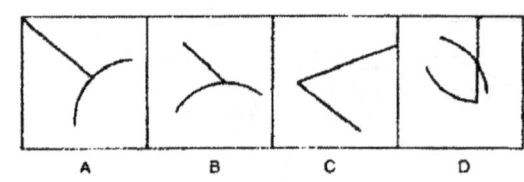

60.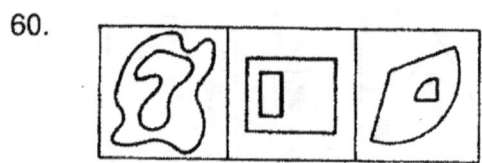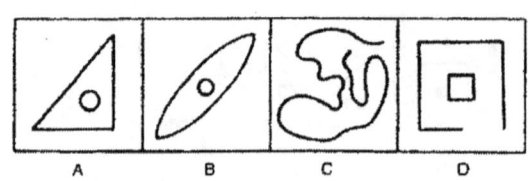

KEY (CORRECT ANSWERS)

1.	C	11.	D	21.	D	31.	C	41.	A	51.	B
2.	B	12.	B	22.	A	32.	C	42.	D	52.	D
3.	A	13.	A	23.	B	33.	D	43.	C	53.	C
4.	C	14.	A	24.	B	34.	B	44.	C	54.	B
5.	D	15.	D	25.	D	35.	C	45.	B	55.	C
6.	B	16.	A	26.	B	36.	D	46.	B	56.	D
7.	C	17.	A	27.	A	37.	B	47.	D	57.	A
8.	C	18.	C	28.	A	38.	B	48.	B	58.	A
9.	D	19.	D	29.	A	39.	B	49.	D	59.	C
10.	A	20.	B	30.	D	40.	C	50.	C	60.	B

BASIC FUNDAMENTALS OF ELECTRICITY

CONTENTS

UNIT 1 – ELECTRICITY	1
UNIT 2 – MAGNETISM	6
UNIT 3 – BATTERIES	13
UNIT 4 – USING ELECTRICITY	17

BASIC FUNDAMENTALS OF ELECTRICITY

Electricity
Unit 1

When you use a small hand drill, the energy that turns the drill comes from your body. When you snap the switch on an electric drill, another form of energy spins the bit of the drill. We call this form of energy *electricity*. Electrical energy plays a vital part in our environment. It lights our houses, cooks our food, runs our factories, and carries messages for us.

Like other forms of energy, electricity is something that we cannot create. We get it by converting another form of energy into electrical energy. The energy in running water is often used to produce, or *generate*, electricity. Waterpower can be used to turn a generator, which converts the energy in running water into electrical energy. Plants which use this process are called *hydroelectric* plants.

In the United States most of our electricity is produced by changing heat energy into electrical energy. A plant which uses this process is called a thermoelectric plant. In a *thermoelectric* plant, heat energy is first changed into mechanical energy. A steam turbine is often used for this purpose. Then the mechanical energy, produced by the turbine, is changed into electrical energy by a large *generator*. Today we produce some electricity also by changing atomic energy into electric energy.

Electrical Charges
Electricity is a form of energy produced when an electrical charge moves along a wire. Let us try to explain what an electrical charge is. If you lift a brick into the air, the brick acquires potential energy. You have separated the brick from the ground by using energy in your body. If you drop the brick, it will move to the ground, expending the energy it picked up when it was lifted. If the brick strikes a pane of glass on the way down, the energy in the brick will break the glass. The moving brick has kinetic energy; it will do work.

Electricity depends on this same principle. Inside the atom the tiny particles called *protons and electrons* are attracted to one another just as the brick is attracted to the ground. The proton and electron are called *charged particles*. The proton carries a *positive* charge. The electron carries a *negative* charge. They attract one another. If we force them apart, we must use energy, just as we use energy to raise a brick. When we release them, the electrons and protons move back together. While they are moving they can do work. For convenience sake, we say that the electrons move toward the protons.

Whenever electrons are moving, electricity is present. As they move, electrons can do work. They have energy. The reason they have energy is the same as the reason the brick has energy. Work must be done to separate electrons and protons. When they come back together, the energy they picked up is released.

Eletrical Energy
Let's take a simple example. Suppose we have a small heap of protons and electrons. We take all the electrons in one hand, and all the protons in the other hand. Then we pull them apart. Since they attract each other, we must use energy when we pull them apart. The electrons and protons then have potential energy. If they can, they will move back together again.

If we connect the two piles with a wire, the electrons will move along the wire and return to the protons. Like the falling brick, the electrons have energy as they move back to the protons. If we put a glass pane under the brick, we can make the brick use some of its energy to break the glass.

If we put a hurdle in front of the electrons, we can make them work as they move back toward the protons. That is the basis of all electricity-powered equipment. Electrons are made to use some of their energy as they try to return to the protons.

Suppose we connect electrons and protons by a wire, but we put in a high hurdle that the electrons must cross. As the electrons move over the hurdle, they release some of their energy. The electron must use energy to jump the hurdle just as we do. This energy is not destroyed. It is converted into heat. A "hot spot" will appear in the wire at the hurdle we placed in the road. If we put the resistance inside a glass bulb, and take out most of the air, the spot will glow white. We will have made an electric light bulb. By making the electrons work as they returned to the protons, we have created a light that we can use.

Electron flow

This illustration is a little too simple. But all electricity works on this general principle. Actually, one electron usually does not move the whole length of a wire. It moves only a short distance. The effect is like one billiard ball striking a long row of billiard balls. The shock is passed from one ball to the next, but each ball does not move very far. Another example is the way a shock runs through a long train when the engine stops. In any electric wire there are millions and millions of electrons that pass the movement along. This is called electron flow. The flow of electrons is the form of energy we call electricity.

The flow of electrons along a wire depends upon the way electrons are placed in an atom. You remember that electrons are arranged in shells around the nucleus of the atom. The nucleus has a positive charge. The electrons have a negative charge. In some atoms the electrons in the outer shell can be knocked loose very easily. Loose electrons are called *free electrons*, and they are the carriers of electrical energy. When the wire connects a supply of protons and a supply of electrons, these free electrons move along the wire-or drift-toward the protons. This movement produces an *electric current*.

Conductors and Insulators

If there are no free electrons, no electric current can be produced. Some materials produce hirge numbers of free electrons. They can carry an electric current very easily. These materials are called *conductors* because they conduct electricity. Other materials contain few free electrons. Little or, no electricity can flow through them. They are called *insulators*. They do not conduct electricity. Materials like silver, copper, aluminum, and gold possess many free electrons. They are good electrical conductors. Because copper is inexpensive, it is used most often for electrical wire. Materials like glass, rubber, wood, air, and paper are *insulators*. They do not carry electricity because they have few free electrons.

Measuring Electricity

When electrons flow along a conductor, we have electrical energy. Energy passes along the wire at the same speed as light, 186,000 miles each second. But how much electrical energy is passing through the wire? How much work can the electricity do? To answer these questions, we must measure electricity. To measure, we must have standards.

To find out how much electricity we have, we need only count the number of electrons available. If there are 6¼ billion billion electrons separated from protons, we have one *coulomb* of electrical charge. This sounds like a large number of electrons. But it is only a small amount of electricity.

A second question we must answer is, "How hard are the electrons trying to get back to the protons? How much pressure do they exert?" If we have electrons in one hand and protons in the other, how hard do they pull? The standard unit used by science to measure electrical pressure is based on the coulomb. If one coulomb of electrons is available, the amount of pressure they produce is defined as one *volt*. This is our standard for electrical pressure. If we have five coulombs of electrons in one hand, they will exert five volts of pressure trying to return to the protons. The volt is often called an *electromotive* force, and abbreviated as *emf*, or just a capital *E*. In our formulas, we will always abbreviate volts as *E*.

The coulomb and the volt measure potential energy. They tell us how many electrons we are holding. This is like weighing a rock we have lifted off the ground. But we would also like to know about electricity when it is in action. How fast are the electrons moving in our wire? To find this, we simply measure the number of electrons that pass one point in one second. If one coulomb of electrons flows past in one second, we say that one *ampere* of electric current is flowing in the wire. In other words, if one coulomb of electrons moves past a point in one second, one ampere of electricity is flowing.

Notice that all of these definitions are tied together. One coulomb is equal to 6¼ billion billion electrons. This number of electrons produces one volt of pressure. If one coulomb of electrons flows each second, the current is called one ampere. Of course, electricity will flow only when two points are connected. It will flow only if there is some separation of electrons and protons. If the number of electrons and the number of protons are equal at the same ends of a wire, no electricity will flow.

Resistance

When you apply energy to a machine like the wheel and axle, you lose some of the energy inside the machine because of friction. If you apply electrical energy to a wire, you also lose some energy in the wire. This loss is due to the *resistance* of the wire. The wire must have free electrons to carry electrical energy through the wire. But the electrons are tied to the nucleus of the atom by a small force. This force must be overcome before the electrons are free. The energy to free the electrons must be supplied from the energy in the electrons moving into the wire.

In a machine we must know how much energy we lose to friction to know the efficiency of the machine. We also measure the amount of loss in an electrical conductor. To do this, we measure the resistance of the conductor. Now, we know that the energy lost was used to pull electrons loose from their shells. And we know that this energy is converted into heat. So if we measure the amount of heat generated in a conductor, we know how much energy we have lost.

The standard unit used to measure resistance is called the ohm. This is the amount of resistance that generates 0.24 calories of heat when one ampere of electrical current flows through a wire. In other words, we run one ampere of current through a wire and measure the heat that is produced. If the heat equals 0.24 calories, then the resistance of the wire is one ohm. This definition of the unit of resistance ties it to all the other measuring standards in electricity. Look at the following table.

NAME OF UNIT	MEANING	UNINT	ABBREVIATION
Voltage	Pressure, or potential difference	Volt	E
Current	Flow of Electrons	Ampere	I
Resistance	Opposition to the flow of electrons	Ohm	R

Ohm's Law

If we separate electrons and protons and keep them separated, we have a potential difference between them. If we connect these two points with a conductor, we have an *electrical circuit*. When the two points are connected, electrons will flow through the conductor. We can find the voltage, the current, and the resistance in any electrical circuit by using a simple formula called *Ohm's Law*. This is one of the basic laws in all electricity, and you should learn it thoroughly. Ohm said that in any electrical circuit:
1. The current flowing is equal to the voltage divided by the resistance.
2. The resistance is equal to the voltage divided by the current.

3. The voltage is equal to the resistance multiplied by the current.

These three rules apply simply because they are defined that way. We know that one volt of electricity will push one ampere of current across a resistance of one ohm. Ohm produced his three rules by combining the definitions into one general rule. The formula is:

$$\text{Current}(I) \frac{(E) \text{voltage}}{(R) \text{resistance}}$$

We can write this in three ways:

1. $I = \frac{E}{R}$ 2. $E = I \times R$ 3. $R \frac{E}{R}$

Learn all three forms of Ohm's Law thoroughly.

Using Ohm's Law

In the United States most of our houses are wired for 110 volts of electricity. Suppose you had a heater that had a resistance of eleven ohms. But you did not know how many amperes of current the heater used. Ohm's Law could tell you the answer easily. You know the voltage and resistance. You want to know the current. Using formula 1 above:

$$I = \frac{E}{R} \quad I = \frac{110}{11} \quad I = 10 \text{ amperes}$$

Your heater would need a ten ampere fuse. You can solve any other problems of this type using the same formula.

Power

If we know the voltage, current, and resistance in an electrical current, we still do not know how much energy the circuit is using. This can be a serious problem when we want to figure out our own electricity bills.

The unit of electrical power is the watt. This is the amount of work done in one second when one volt of electricity moves one ampere of current through a circuit. In other words, if we have one volt of pressure and it moves one ampere of current through the circuit, we are using one watt of electrical energy. When larger units are needed, we use the unit called the kilowatt which is equal to one thousand watts.

To find the power (in watts) used in a circuit, simply multiply the voltage of the circuit by the current flowing through a circuit. The power formula is written:

$$\text{Power }(W) = (E) \text{ Voltage} \times (I) \text{ Current}$$

Almost every electrical problem can be solved by using the power formula, or combining the power formula with Ohm's Law.

Examples

1. An air conditioner has a tag which states that the unit uses 2,200 watts of power. The unit plugs into 110 volt electricity. How large must the fuse be in the line?

   a. $W = E \times I$ or $2,200 = 110 \times I$

   b. $I = \frac{2,200}{110}$ or $I = 20$ ampers

The air conditioner will use a twenty ampere fuse. This is a very heavy load for house wiring, and the wiring should be checked before adding this much current to a line.

2. You have just bought a new electric heater. It operates on 110 volt electricity, and it has a resistance of ten ohms. You pay five cents for each kilowatt of electricity. How much will it cost to run the heater for thirty days?

a. First, you must use Ohm's Law to find the current that flows through the heater:

$$I = \frac{E}{R} \qquad I = \frac{110}{10} \qquad I = 11 \text{ amperes}$$

b. Then you find the number of watts the heater uses, using the power formula:

$$W = E \times I \qquad W = 110 \times 11 \qquad W = 1{,}210 \text{ watts}$$

c. Now you know that the heater uses 1.21 kilowatts every hour. This electricity costs five cents for each kilowatt hour. You can figure that the heater will cost about six cents per hour to run. If it ran day and night for thirty days, the total cost would be approximately forty-three dollars ($43.56, to be exact). This is the way you can use the two formulas to work out electrical problems in the home.

Words Used in Unit 1

abbreviated (ə brē′vĭ āt əd), shortened
convenience (kən vēn′ yəns), saving of trouble
electron (ĭ lĕk′trŏn), a tiny particle carrying one unit of negative electricity
expending (ĕks pĕnd′ĭng), i using up
hurdle (hər′ dəl), an obstacle in one's way
illustration (ĭl əs tră′shən), story, example
proton (prō′tŏn), tiny particle carrying one unit of positive electricity
thermoelectric (thər mō ĭ lĕk′trĭk), having to do with electricity produced by heat

Magnetism
Unit 2

If you take a small piece of the mineral magnetite and hold it near some iron filings, the iron filings will cling to the magnetite. This material is called a *natural magnet.* Since this magnet actually pulls the iron filings toward it, we know that it can do work. So we know that a magnet contains energy of some sort.

We can make a magnet with electricity, too. If we wrap some wire around an iron spike and run an electric current through the wire, the spike will also attract iron filings. But the spike will attract iron only while the electric current is flowing. When the current is shut off, the spike loses its magnetism. Such a magnet is called an electromagnet.

What is this mysterious force that draws the iron to the magnet? We know that it is related to electricity because we can produce magnetism by electricity.

What's a Magnet?

Like most basic questions about our universe, this isa hard question to answer. We know that the molecules inside a magnet are organized. They are so arranged that there is potential difference between the two ends of the magnet. That is, one end has a positive charge and the other end has a negative charge. We know that energy must have been used to make this arrangement. Each end of the magnet is called a pole. We say that one pole is positive and the other is negative. The two poles act like electrons and protons. That is, likes repel each other; opposites attract. Two positive poles repel each other, and two negative poles repel each other. But a positive pole and a negative pole will attract one another.

The charges at the poles of a magnet are probably due to the movement of electrons inside the magnet. We are not exactly certain what bring this about. But we do know a great deal about the way magnets work. And we know many of the relations between magnetism and electricity. These are the things we will study in this unit.

Magnetic fields

A magnet attracts an iron filing *before* it touches the filing. The area around a magnet is charged, and the charge around the magnet pulls the iron toward the magnet. This charged area is called a magnetic field. Without these magnetic fields there could be no electricity as we know it.

The magnetic field increases in strength as we move closer to the surface of the magnet. If we place a magnet beneath a sheet of paper, and sprinkle tiny iron particles on the paper, the iron particles will arrange themselves along field lines of the magnet. Notice the pattern the lines form. Near the poles the lines are close together. The field is very strong here. At the center point between the poles, the lines are spread apart. The field is weakest here.

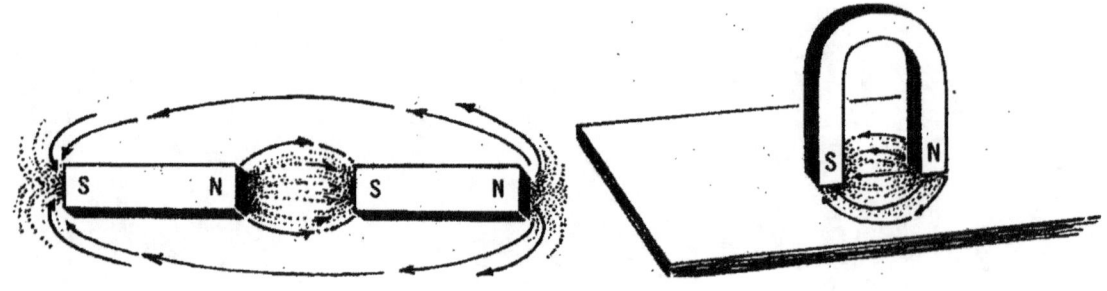

Fig. 1 a

Fig. 1 b

Figures 1a, 1 b Magnetic Lines of Force-Bar Magnet and Horseshoe Magnet.

The strength of the magnet determines the strength of the field. If we place a pieee of iron in the field, it concentrates the lines of force and increases the strength of the field. A magnetic field can attract certain objects through solid wood and some other materials. It can exert force through a perfect vacuum. Every magnet or electromagnet produces a magnetic field.

Induction

We have the whole science of electronics because a magnet produces a magnetic field. Yet we cannot really explain magnetism very well. We can only say how magnetism works, not why it works. One property of a magnetic field is of outstanding importance. If a small piece of wire is moved across the lines of force of a magnetic field, a small electric current flows in the wire. The kinetic energy of the moving wire is changed into electrical energy. The wire does not have to touch the magnet. All it must do is cut *across* the lines of force. The faster the wire moves the more electrical current runs in the wire. The more lines of force the wire cuts, the more electric current runs in the wire. This principle is called *induction*. An electric current is *induced* in the moving wire. Actually, the magnetic field is able to change mechanical energy into elctrical energy. Every electric motor, every electric generator, and every transformer depends upon this principle of induction.

REMEMBER

- A moving wire cutting the lines of force in a magnetic field produces an electric current in the wire.

- The more lines of force the wire cuts, the more current generated.

- The faster the wires move, the more electric current generated.

Electromagnetism

If a wire is passed through a magnetic field, an electric current is produced. To reverse the process, if an electric current is run through a wire, a magnetic field is produced. This is called an electromagnet. You can test this principle by connecting the two terminals on a small battery with a bare wire. The wire will pick up iron filings while it is connected. If the wire is shaped into a loop, the shape of the magnetic field changes. Figure100 (A) shows the effect of the loop. Th lines of force are increased inside the loop. If more loops are added, the magnetic field grows stronger. A coiled wire carrying electricity that has more than one loop is usually called a *solenoid, or coil*. The coil will act like any other magnet. One end of the coil is positive; the other end is negative. Because the coil has two poles, we say that it shows *polarity*.

A solenoid acts just like a bar magnet. The strength of the magnet depends upon the size of the wire, the number of turns of wire, and the amount of electrical current running through the wire. An increase in any of these factors makes the magnet stronger. If an iron bar is placed inside the coiled wire, it concentrates the lines of force and makes the magnet much stronger. Most electromagnets have an Iron core.

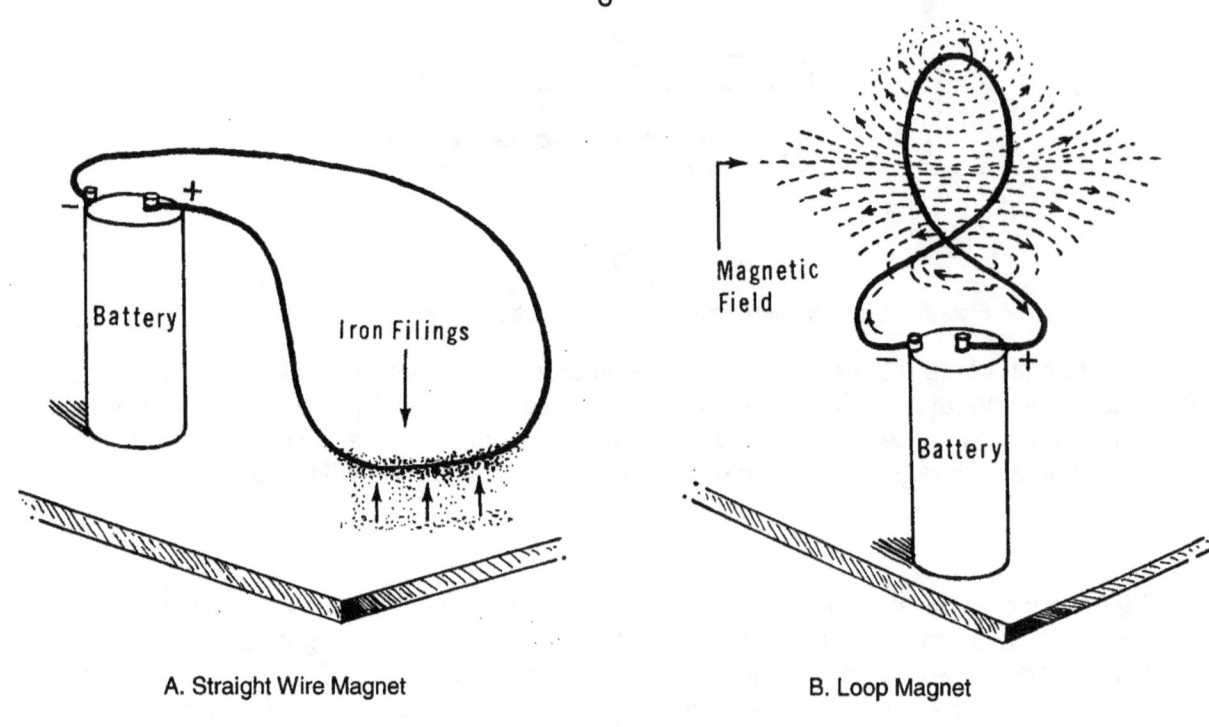

A. Straight Wire Magnet   B. Loop Magnet

FIGURE 2

Making Electricity

When electrons flow through wire, an electric current is present. That is what we mean by electricity. Before electrons will flow, there must be an excess of electrons in one place, separated from an excess of protons. This makes a potential difference between the two points. To make electricity we must create a potential difference between two points. We can do this with a magnet and a length of wire.

Let us place a large U-shaped magnet in a vice. Then we take a piece of copper wire and attach the wire to a sensitive meter that measures electric current. Now we move the wire down between the poles of the magnet. We have cut the lines of force, and we have created a potential difference inside the wire. For electrons will move from one end of the wire to the other. An electric current flows in the wire. If we move the wire back up between the poles of the magnet, the electrons flow back in the other direction. The magnetic field holds the electrons in position. When the wire moves, the electrons are strained apart. This produces the potential difference that causes electrical current to flow. And this is the way we change the mechanical energy of the moving wire into electrical energy.

The Alternating Current Generator

Now let us put this principle to work. In figure 101, a simple electric generator is shown. There is a large magnet, with a loop of wire that rotates between the poles of the magnet. We must have some source of energy to spin the wire loop. The energy that spins the loop is converted into electrical energy by the generator. The generator is called an *alternating current generator*. The electrons flow first in one direction along the wire and then in the reverse direction.

Each complete turn of the wire loop is called one *cycle*. As the loop turns, the amount of electric current flowing in the wire varies in a regular pattern. If we follow the wire loop through one complete turn, or cycle, we can see how this change takes place.

In position A the wire loop is horizontal. It is not cutting any lines of force in the magnetic field. Therefore no electric current is flowing in the wire. As the loop turns from A to B, it begins to cut lines of force. More and more electric current flows in the wiare. When the loop reaches position

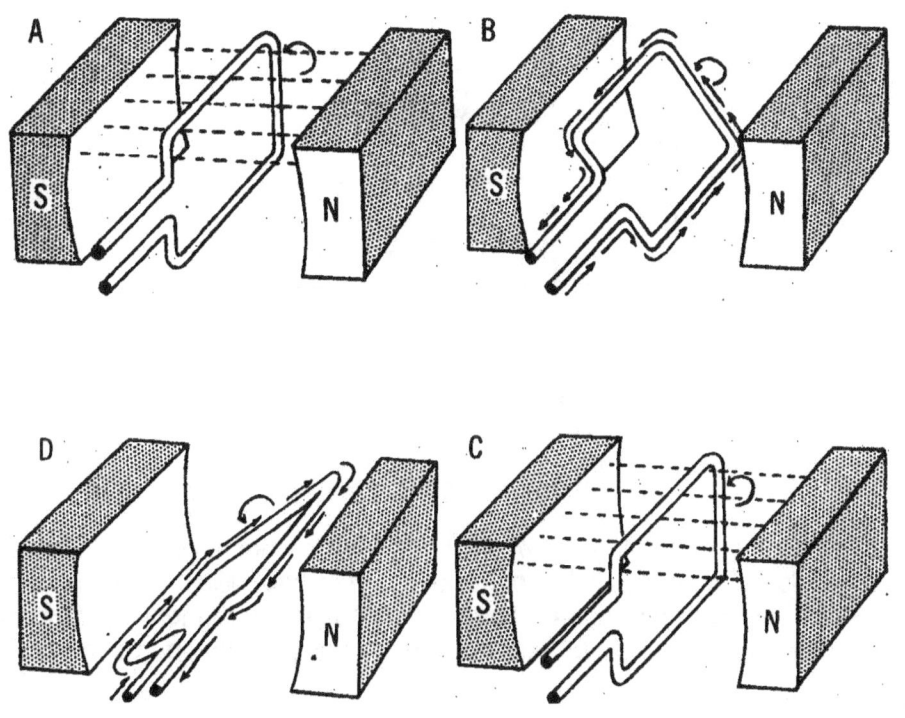

FIGURE 3. Loop Generator-Four Positions.

B, it is cutting all of the lines of force, and the current in the wire reaches a peak. Moving from B to C, the amount of current in the wire drops away to zero. The number of lines of force cut by the wire drops away to zero. When the wire is in position C, no current is flowing in the wire

The wire loop continues to turn from position C to position D. But this time the wires are reversed, and the current is flowing in the opposite direction. The amount of current increases once again to a peak at position D, but the current is flowing in the opposite direction in the wire. From position D back to position A, the current drops off once again. Back at position A, the current in the wire is zero, and one full cycle is complete.

Tile Current Cycle

We can draw a graph to show the amount of current flowing in the wire loop at different parts of the cycle. This graph is shown in figure 102. The graph begins at position A in figure 101. Each quarter turn of the loop is marked. Notice that the current reaches a peak after one quarter turn, and then returns to zero. In the next quarter turn, it reaches a second peak--*in the opposite direction*. Then it returns again to zero. Alternating current always has peaks in both directions because the current flows in both directions in the wire loop. The graph in figure 102 is called a sine wave. It shows one full cycle of electric current, produced by an alternating current generator.

The number of cycles of current produced each second is called the *frequency* of the electricity. In the United States most generators produce sixty full cycles of current each second. This is written sixty cps. For radio broadcasting, much higher frequencies are used. The radio

10

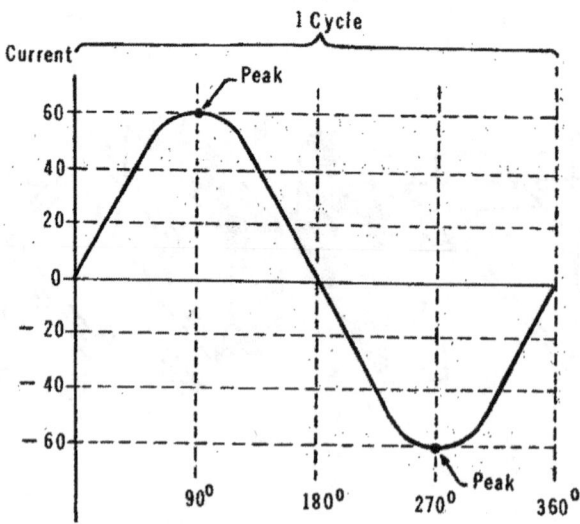

FIGURE 4. Graph: Sine Wave.

broadcasting band begins at 550 kilocycles, or 550,000 cycles per second. One kilocycle is equal to one thousand cycles. For special types of radio, a unit of one million cycles is used. This is called a *megacycle*. The human ear cannot hear these electrical frequencies. Our ears can be stimulated by mechanical energy only. Electrical energy has no effect on the ear.

The Electric Generator

An electric motor and electric generator are nearly the same. The electric generator converts mechanical energy into electrical energy. An electric motor converts electrical energy into mechanical energy. Actually, electricity is not very useful until it is changed into another form. But it is easy to transport and store, and cheap to produce. This makes it an ideal form of energy for many purposes.

The magnetic field in an electric generator is supplied by an electromagnet called the field coil. This coil lies just inside the housing of the generator. The moving part of the generator (the loop) is called the *armature*. The armature is wound with many loops of wire. Some wire is always cutting the lines of force of the magnetic field and producing electric current. The ends of the loop of wire wound on the armature are attached to two *slip rings*. The electric current generated in the generator is taken off the armature from these two rings. They are in contact with two *brushes* which carry the current away from the rings. When the generator is used to produce *direct current*, which flows in only one direction, a device is used to reverse the connections after each half turn of the armature. This device is called a *commutator*.

The generator cannot produce energy. It can only convert mechanical energy into electrical energy. Some outside power must turn the armature. In large electric plants a steam turbine is used to turn the armature in a very heavy generator. In an automobile, the small generator is attached to the drive shaft of the car.

The Electric Motor

The electric generator changes mechanical energy into electrical energy. The electric motor changes electrical energy into mechanical energy. The parts in a motor and a generator are nearly the same. But an electric motor depends on a different principle. A pole that has a positive charge is attracted to a pole with a negative charge. But it is repelled by another positive pole. This is the principle that runs an electric motor.

In an electric motor, electricity is fed into the field coil and into the winding of the armature. This creates two electromagnets, each with a positive pole and a negative pole. When the electricity is connected, the positive pole of the armature moves toward the negative pole of the field coil. This turns the armature. But the turning would stop as soon as the positive armature pole reached the negative field coil pole. So, when the positive pole has nearly reached its goal, the commutator on the motor reverses the current.

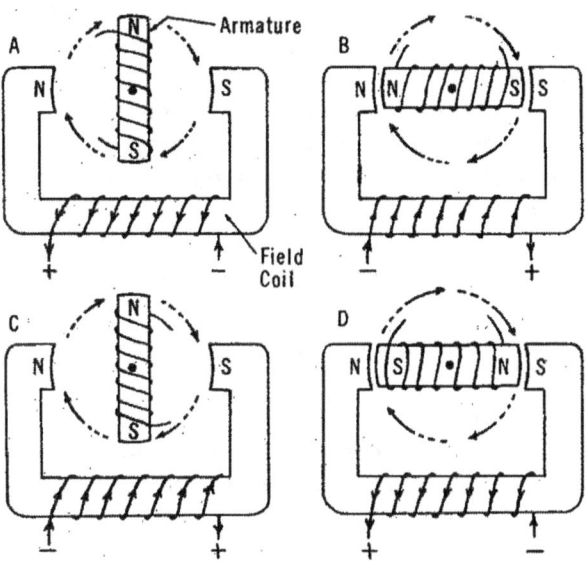

FIGURE 5. Electric Motor Showing Rotation

The positive pole on the armature is now facing a positive pole and is pushed away toward the negative pole. Again, just as it reaches its goal, the commutator reverses the connections. Again the armature pole is shoved away. So the armature keeps turning, trying to bring a positive and negative pole together. Because of the commutator it never succeeds. The pole on the armature is like a dog chasing a mechanical rabbit at a race track. Just as the dog reaches the rabbit, the rabbit's speed is increased and the dog falls bechind. The turning armature of the motor produces mechanical energy which can be used to do work.

Transformers

The electric line that passes your house carries about eighteen thousand volts. But inside the house it is a safe 110 volts. This voltage is produced by a transformer. A transformer also uses the principle of induction. But it uses it to move electricity from one wire to another even though the two wires are not touching. Inside a transformer there are two solenoids or coils. They are often wound around the same center.

One solenoid is connected to a source of alternating current. As the current moves through the coil, it produces an electric field around the coil. The electric field passes through the second coil nearby. As the current moving through the coil rises and falls with each cycle, the magnetic field

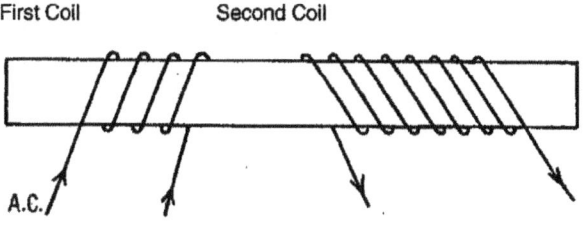

FIGURE 6. Principle of the Transformer.

around the coil also rises and falls. This produces an electric current in the second coil which is an exact duplicate of the electric current in the first coil. Although neither of the coils moves, the lines of force move as the field expands and collapses. As the lines of force cut across the wire in the second coil, they induce an electric current in the second coil.

The voltage in the second coil depends upon the number of turns of wire used in each coil. If there is the same number of turns in each coil, the voltage will not change as it moves from one to the other. If the second coil has ten times as many turns as the first coil, the voltage will be increased ten times. This is called a *step-up* transformer. If the number of turns in the second coil is 1/10 as large as the number in the first coil, only 1/10 as much voltage will be produced in the second coil. This is called a *step-down* transformer. Transformers can be used any time the voltage must be changed in an electric circuit. They are manufactured in a wide variety of sizes for different types of voltage changes.

Words Used in Unit 2

armature (ăr´məchər), the moving part of a generator
arranged (ərănjd´), put into proper order
collapses (kə lăps´əz), shrinks together
commutator (kŏm´ū tă tər), device which reverses the direction of flow of electricity
concentrates (kŏn´sən trăts), brings together to one place
induced (in dūst´), produced, caused to appear
organized (ŏr´gən īzd), put into working order
repel (rĭ pĕl´), force back, move away from
terminals (tər´mə nəlz), the ends of a battery where an electrical connection is made

Batteries

Unit 3

Science is full of surprises. We learned in the last unit that a spinning loop of wire in a magnetic field can produce electricity. It does this by separating electrons and protons to produce an electrical potential in the spinning wire. No liquids are used. No chemical reaction takes place. Yet electricity is produced. This seems to be a long way from the chemist's laboratory. Yet the chemist only smiles to himself. He fills a glass with a few chemicals dissolved in water. He places a rod of carbon and a rod of zinc in the water and attaches a wire to each rod. When the two wires are connected, an electric current flows through the wires. The chemist too can produce electricity.

There is a useful lesson in this for anyone who studies science. The chemist and the physicist start from different points. But they both deal with electricity, even though they use different approaches. You see nature is not divided into only chemistry and physics. Our environment is all one. We have divided our world into physical and chemical things. But electricity is only the flow of electrons along a wire. It does not matter how you cause the electrons to flow. The physicist does it one way; the chemist does it another. Both men produce electricity.

The Voltaic Cell

When you start your car, you must use a battery to turn the engine over until the small electrical generator gets going. This battery produces electricity by a chemical reaction. We know that electricity is produced when there is a potential difference between two points. This occurs when electrons and protons, or positive and negative charges, are separated. The chemist separates his charges in a unit called the *voltaic cell*. All batteries are a variation of this basic unit.

The voltaic cell consists of three parts:

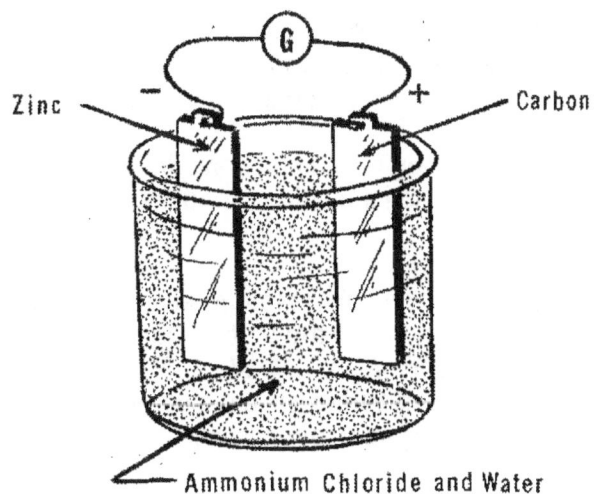

FIGURE 7. Voltaic cell

(1) a container made of insulating material-some material that will not conduct electricity; (2) a chemical solution called an electrolyte; and (3) two metal plates, called electrodes, which are placed in the solution. The electrodes must be conductors of electricity. When the electrodes are joined by a wire, electrons will flow along the wire. The voltaic cell will produce an electric current.

What happens inside the cell to produce electricity? One of the electrodes is made of the metal zinc. The other is made of pure carbon. The electrolyte is usually a mixture of water and sulfuric acid. Water is not a good electrical conductor the sulfuric acid makes the solution a conducting material.

Chemical Action in Cell

When the electrodes are placed in the electrolyte, the zinc plate dissolves. It forms charged particles called irns. Ions can be either positively charged or negatively charged. If there is a surplus of eleetrons on the ion, it is negatively charged. If there is a shortage of electrons on the ion, it is positively charged. You can probably see the connection already. Electricity is produced by a flow of surplus electrons. Anyhow, the zinc forms ions with a surplus of electrons. These surplns electrons gather on the zinc electrode. This gives the zinc electrode a negative charge.

The electrons taken from zinc are added to the zinc strip. So the zinc electrode acquires a surplus of electrons. There is still one more step. The water in the electrolyte produces hydrogen ions, or negative charges. These hydrogen ions move to the carbon rod and collect electrons from it. So the carbon rod gets a surplus of protons, or positive charges.

By chemical action we thus produce a positive charge on the carbon rod and a negative charge on the zinc rod. The zinc rod has an excess of electrons. And so there is a potential difference between the carbon rod and the zinc rod. If we conned these two points, electrons will flow from the zinc rod to the carbon rod. An electric current will be produced in the wire. As the electrons move from the zinc plate, more zinc dissolves and the potential difference is maintained. Eleetric current will flow from zinc to carbon until the zinc has completely dissolved. Then the voltaic cell will be worn out. A new zinc rod must be added to make it work again.

This is the basic method which the chemist uses to produce electricity. He dissolves zinc and uses the energy to produce electricity. Many kinds of material can be used to make a voltaic cell. Usually electrodes are made of zinc and carbon because both minerals are cheap. The electrolyte is often a compound of ammonia and chlorine called *ammonium chloride.*

Primary Cells and Secondary Cells

When the zinc in the voltaic cell is used up, the battery is dead. A cell of this sort is called a *primary cell*. The chemical action inside the battery moves only in one direction. When the cell is unable to produce more electricity, nothing can be done to make the battery useful again.

There is another type of battery, however, which can solve this problem. The chemical action inside this battery cell can be reversed. When the cell is producing electricity, a chemical reaction takes place.

When the cell runs down, the chemical action can be reversed. We say that the battery is *discharging* when it is producing electricity. When the process is reversed, the cell is being charged. This type of battery is called a *secondary cell.* We know many examples of both batteries. A flashlight battery is a primary cell. When it is used up, we throw it away. An automobile battery is a secondary cell. It can be recharged again and again before it must be thrown away.

The Primary Cell --- A Dry Cell Battery

The most common primary cell is the small battery we use in a flashlight. Usually it is made in the shape of a small cylinder. The outer shell of the battery is a small can made of zinc. This is the negative electrode of the battery. The positive electrode is a solid carbon rod suspended in the can. The carbon rod is insulated from the zinc can-they do not touch. Inside the can there is a damp paste of ammonium chloride and water. The cell is not completely dry, but it can be turned upside down without spilling. The top of the can is sealed with some plastic insulating material. This separates the carbon rod from the zinc can and holds in the electrolyte.

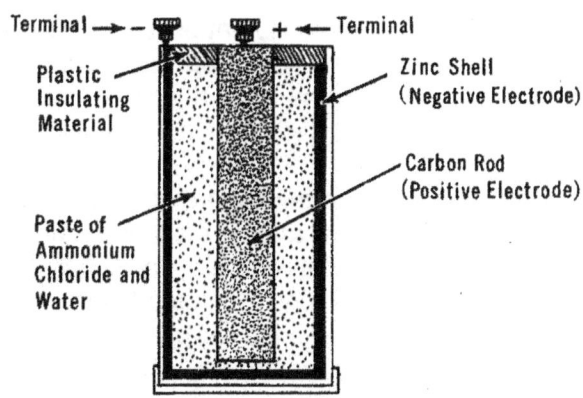

FIGURE 8. Dry Cell Battery

The dry cell works just like the voltaic cell. The zinc dissolves, and excess electrons form on the zinc can, and hydrogen ions take electrons from the carbon rod, creating a shortage of electrons on the rod. This produces a potential difference between the two points. When they are connected, electricity is produced in the connecting wire. When all of the zinc has dissolved, the cell is used up. These cells produce about one volt of electrical pressure and a small amount of electrical current.

Electrolysis

The secondary battery cell is based on another principle. When an electric current is passed through a solution of water, the process is called *electrolysis*. The results of *electrolysis* depend on the dissolved materials in the solution. If the solution is a mixture of water and sulfuric acid, electrolysis produces hydrogen at one electrode and oxygen at the other electrode. In other words, electrolysis separates water into hydrogen and oxygen molecules. If the solution contains copper sulfate, electrolysis will produce pure copper on the negative electrode. The electric current separates the dissolved materials so they have an electrical charge. They then move toward the terminal of the opposite polarity, or opposite charge.

Because electrolysis will separate dissolved materials, it is often used to place a thin metal coating on a metal base. Silver plating and chromium plating are done by electrolysis. This is called *electroplating*. Let us look at one example of the process. When electricity is passed through a solution of copper sulfate, copper ions and sulfate ions are formed. The copper ions have a positive charge; the sulfate ions have a negative charge. The positive copper ions move to the negative plate, and the negative sulfate ions move to the positive plate. This movement takes place when electric current is flowing.

Direct current must always be used for electrolysis to keep the current moving in just one direction. If the negative plate in the tank is a piece of metal, a layer of pure copper will be deposited on the plate. Because the ions of copper are pure, this is a good method for separating copper from any impurities it may contain. So electrolysis is widely used in the copper industry to produce pure metal.

The Storage Battery

The principle of electrolysis is used by the secondary cell to produce electricity. Electrolysis is made to produce a chemical change in a battery. When this chemical change is reversed, electricity is produced by the battery. Actually, the battery gives up the energy that caused the first chemical change. That is why it is often called a storage battery. It "stores" the electrical energy until its chemical process is reversed. Then it releases the energy.

How is this done? Let us take the automobile battery as an example. This is called a lead-acid battery because its main parts are lead and acid. This battery is an insulated case, containing an electrolyte and two plates. Both plates are made of the same material-lead. The electrolyte is a mixture of sulfuric acid and water.

Now, when the battery is made, both terminals are attached to lead plates. There is no potential difference between the two plates, and no electricity can be produced by the cell. Before the cell will produce electricity, it must go through electrolysis. A direct current is run through the battery. This causes a chemical change in one of the lead plates. It creates a potential difference between the two plates. This potential difference will produce electricity when the chemical reaction is reversed. Electrolysis is called *charging the battery*.

Grouping Battery Cells

A single battery cell provides a small voltage and a little current. A commercial battery usually contains several separate cells, tied together into one unit. There are various ways to tie the batteries together. Each method gives different voltage and current ratings for the battery. If all the positive terminals and all the negative terminals are tied together, the connection is called a *parallel* connection. If the positive terminal of one cell is tied to the negative terminal of the next cell, the connection is called a *series* connection. If a combination of the two eonncctions is used, it is called a *series-parallel* connection. Each method has advantages and disadvantages. In general, a parallel circuit supplies high current rating, but no increase in voltage. A series circuit supplies high voltage and low current ratings. A series-parallel circuit can combine the advantages of both types of connection.

Batteries

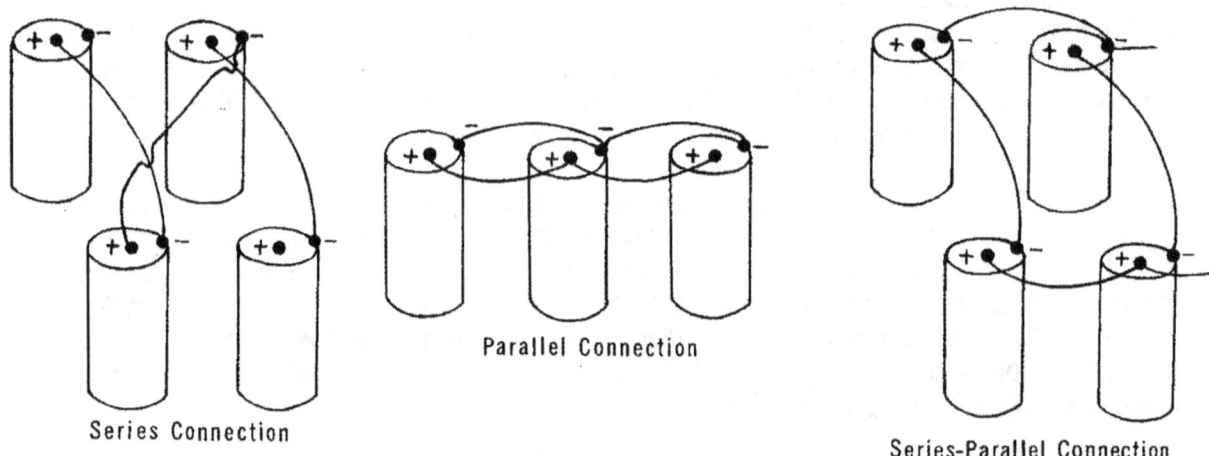

FIGURE 9. Series, Parallel, and Series-Parallel Connections.

Words Used in Unit 3

approaches (əprōch´əz), ways of getting to something
commercial (kə mėr´shăl), made to be sold
electrolysis (ĭ lĕktr´ōlə sĭs), the passing of an electric current through a solution of water
ions (ī´ənz), electrically charged particles
laboratory (lăb´rə tō rĭ), place equipped for scientists to work
surplus (sėr´pləs), amount over and above what is needed
voltaic (vŏl tā´ĭk), basic type of battery

Using Electricity

Unit 4

Electricity is energy. It can be used to do work. Electricity is probably the most convenient form of energy we have. It can be produced easily and cheaply. It can be transported from place to place rapidly and, economically. It can be changed into mechanical energy by a simple and inexpensive electric motor. Electric heat is clean and quickly produced. In many ways electricity is an ideal form of energy.

Producing Electricity
Every year the United States uses about 600 billion kilowatt-hours of electricity. One kilowatt-hour is the amount of electricity needed to burn a thousand watt bulb for one full hour. Some of our electricity is produced by converting water power into electric power. Running or falling water is used to spin a large turbine. A generator converts this spinning energy into electrical energy.

Most of the electricity used in the United States is produced by burning coal. In the last few years, we have begun to use atomic power to produce electricity. Most atomic plants use the heat energy in a nuclear reactor to produce steam. The steam is used in a turbine, and the turbine spins a large generator. The generators used to make electricity commercially are very large and heavy. The armature may weigh thousands of pounds. The coils are made of thick heavy wire. A large generator can produce thousands of amperes of electric current under a pressure of ten thousand to fifteen thousand volts.

Transporting Electricity
When electricity is transmitted for long distances, the voltage is always increased. The electricity is run through a step-up transformer. Then high voltage electricity is sent along heavy wires. This reduces the loss of energy in the transmission lines.

Electricity can also be transmitted without wires. But air has a very high resistance to electricity, and the losses are high. Wireless transmission of electric power is not yet practical. Radio waves are really electrical energy moving through air. But they must be produced at high frequencies. And the amount of energy that reaches a radio receiver is very small.

Long-distance electric power lines usually carry electricity at about 300,000 volts pressure. This high pressure cuts down losses. But it is too dangerous to use in the home. Three hundred thousand volts of pressure can force electricity through several inches of air, and cause an arc. This can be very dangerous. So the voltage is dropped for home use to 110 volts or 220 volts. Heavy appliances like stoves use 220 volt electricity because this reduces the relative amount of current flowing in the wires of the house. If a stove needs twenty amperes of 110 volt electricity, it needs only ten amperes of 220 volt electricity to produce the same energy. You can prove this by looking at Ohm's Law again. When the voltage is doubled, the current needed to produce the same power is cut in half. This makes for safer electrical operation.

Heating with Electricity
Electricity is produced when electrons flow through a wire. The electrons are carrying energy, and they can do work as they flow. If we place a high resistance in the path of the electrons, they will work hard to get past it. This work generates heat. This is the basic principle behind all electrical heating systems. The higher the resistance, the more work the electrons must do to pass. This produces more heat. An English physicist named Joule studied the relation between resistance and heating power in electricity. He discovered three basic laws that seem to explain what happens when we heat by electricity. The three laws are:
- ❖ The amount of heat produced is directly proportional to resistance.
    - o If one ohm of resistance in a cir- cuit produces one joule of heat, ten ohms of resistance will produce ten joules of heat. One joule is equal to 0.24 calories.

- ❖ The amount of heat produced is directly proportional to the time the current flows.
  - ○ If one joule of heat is produced in one second, ten joules of heat will be produced in ten seconds.
- ❖ Heat produced in a circuit is directly proportional to the square of the current flowing in the circuit.
  - ○ If two amperes of current produce four joules of heat, three amperes of current will produce nine joules of heat.

These three laws tell us that we can increase the amount of heat that is produced by an electrical circuit if we:
1. increase the resistance in the circuit.
2. increase the current in the circuit.
3. increase the time that current flows in the circuit.

Notice that an increase in current causes the greatest change in the amount of heat produced. That is why 220 volt electricity is used for heavy appliances. It reduces the current in the house wiring and reduces the amount of heat produced in the wires. This cuts down the danger of fire in the house.

Lighting

The electric light bulb was invented by an American, Thomas A. Edison. A light bulb is simply a piece of wire with a very high resistance and a high melting point which is placed inside an evacuated glass bulb. When electrons pass through the wire, they heat it white hot. The material must have a high resistance to produce the white heat. So it must have a high melting point too, or it will melt in the high temperature. Most light bulb filaments are made of tungsten wire. The filament is placed in a glass bulb, and most of the air is pumped out of the bulb. If the air remained in the bulb, the oxygen would burn the hot filament. Usually some inert gas like argon or nitrogen is placed in the bulb. This saves the filament and allows the use of higher temperatures.
Inert Gas

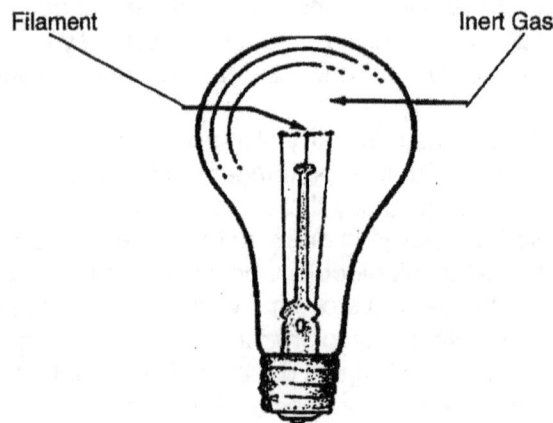

FIGURE 10. Light Bulb.

The Telegraph

Electricity travels at the speed of light --186,000 miles per second. This makes it an ideal carrier for messages. The first method of using electricity to carry messages was invented by Samuel F. B. Morse in 1837. Morse called his invention the *telegraph*. It uses the principle of an electromagnet. When an electric current flows through a coil of wire, the coil becomes a magnet, and it will attract metal. When the current is shut off, the magnet stops working. Morse used this simple principle to send his messages along electric wires.

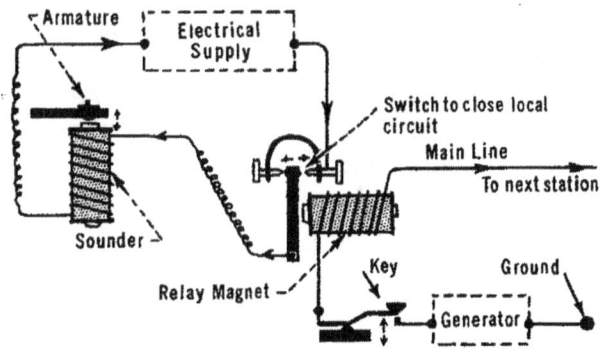

FIGURE 11. Simplified Telegraph with Key.

The main parts of a telegraph system are the key, the sounder, the wires, and a supply of electricity. These parts are shown in figure 109. When the key is pushed down, electricity flows through the wires and produces an electromagnet in the coil. This draws the sounder down with a sharp click. When the key is released, the magnet releases the sounder. By spacing the sounds made on the sounder, we can send messages. Morse also invented an alphabet made of long and short signals which is called the *Morse Code*. Using this code, we can send messages from one place to another. Of course, both the sender and the receiver must understand the Morse Oode-but it can be learned in a short time.

The old key and sounder system is not used much today. Instead, we use a machine that looks like a typewriter to send and receive messages. Each key of the machine sends a special signal along the wire. When that signal is received, the receiving machine types out the same message. These machines are called *teletype* machines. They are much faster and more accuurate than a key and sounder. They are used by the Armed Forces, police, news services, and many other organizations.

The Telephone
The telephone is more complex than the telegraph. The telegraph works by changing the *amount* of energy sent over a wire. The telephone must do more than this. First, it must change mechanical energy, produced by the voice, into electrical energy. Then the electrical energy is transmitted over a wire. Finally, the telephone must change the electrical energy back to mechanical energy that our ears can hear.

The principle that a telephone uses to change mechanical energy into electrical energy is a simple one. According to Ohm's Law, when the resistance in a circuit changes, the amount of current flowing through the circuit changes. A telephone transmitter uses the mechanical energy in sound to change the electrical resistance in a circuit. The method is quite simple.

A round disc, or diaphragm, is attached to a small box filled with carbon particles. Carbon is a resistor, and it is part of the electrical circuit of the telephone. When the sound waves strike the disc, it vibrates. This compresses the particles of carbon. As the carbon particles are pressed together, the resistance in the circuit drops. When the pressure is released, the resistance in the circuit rises. This causes changes in the current flowing in the circuit. They follow the same pattern as the vibrations of the disc

The telephone receiver must change the electrical energy carried by the electric current into mechanical energy. We cannot hear electrical waves. Our ears respond only to mechanical waves in the air. The telephone receiver uses the principle of the electromagnet. The variations in electric current produced by the transmitter cause variations in the strength of the electromagnet in the receiver.

In a telephone receiver there is a small electromagnet. This magnet holds the thin disc in place. As the strength of the magnet varies, the disc vibrates. Since the strength of the magnet is varied by the electric current produced by the vibrating disc in the transmitter, the disc in the receiver vibrates in exactly the same way. These vibrations produce mechanical sound waves exactly like those that activated the transmitter. Electrical energy is changed into mechanical energy, and our ears hear the sound coming from the receiver.

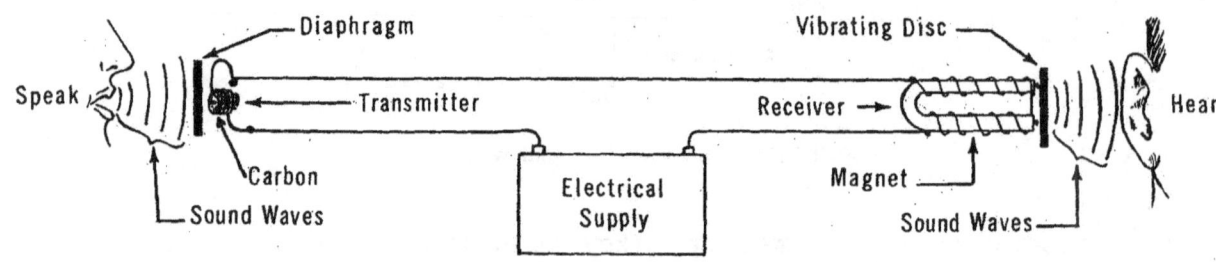

FIGURE 12 Simplified Telephone Circuit

Arc Welding

There are so many possible uses of electricity that we can cover only a very few of them. In this unit we are looking at a few nonelectronic uses of electricity. One of the most important of these uses is arc welding. In modern industry arc welding is a very important process. It is employed to build auto bodies, airplanes, and thousands of other things that we use every day.

Electric welding works on the same principle as the electric arc light. High voltage and very heavy electric currents are needed for welding. Usually this requires a special transformer and a special electric line into the building. One end of the electric line is attached to the material to be welded. The other end is run through a special tip or rod made of high resistance metal. This rod is held by the man who does the welding.

There are different kinds of welding rods for each type of welding, depending upon the material to be welded. The composition of the tip or rod determines the strength of the joint and the temperature at the arc. A skilled welder chooses the rod that will best do the particular job. When the metal rod is touched against the material to be welded, the electric circuit is closed and electric current runs through the rod. The high resistance produces a high temperature, and the material in the rod is vaporized. This produces a trail of metal vapor between the rod and the material being welded. The heavy electric current runs through this vapor arc, producing a white heat.

As in the carbon arc light, the metal tip keeps melting as electricity flows along the rod. The vaporized metal forms a solid deposit on the joint, called a "bead." The tip of the rod must be kept an even distance from the material to produce a smooth, even joint. This takes experience and a steady hand. When the metal hardens and cools, it produces a joint that is very strong. In fact, the welded part of a joint is often stronger than the metal that is joined together.

Other Uses of Electricity

Some of the special uses of electricity are often overlooked. It can be used to reduce smoke in cities, for example. If an electric device is placed inside a large chimney, it can be used to charge dirt particles as they move up the chimney. A collector higher up the chimney that has an opposite charge will collect the particles as they pass by. The amount of smoke and dirt that leaves the chimney is, thus, cut to a minimum. The collector must be emptied from time to time.

Electricity is very useful in the field of medicine. Special light bulbs are used to kill germs in hospitals. These lights produce energy of a particular frequency that is deadly to germs. Electric energy is used to provide heating for therapy machines, used to ease the pain when bones or muscles are seriously injured. There is even an electric knife that seals as it cut, thus eliminating the need for sewing. It is an excellent instrument for certain kinds of operations.

Radar and television, calculating machines, and weather satellites all come under the area of *electronics*. Yet all of these complex machines are built upon the same principles that are stated in Ohm's Law. The study of electronics is based on our study of electricity. The one great difference between electricity and electronics lies in making use of the effect that can be produced by a vacuum tube. But all electricity, whether it is passed through a vacuum tube or not, must obey the same general law.

Words Used in Unit 4

economically (ē kə nŏm´ĭk lĭ), inexpensively
evacuated (ĭ văk´ū ăt əd), emptied
filament (fil´ə mənt), the wire in a light bulb
inert (ĭn ərt´), not active
reduces (rĭ dūs´əs), makes less
transformer (trăns form´ər), an apparatus for increasing or decreasing voltage
vaporized (vă´pər ĭzd), changed into vapor, or a gas
welded (wĕld´əd), joined together by pressing while soft and hot

BASIC ELECTRICITY

FUNDAMENTAL CONCEPTS OF ELECTRICITY
What is Electricity?

The word "electric" is actually a Greek-derived word meaning AMBER. Amber is a translucent (semitransparent) yellowish mineral, which, in the natural form, is composed of fossilized resin. The ancient Greeks used the words "electric force" in referring to the mysterious forces of attraction and repulsion exhibited by amber when it was rubbed with a cloth. They did not understand the fundamental nature of this force. They could not answer the seemingly simple question, "What is electricity?". This question is still unanswered. Though you might define electricity as "that force which moves electrons," this would be the same as defining an engine as "that force which moves an automobile." You would have described the effect, not the force.

We presently know little more than the ancient Greeks knew about the fundamental nature of electricity, but tremendous strides have been made in harnessing and using it. Elaborate theories concerning the nature and behavior of electricity have been advanced, and have gained wide acceptance because of their apparent truth and demonstrated workability.

From time to time various scientists have found that electricity seems to behave in a constant and predictable manner in given situations, or when subjected to given conditions. These scientists, such as Faraday, Ohm, Lenz, and Kirchhoff, to name only a few, observed and described the predictable characteristics of electricity and electric current in the form of certain rules. These rules are often referred to as "laws." Thus, though electricity itself has never been clearly defined, its predictable nature and easily used form of energy has made it one of the most widely used power sources in modern time. By learning the rules, or laws, applying to the behavior of electricity, and by learning the methods of producing, controlling, and using it, you will have "learned" electricity without ever having determined its fundamental identity.

THE MOLECULE

One of the oldest, and probably the most generally accepted, theories concerning electric current flow is that it is comprised of moving electrons. This is the ELECTRON THEORY. Electrons are extremely tiny parts, or particles, of matter. To study the electron, you must therefore study the structural nature of matter itself. (Anything having mass and inertia, and which occupies any amount of space, is composed of matter.) To study the fundamental structure or composition of any type of matter, it must be reduced to its fundamental fractions. Assume the drop of water in figure 1-1 (A) was halved again and again. By continuing the process long enough, you would eventually obtain the smallest particle of water possible-the molecule. All molecules are composed of atoms.

A molecule of water (H_2O) is composed of one atom of oxygen and two atoms of hydrogen, as represented in figure 1-1 (B). If the molecule of water were further subdivided, there would remain only unrelated atoms of oxygen and hydrogen, and the water would no longer exist as such. This example illustrates the following fact-the molecule is the smallest particle to which a substance can be reduced and still be called by the same name. This applies to all substances-liquids, solids, and gases.

When whole molecules are combined or separated from one another, the change is generally referred to as a PHYSICAL change. In a CHEMICAL change the molecules of the substance are altered such that

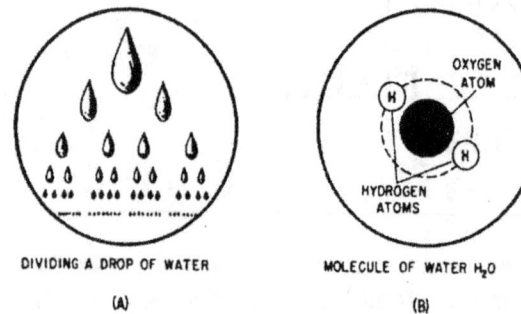

Figure 1-1.—Matter is made up of molecules.

new molecules result. Most chemical changes involve positive and negative ions and thus are electrical in nature. All matter is said to be essentially electrical in nature.

THE ATOM

In the study of chemistry it soon becomes apparent that the molecule is far from being the ultimate particle into which matter may be subdivided. The salt molecule may be decomposed into radically different substances—sodium and chlorine. These particles that make up molecules can be isolated and studied separately. They are called ATOMS.

The atom is the smallest particle that makes up that type of material called an ELEMENT. The element retains its characteristics when subdivided into atoms. More than 100 elements have been identified. They can be arranged into a table of increasing weight, and can be grouped into families of material having similar properties. This arrangement is called the PERIODIC TABLE OF THE ELEMENTS.

The idea that all matter is composed of atoms dates back more than 2,000 years to the Greeks. Many centuries passed before the study of matter proved that the basic idea of atomic structure was correct. Physicists have explored the interior of the atom and discovered many subdivisions in it. The core of the atom is called the NUCLEUS. Most of the mass of the atom is concentrated in the nucleus. It is comparable to the sun in the solar system, around which the planets revolve. The nucleus contains PROTONS (positively charged particles) and NEUTRONS which are electrically neutral.

Most of the weight of the atom is in the protons and neutrons of the nucleus. Whirling around the nucleus are one or more smaller particles of negative electric charge. THESE ARE THE ELECTRONS. Normally there is one proton for each electron in the entire atom so that the net positive charge of the nucleus is balanced by the net negative charge of the electrons whirling around the nucleus. THUS THE ATOM IS ELECTRICALLY NEUTRAL.

The electrons do not fall into the nucleus even though they are attracted strongly to it. Their motion prevents it, as the planets are prevented from falling into the sun because of their centrifugal force of revolution.

The number of protons, which is usually the same as the number of electrons, determines the kind of element in question. Figure 1-2 shows a simplified picture of several atoms of different materials based on the conception of planetary electrons describing orbits about the nucleus. For example, hydrogen has a nucleus consisting of 1 proton, around which rotates 1 electron. The helium atom has a nucleus containing 2 protons and 2 neutrons with 2 electrons encircling the nucleus. Near the other extreme of the list of elements is curium (not shown in the figure), an element discovered in the 1940's, which has 96 protons and 96 electrons in each atom.

The *Periodic Table of the Elements* is an orderly arrangement of the elements in ascending atomic number (number of planetary electrons) and also in atomic weight (number of protons and neutrons in the nucleus). The various kinds of atoms have distinct masses or

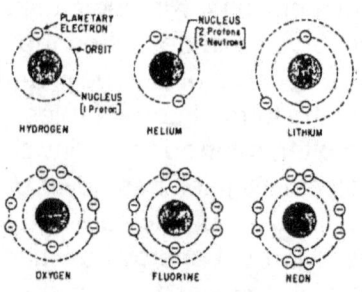

Figure 1-2.—Atomic structure of elements.

weights with respect to each other. The element most closely approaching unity (meaning 1) is hydrogen whose atomic weight is 1.008 as compared with oxygen whose atomic weight is 16. Helium has an atomic weight of approximately 4, lithium 7, fluorine 19, and neon 20, as shown in figure 1-2.

Figure 1-3 is a pictorial summation of the discussion that has just been presented. Visible matter, at the left of the figure, is broken down first to one of its basic molecules, then to one of the molecule's atoms. The atom is then further reduced to its subatomic particles—the protons, neutrons, and electrons. Subatomic particles are electric in nature. That is, they are the particles of matter most affected by an electric force. Whereas the whole molecule or a whole atom is electrically neutral, most subatomic particles are not neutral (with the exception of the neutron). Protons are inherently positive, and electrons are inherently negative. It is these inherent characteristics which make subatomic particles sensitive to electric force.

When an electric force is applied to a conducting medium, such as copper wire, electrons in the outer orbits of the copper atoms are forced out of orbit and impelled along the wire. The direction of electron movement is determined by the direction of the impelling force. The protons do not move, mainly because they are extremely heavy. The proton of the lightest element, hydrogen, is approximately 1,850 times as heavy as an electron. Thus, it is the relatively light electron that is most readily moved by electricity.

When an orbital electron is removed from an atom it is called a FREE ELECTRON. Some of the electrons of certain metallic atoms are so loosely bound to the nucleus that they are comparatively free to move from atom to atom. Thus, a very small force or amount of energy will cause such electrons to be removed from the atom and become free electrons. It is these free electrons that constitute the flow of an electric current in electrical conductors.

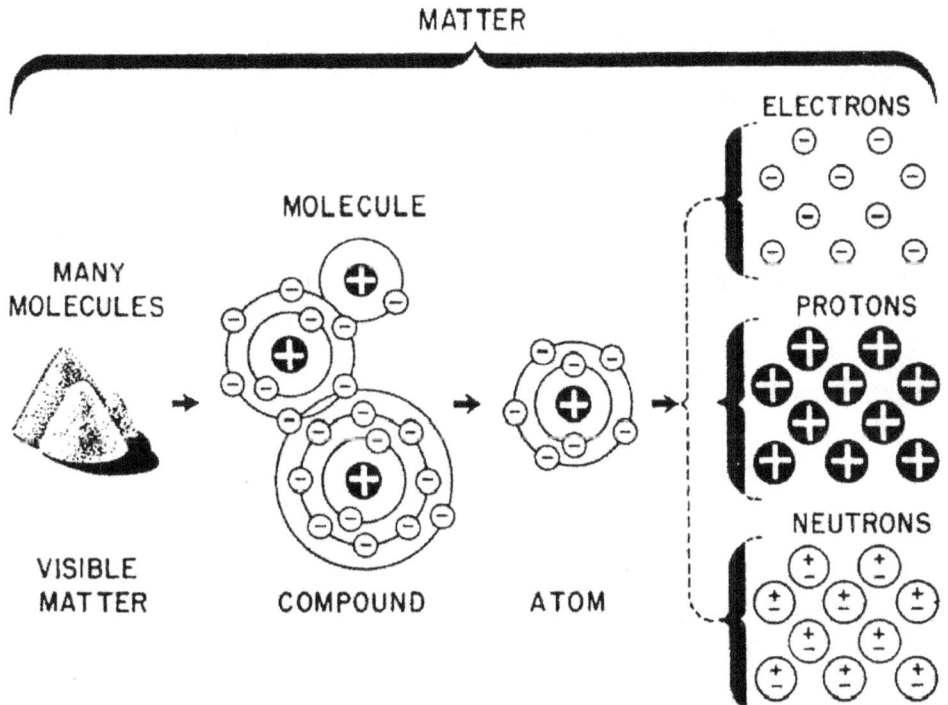

Figure 1-3.—Breakdown of visible matter to electric particles.

If the internal energy of an atom is raised above its normal state, the atom is said to be EXCITED. Excitation may be produced by causing the atoms to collide with particles that are impelled by an electric force. In this way, energy is transferred from the electric source to the atom. The excess energy absorbed by an atom may become sufficient to cause loosely bound outer electrons to leave the atom against the force that acts to hold them within. An atom that has thus lost or gained one or more electrons is said to be IONIZED. If the atom loses electrons it becomes positively charged and is referred to as a POSITIVE ION. Conversely, if the atom gains electrons, it becomes negatively charged and is referred to as a NEGATIVE ION. Actually then, an ion is a small particle of matter having a positive or negative charge.

Conductors and Insulators

Substances that permit the free motion of a large number of electrons are called CONDUCTORS. Copper wire is considered a good conductor because it has many free electrons. Electrical energy is transferred through conductors by means of the movement of free electrons that migrate from atom to atom inside the conductor. Each electron moves a very short distance to the neighboring atom where it replaces one or more electrons by forcing them out of their orbits. The replaced electrons repeat the process in other nearby atoms until the movement is transmitted throughout the entire length of the conductor. The greater the number of electrons that can be made to move in a material under the application of a given force the better are the conductive qualities of that material. A good conductor is said to have a low opposition or low resistance to the current (electron) flow.

In contrast to good conductors, some substances such as rubber, glass, and dry wood have very few free electrons. In these materials large amounts of energy must be expended in order to break the electrons loose from the influence of the nucleus. Substances containing very few free electrons are called POOR CONDUCTORS, NON-CONDUCTORS, or INSULATORS. Actually, there is no sharp dividing line between conductors and insulators, since electron motion is known to exist to some extent in all matter. Electricians simply use the best conductors as wires to carry current and the poorest conductors as insulators to prevent the current from being diverted from the wires.

Listed below are some of the best conductors and best insulators arranged in accordance with their respective abilities to conduct or to resist the flow of electrons.

Conductors	Insulators
Silver	Dry air
Copper	Glass
Aluminum	Mica
Zinc	Rubber
Brass	Asbestos
Iron	Bakelite

Static Electricity

In a natural, or neutral state, each atom in a body of matter will have the proper number of electrons in orbit around it. Consequently, the whole body of matter comprised of the neutral atoms will also be electrically neutral. In this state, it is said to have a "zero charge," and will neither attract nor repel other matter in its vicinity. Electrons will neither leave nor enter the neutrally charged body should it come in contact with other neutral bodies. If, however, any number of electrons are removed from the atoms of a body of matter, there will remain more protons than electrons, and the whole body of matter will become electrically positive. Should the positively charged body come in contact with another body having a normal charge, or having a negative (too many electrons) charge, an electric current will flow between them. Electrons will leave the more negative body and enter the positive body. This electron flow will continue until both bodies have equal charges.

When two bodies of matter have unequal charges, and are near one another, an electric force is exerted between them because of their unequal charges. However, since they are not in contact, their charges cannot equalize. The existence of such an electric force, where current cannot flow, is referred to as static electricity. "Static" means "not moving." This is also referred to as an ELECTROSTATIC FORCE.

One of the easiest ways to create a static charge is by the friction method. With the friction method, two pieces of matter are rubbed together and electrons are "wiped off" one onto the other. If materials that are good conductors are used, it is quite difficult to obtain a detectable charge on either. The reason for this is that equalizing currents will flow easily in and between the conducting materials. These currents equalize the charges almost as fast as they are created. A static charge is easier to obtain by rubbing a hard nonconducting material against a soft, or fluffy, nonconductor. Electrons are rubbed off one material and onto the other material. This is illustrated in figure 1-4.

When the hard rubber rod is rubbed in the fur, the rod accumulates electrons. Since both fur and rubber are poor conductors, little equalizing current can flow, and an electrostatic charge is built up. When the charge is great enough, equalizing currents will flow in spite of the material's poor conductivity. These currents will cause visible sparks, if viewed in darkness, and will produce a crackling sound.

CHARGED BODIES

One of the fundamental laws of electricity is that LIKE CHARGES REPEL EACH OTHER and UNLIKE CHARGES ATTRACT EACH OTHER. A positive charge and negative charge, being unlike, tend to move toward each other. In the atom the negative electrons are drawn toward the positive protons in the nucleus. This attractive force is balanced by the electron's centrifugal force caused by its rotation about the nucleus. As a result, the electrons remain in orbit and are not drawn into the nucleus. Electrons repel each other because of their like negative charges, and protons repel each other because of their like positive charges.

The law of charged bodies may be demonstrated by a simple experiment. Two pith (paper pulp) balls are suspended near one another by threads, as shown in figure 1-5.

If the hard rubber rod is rubbed to give it a negative charge, and then held against the right-hand ball in part (A), the rod will impart a negative charge to the ball. The right-hand ball will be charged negative with respect to the left-hand ball. When released, the two balls will be drawn together, as shown in figure 1-5 (A). They will touch and remain in contact until the left-hand ball acquires a portion of the negative charge of the right-hand ball, at which time they will swing apart as shown in figure 1-5 (C). If positive charges are placed on both balls (fig. 1-5 (B)), the balls will also be repelled from each other.

COULOMB'S LAW OF CHARGES

The amount of attracting or repelling force which acts between two electrically charged bodies in free space depends on two things(1) their charges, and (2) the distance between them. The relationship of charge and distance to electrostatic force was first discovered and written by a French scientist named Charles A. Coulomb. Coulomb's Law states that CHARGED BODIES ATTRACT OR REPEL EACH OTHER WITH A FORCE THAT IS DIRECTLY PROPORTIONAL TO THE PRODUCT OF THEIR CHARGES, AND IS INVERSELY PROPORTIONAL TO THE SQUARE OF THE DISTANCE BETWEEN THEM.

ELECTRIC FIELDS

The space between and around charged bodies in which their influence is felt is called an ELECTRIC FIELD OF FORCE. The electric field is always terminated on material objects and extends between positive and negative charges. It can exist in air, glass, paper, or a vacuum. ELECTROSTATIC FIELDS and DIELECTRIC FIELDS are other names used to refer to this region of force.

Fields of force spread out in the space surrounding their point of origin and, in general, DIMINISH IN PROPORTION TO THE SQUARE OF THE DISTANCE FROM THEIR SOURCE.

The field about a charged body is generally represented by lines which are

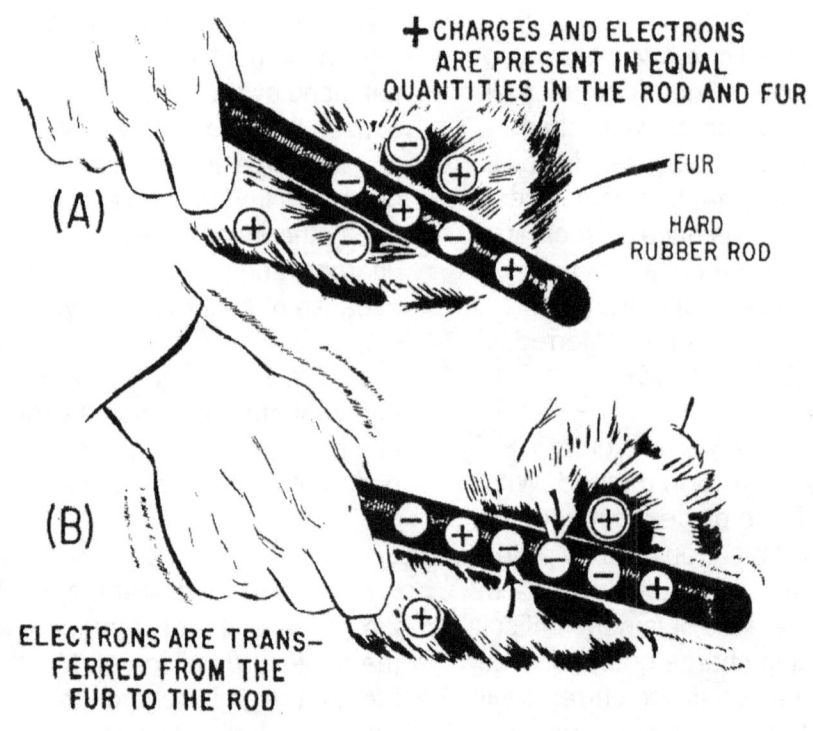

Figure 1-4.—Producing static electricity by friction.

referred to as ELECTROSTATIC LINES OF FORCE. These lines are imaginary and are used merely to represent the direction and strength of the field. To avoid confusion, the lines of force exerted by a positive charge are always shown leaving the charge, and for a negative charge they are shown as entering. Figure 1-6 illustrates the use of lines to represent the field about charged bodies.

Figure 1-6 (A) represents the repulsion of like-charged bodies and their associated fields. Part (B) represents the attraction between unlike-charged bodies and their associated fields.

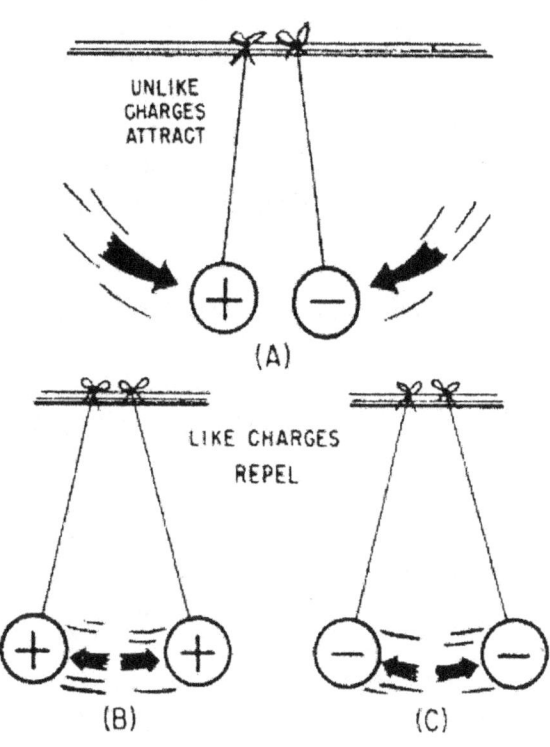

Figure 1-5.—Reaction between charged bodies.

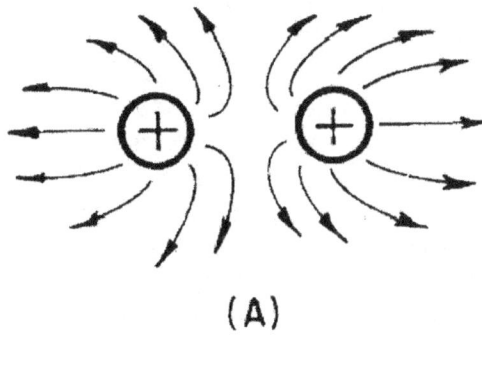

(A)

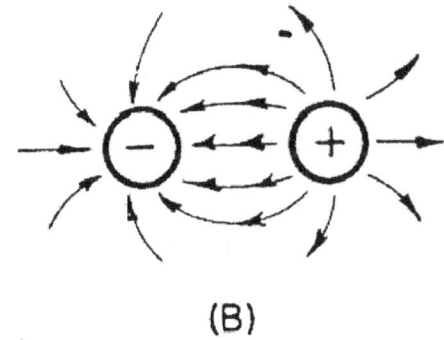

(B)

Figure 1-6.—Electrostatic lines of force.

Magnetism

A substance is said to be a magnet if it has the property of magnetism-that is, if it has the power to attract such substances as iron, steel, nickel, or cobalt, which are known as MAGNETIC MATERIALS. A steel knitting needle, magnetized by a method to be described later, exhibits two points of maximum attraction (one at each end) and no attraction at its center. The points of maximum attraction are called MAGNETIC POLES. All magnets have at least two poles. If the needle is suspended by its middle so that it rotates freely in a horizontal plane about its center, the needle comes to rest in an approximately north-south line of direction. The same pole will always point to the north, and the other will always point toward the south. The magnetic pole that points northward is called the NORTH POLE, and the other the SOUTH POLE.

A MAGNETIC FIELD exists around a simple bar magnet. The field consists of imaginary lines along which a MAGNETIC FORCE acts. These lines emanate from the north pole of the magnet, and enter the south pole, returning to the north pole through the magnet itself, thus forming closed loops.

A MAGNETIC CIRCUIT is a complete path through which magnetic lines of force may be established under the influence of a magnetizing force. Most magnetic circuits are composed largely of magnetic materials in order to contain the magnetic flux. These circuits are similar to the ELECTRIC CIRCUIT, which is a complete path through which current is caused to flow under the influence of an electromotive force.

Magnets may be conveniently divided into three groups.

1. NATURAL MAGNETS, found in the natural state in the form of a mineral called magnetite.

2. PERMANENT MAGNETS, bars of hardened steel (or some form of alloy such as alnico) that have been permanently magnetized.

3. ELECTROMAGNETS, composed of soft-iron cores around which are wound coils of insulated wire. When an electric current flows through the coil, the core becomes magnetized. When the current ceases to flow, the core loses most of its magnetism.

Permanent magnets and electromagnets are sometimes called ARTIFICIAL MAGNETS to further distinguish them from natural magnets.

NATURAL MAGNETS

For many centuries it has been known that certain stones (magnetite, Fe_3O_4) have the ability to attract small pieces of iron. Because many of the best of these stones (natural magnets) were found near Magnesia in Asia Minor, the Greeks called the substance MAGNETITE, or MAGNETIC.

Before this, ancient Chinese observed that when similar stones were suspended freely, or floated on a light substance in a container of water, they tended to assume a nearly north-and-south position. Probably Chinese navigators used bits of magnetite floating on wood in a liquid-filled vessel as crude compasses. At that time it was not known that the earth itself acts like a magnet, and these stones were regarded with considerable superstitious awe. Because bits of this substance were used as compasses they were called LOADSTONES (or lodestones), which means "leading stones."

Natural magnets are also found in the United States, Norway, and Sweden. A natural magnet, demonstrating the attractive force at the poles, is shown in figure 1-7 (A).

ARTIFICIAL MAGNETS

Natural magnets no longer have any practical value because more powerful and more conveniently shaped permanent magnets can be produced artificially. Commercial magnets are made from special steels and alloysfor example, alnico, made principally of aluminum, nickel, and cobalt. The name is derived from the first two letters of the three principal elements of which it is composed. An artificial magnet is shown in figure 1-7 (B).

An iron, steel, or alloy bar can be magnetized by inserting the bar into a coil of insulated wire and passing a heavy direct current through the coil, as shown in figure 1-8 (A). This aspect of magnetism is

Artificial magnets may be classified as "permanent" or "temporary" depending on their ability to retain their magnetic strength after the magnetizing force has been removed. Hardened steel and certain alloys are relatively difficult to magnetize and are said to have a LOW PERMEABILITY because the magnetic lines of force do not easily permeate, or distribute themselves readily through the steel. Once magnetized, however, these materials retain a large part of their magnetic strength and are called PERMANENT MAGNETS. Permanent magnets are used extensively in electric instruments, meters, telephone receivers, permanent-magnet loudspeakers, andmagnetos. Conversely, substances

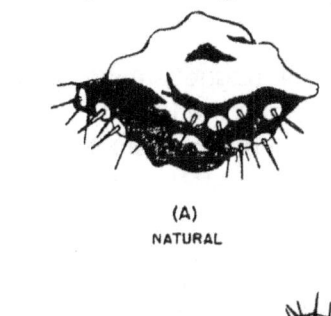

(A) NATURAL

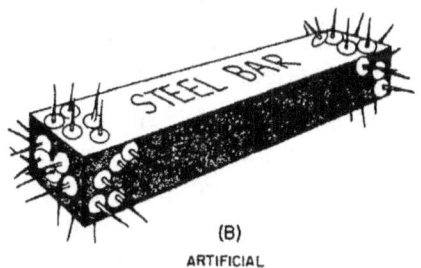

(B) ARTIFICIAL

Figure 1-7.-(A) Natural magnet; (B) artificial magnet.

treated later in the chapter. The same bar may also be magnetized if it is stroked with a bar magnet, as shown in figure 1-8 (B). It will then have the same magnetic property that the magnet used to induce the magnetism-has namely, there will be two poles of attraction, one at either end. This process produces a permanent magnet by INDUCTION-that is, the magnetism is induced in the bar by the influence of the stroking magnet.

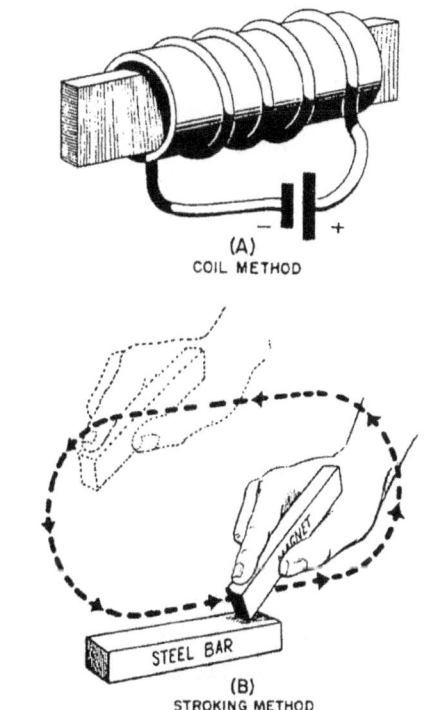

Figure 1-8.Methods of producing artificial magnets.

that are relatively easy to magnetizesuch as soft iron and annealed silicon steelare said to have a HIGH PERMEABILITY. Such substances retain only a small part of their magnetism after the magnetizing force is removed and are called TEMPORARY MAGNETS. Silicon steel and similar materials are used in transformers where the magnetism is constantly changing and in generators and motors where the strengths of the fields can be readily changed.

The magnetism that remains in a temporary magnet after the magnetizing force is removed is called RESIDUAL MAGNETISM. The fact that temporary magnets retain even a small amount of magnetism is an important factor in the buildup of voltage in self-excited d-c generators.

NATURE OF MAGNETISM

Weber's theory of the nature of magnetism is based on the assumption that each of the molecules of a magnet is itself a tiny magnet. The molecular magnets that compose an unmagne-tized bar of iron or steel are arranged at random, as shown by the simplified diagram of figure 1-9 (A). With this arrangement, the magnetism of each of the molecules is neutralized by that of adjacent molecules, and no external magnetic effect is produced. When a magnetizing force is applied to an unmagnetized iron or steel bar, the molecules become alined so that the north poles point one way and the south poles point the other way, as shown in figure 1-9 (B).

If a bar magnet is broken into several parts, as in figure 1-10, each part constitutes a magnet. The north and south poles of these small magnets are in the same respective directions as those of the original magnet. If each of these parts is again broken, the resulting parts are likewise magnets, and the magnetic orientation is the same. If this breaking process could be continued, smaller and smaller pieces would retain their magnetism until each part was reduced to a molecule. It is therefore logical to assume that each of these molecules is a magnet.

A further justification for this assumption results from the fact that when a bar magnet is held out of alinement with the earth's field and is repeatedly jarred, heated, or exposed to a powerful alternating field, the molecular alinement is disarranged and the magnet becomes demagnetized. For example, electric measuring instruments become inaccurate if their permanent magnets lose some of their magnetism because of severe jarring or exposure to opposing magnetic fields.

A theory of magnetism that is perhaps more adequate than the MOLECULAR theory is the DOMAIN theory. Much simplified, this theory may be stated as follows:

In magnetic substances the "atomic" magnets, produced by the movement of the planetary electrons around the nucleus, have a strong tendency to line up together in groups of from 10^{14} to 10^{15} atoms. This occurs without the influence of any external magnetic field. These groups of atoms having their poles orientated in the same direction are called DOMAINS. Therefore,

UNMAGNETIZED STEEL
(A)

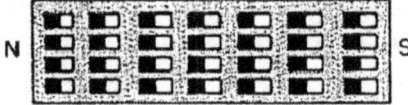

MAGNETIZED STEEL
(B)

Figure 1-9.—Molecular theory of magnetism.

throughout each domain an intense magnetic field is produced. These fields are normally in a miscellaneous arrangement so that no external field is apparent when the substance as a whole is unmagnetized.

Each tiny domain (10^6 of them may be contained in 1 cubic millimeter) is always magnetized to saturation, and the addition of an external magnetic field does not increase the inherent magnetism of the individual domains.

However, if an external field that is gradually increased in strength is applied to the magnetic substance the domains will line up one by one (or perhaps several at a time) with the external field.

MAGNETIC FIELDS AND LINES OF FORCE

If a bar magnet is dipped into iron filings, many of the filings are attracted to the ends of the magnet, but none are attracted to the center of the magnet. As mentioned previously, the ends of the magnet where the attractive force is the greatest are called the POLES of the magnet. By using a compass, the line of direction of the magnetic force at various points near the magnet may be observed. The compass needle itself is a magnet. The north end of the compass needle always points toward the south pole, S, as shown in figure 1-11 (A), and thus the sense of direction (with respect to the polarity of the bar magnet) is also indicated. At the center, the compass needle points in a direction that is parallel to the bar magnet.

When the compass is placed successively at several points in the vicinity of the bar magnet the compass needle alines itself with the field at each position. The direction of the field is indicated by the arrows and represents the direction in which the north pole of the compass needle will point when the compass is placed in this field. Such a line along which a compass needle alines itself is called a MAGNETIC LINE OF FORCE. As mentioned previously, the magnetic lines of force are assumed to emanate from the north pole of a magnet, pass through the surrounding space, and enter the south pole. The lines of force then pass from the south pole to the north pole inside the magnet to form a closed loop. Each line of force forms an independent closed loop and does not merge with or cross other lines of force. The lines of force between the poles of a horseshoe magnet are shown in figure 1-11 (B).

The space surrounding a magnet, in which the magnetic force acts, is called a MAGNETIC FIELD. Michael Faraday was the first scientist to visualize the magnet field as being in a state of stress and consisting of uniformly distributed lines of force. The entire quantity of magnetic lines surrounding a magnet is called MAGNETIC FLUX. Flux in a magnetic circuit corresponds to current in an electric circuit.

The number of lines of force per unit area is called FLUX DENSITY and is measured in lines per square inch or lines per square centimeter. Flux density is expressed by the equation

$$B = \frac{\phi}{A}$$

where B is the flux density, ϕ (Greek phi) is the total number of lines of flux, and A is the cross-sectional area of the magnetic circuit. If A is in square centimeters, B is in lines per square centimeter, or GAUSS. The terms FLUX and FLOW of magnetism are frequently used in textbooks. However, magnetism itself is not thought to be a stream of particles in motion, but is simply a field of force exerted in space. A visual representation pf the magnetic field around a magnet can be obtained by placing a plate of glass over a magnet and sprinkling iron filings onto

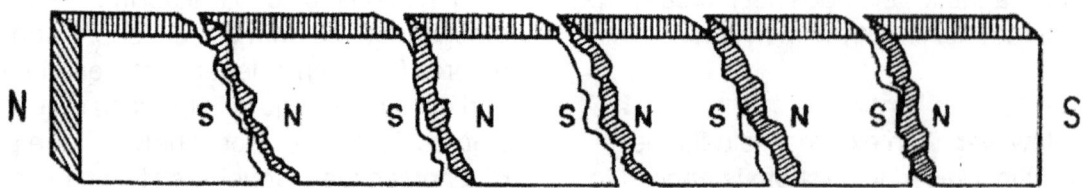

Figure 1-10.—Magnetic poles of a broken magnet.

the glass. The filings arrange themselves in definite paths between the poles.

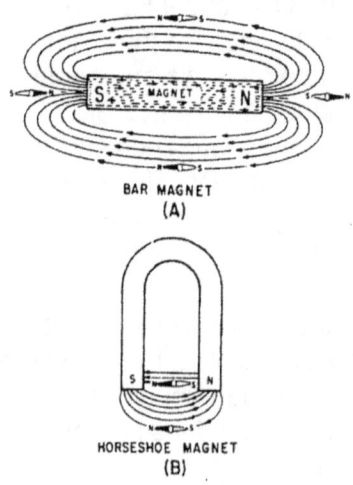

Figure 1-11.—Magnetic lines of force.

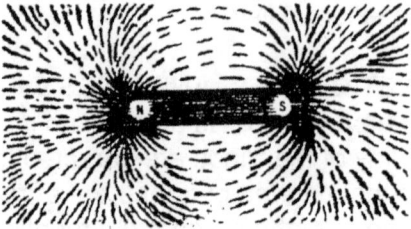

Figure 1-12.—Magnetic field pattern around a magnet.

This arrangement of the filings shows the pattern of the magnetic field around the magnet, as in figure 1-12.

The magnetic field surrounding a symmetrically shaped magnet has the following properties:

1. The field is symmetrical unless disturbed by another magnetic substance.

2. The lines of force have direction and are represented as emanating from the north pole and entering the south pole.

LAWS OF ATTRACTION AND REPULSION

If a magnetized needle is suspended near a bar magnet, as in figure 1-13, it will be seen that a north pole repels a north pole and a south pole repels a south pole. Opposite poles, however, will attract each other.

Thus, the first two laws of magnetic attraction and repulsion are:

1. LIKE magnetic poles REPEL each other.

2. UNLIKE magnetic poles ATTRACT each other.

The flux patterns between adjacent UNLIKE poles of bar magnets, as indicated by lines, are shown in figure 1-14 (A). Similar patterns for adjacent LIKE poles are shown in figure 1-14 (B). The lines do not cross at any point and they act as if they repel each other.

Figure 1-15 shows the flux pattern (indicated by lines) around two bar magnets placed close together and parallel with each other. Figure 1-15 (A) shows the flux pattern when opposite poles are adjacent; and figure 1-15 (B) shows the flux pattern when like poles are adjacent.

The THIRD LAW of magnetic attraction and repulsion states in effect that the force of attraction or repulsion existing between two magnetic poles decreases rapidly as the poles are separated from each other. Actually, the force of attraction or repulsion varies directly as the product of the separate pole strengths and inversely as the square of the distance separating the magnetic poles, provided the poles are small enough to be considered as points. For example, if the distance between two north poles is increased from 2 feet to 4 feet, the force of

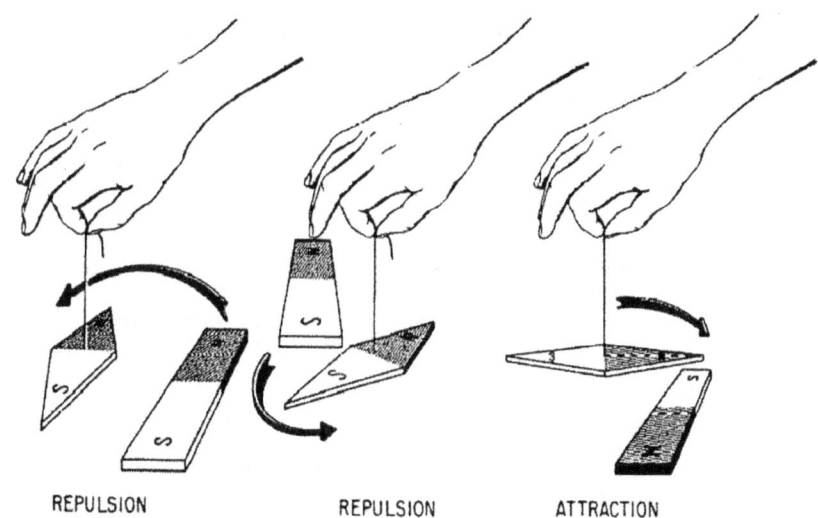

Figure 1-13.—Laws of attraction and repulsion.

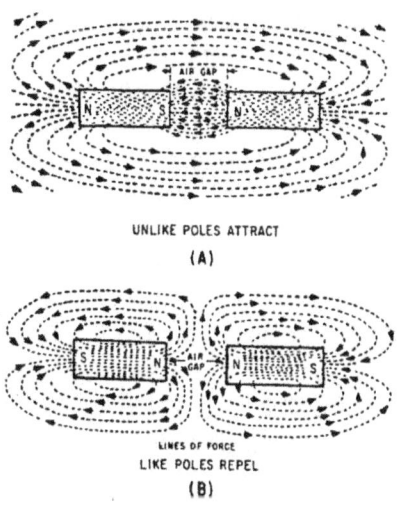

Figure 1-14.—Lines of force between unlike and like poles.

repulsion between them is decreased to one-fourth of its original value. If either pole strength is doubled, the distance remaining the same, the force between the poles will be doubled.

THE EARTH'S MAGNETISM

As has been stated, the earth is a huge magnet; and surrounding the earth is the magnetic field produced by the earth's magnetism. The magnetic polarities of the earth are as indicated in figure 1-16. The geographic poles are also shown at each end of the axis of rotation of the earth. The magnetic axis does not coincide with the geographic axis, and therefore the magnetic and geographic poles are not at the same place on the surface of the earth.

The early users of the compass regarded the end of the compass needle that points in a northerly direction as being a north pole. The other end was regarded as a south pole. On some maps the magnetic pole of the earth towards which the north pole of the compass pointed was designated a north magnetic pole. This magnetic pole was obviously called a north pole because of its proximity to the north geographic pole.

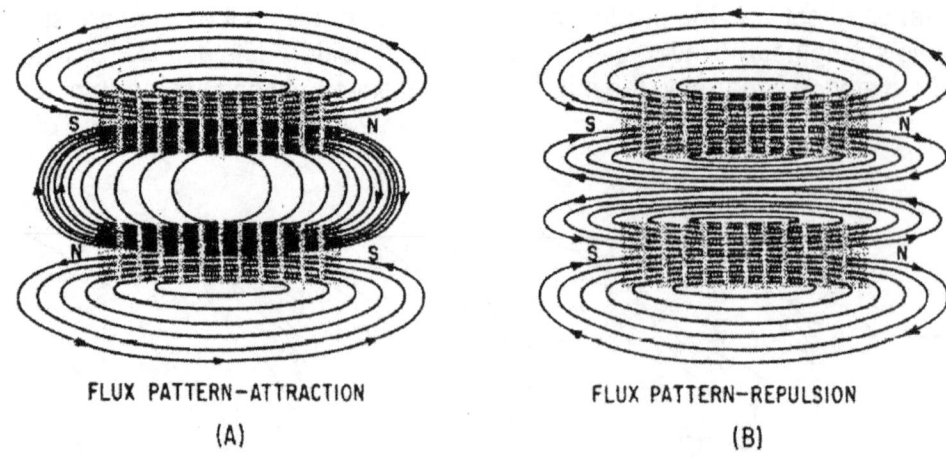

Figure 1-15.—Flux patterns of adjacent parallel bar magnets.

When it was learned that the earth is a magnet and that opposite poles attract, it was necessary to call the magnetic pole located in the northern hemisphere a SOUTH MAGNETIC POLE and the magnetic pole located in the southern hemisphere a NORTH MAGNETIC POLE. The matter of naming the poles was arbitrary. Obviously, the polarity of the compass needle that points toward the north must be opposite to the polarity of the earth's magnetic pole located there.

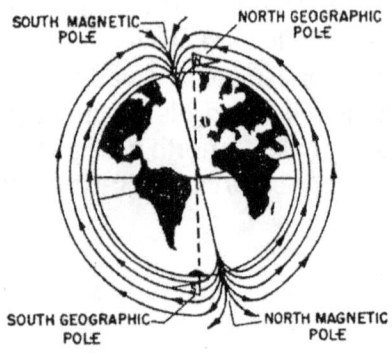

Figure 1-16.—Earth's magnetic poles.

As has been stated, magnetic lines of force are assumed to emanate from the north pole of a magnet and to enter the south pole as closed loops. Because the earth is a magnet, lines of force emanate from its north magnetic pole and enter the south magnetic pole as closed loops. The compass needle alines itself in such a way that the earth's lines of force enter at its south pole and leave at its north pole. Because the north pole of the needle is defined as the end that points in a northerly direction it follows that the magnetic pole in the vicinity of the north geographic pole is in reality a south magnetic pole, and vice versa.

Because the magnetic poles and the geographic poles do not coincide, a compass will not (except at certain positions on the earth) point in a true (geographic) north-south direction-that is, it will not point in a line of direction that passes through the north and south geographic poles, but in a line of direction that makes an angle with it. This angle is called the angle of VARIATION OR DECLINATION.

MAGNETIC SHIELDING

There is not a known INSULATOR for magnetic flux. If a nonmagnetic material is placed in a magnetic field, there is no appreciable change in flux-that is, the flux penetrates the nonmagnetic material. For example, a glass plate placed between the poles of a horseshoe magnet will have no appreciable effect on the field although glass itself is a good insulator in an electric circuit. If a magnetic material (for example, soft iron) is placed in a magnetic field, the flux may be redirected to take advantage of the greater permeability of the magnetic material as shown in figure 1-17. Permeability is the quality of a substance which determines the ease with which it can be magnetized.

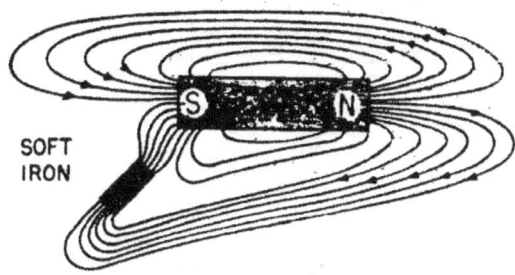

Figure 1-17.—Effects of a magnetic substance in a magnetic field.

The sensitive mechanism of electric instruments and meters can be influenced by stray magnetic fields which will cause errors in their readings. Because instrument mechanisms cannot be insulated against magnetic flux, it is necessary to employ some means of directing the flux around the instrument. This is accomplished by placing a soft-iron case, called a MAGNETIC SCREEN OR SHIELD, about the instrument. Because the flux *is* established more readily through the iron (even though the path is longer) than through the air inside the case, the instrument is effectively shielded, as shown by the watch and soft-iron shield in figure 1-18.

The study of electricity and magnetism, and how they affect each other, is given more thorough coverage in later chapters of this course.

The discussion of magnetism up to this point has been mainly intended to clarify terms and meanings, such as "polarity," "fields," "lines of force," and so forth. Only one fundamental relationship between magnetism and electricity is discussed in this chapter. This relationship pertains to magnetism as used to generate a voltage and it is discussed under the headings that follows.

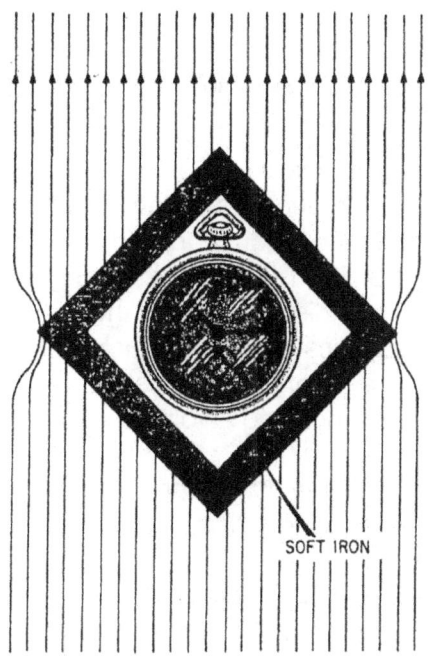

Figure 1-18.—Magnetic shield.

Difference in Potential

The force that causes free electrons to move in a conductor as an electric current is called (1) an electromotive force (e.m.f.), (2) a voltage, or (3) a difference in potential. When a difference in potential exists between two charged bodies that are connected by a conductor, electrons will flow along the conductor. This flow will be from the negatively charged body to the positively charged body until the two charges are equalized and the potential difference no longer exists.

An analogy of this action is shown in the two water tanks connected by a pipe and valve in figure 1-19. At first the valve is closed and all the water is in tank A. Thus, the water pressure across the valve is at maximum. When the valve is opened, the water flows through the pipe from A to B until the water level becomes the same in both tanks. The water then stops flowing in the pipe, because there is no longer a difference in water pressure between the two tanks.

Current flow through an electric circuit is directly proportional to the difference in potential across the circuit, just as the flow of water through the pipe in figure 1-19 is directly proportional to the difference in water level in the two tanks.

A fundamental law of current electricity is that the CURRENT IS DIRECTLY PROPORTIONAL TO THE APPLIED VOLTAGE.

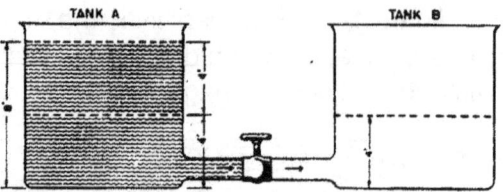

Figure 1-19.—Water analogy of electric difference in potential.

Primary Methods of Producing a Voltage

Presently, there are six commonly used methods of producing a voltage. Some of these methods are much more widely used than others. The methods of utilizing each source will be discussed, and their most common applications will be included. The following is a list of the six most common methods of producing a voltage.

1. FRICTION.-Voltage produced by rubbing two materials together.

2. PRESSURE (Piezoelectricity).-Voltage produced by squeezing crystals of certain substances.

3. HEAT (Thermoelectricity).-Voltage produced by heating the joint (junction) where two unlike metals are joined.

4. LIGHT (Photoelectricity).-Voltage produced by light striking photosensitive (light sensitive) substances.

5. CHEMICAL ACTION.-Voltage produced by chemical reaction in a battery cell.

6. MAGNETISM.-Voltage produced in a conductor when the conductor moves through a magnetic field, or a magnetic field moves through the conductor in such a manner as to cut the magnetic lines of force of the field.

VOLTAGE PRODUCED BY FRICTION

This is the least used of the six methods of producing voltages. Its main application is in Van de Graf generators, used by some laboratories to produce high voltages. As a rule, friction electricity (often referred to as static electricity) is a nuisance. For instance, a flying aircraft accumulates electric charges from the friction between its skin and the passing air.

These charges often interfere with radio communication, and under some circumstances can even cause physical damage to the aircraft. You have probably received unpleasant shocks from friction electricity upon sliding across dry seat covers or walking across dry carpets, and then coming in contact with some other object.

VOLTAGE PRODUCED BY PRESSURE

This action is referred to as piezoelectricity. It is produced by compressing or decompressing crystals of certain substances. To study this form of electricity, you must first understand the meaning of the word "crystal." In a crystal, the molecules are arranged in an orderly and uniform manner. A substance in its crystallized state and in its noncrystallized state is shown in figure 1-20.

For the sake of simplicity, assume that the molecules of this particular substance are spherical (ball-shaped). In the noncrystallized state, in part (A), note that the molecules are arranged irregularly. In the crystallized state, part (B), the molecules are arranged in a regular and uniform manner. This illustrates the major physical difference between crystal and noncrystal forms of matter. Natural crystalline matter is rare; an example of matter that is crystalline in its natural form is diamond, which is crystalline carbon. Most crystals are manufactured.

Crystals of certain substances, such as Rochelle salt or quartz, exhibit peculiar electrical characteristics. These characteristics, or effects, are referred to as "piezoelectric." For instance, when a crystal of quartz is compressed, as in figure 1-20 (C), electrons tend

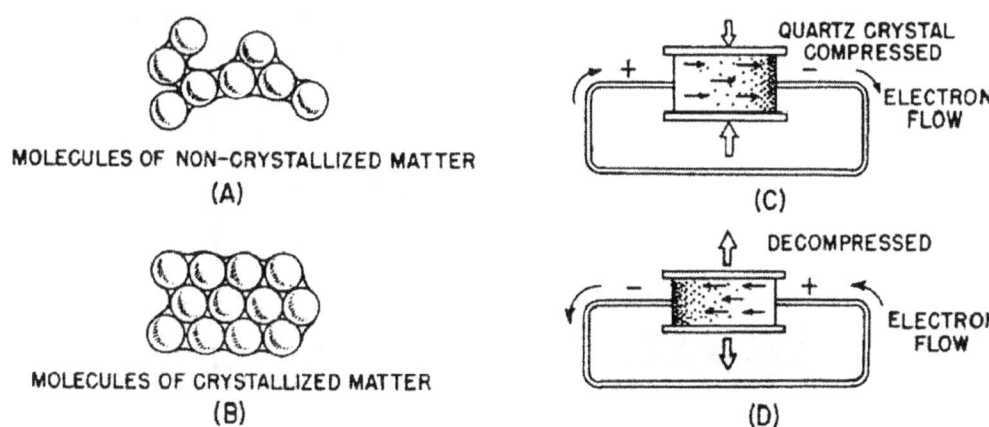

Figure 1-20.—(A) Noncrystallized structure, (B) crystallized structure, (C) compression of a crystal, (D) decompression of a crystal.

to move through the crystal as shown. This tendency creates an electric difference of potential between the two opposite faces of the crystal. (The fundamental reasons for this action are not known. However, the action is predictable, and therefore useful.) If an external wire is connected while the pressure and e.m.f. are present, electrons will flow. If the pressure is held constant, the electron flow will continue until the charges are equalized. When the force is removed, the crystal is decompressed, and immediately causes an electric force in the opposite direction, as shown in part (D). Thus, the crystal is able to convert mechanical force, either pressure or tension, to electrical force.

The power capacity of a crystal is extremely small. However, they are useful because of their extreme sensitivity to changes of mechanical force or changes in temperature. Due to other characteristics not mentioned here, crystals are most widely used in radio communication equipment. The more complicated study of crystals, as they are used for practical applications, is left for those courses that pertain to the special ratings concerned with them.

VOLTAGE PRODUCED BY HEAT

When a length of metal, such as copper, is heated at one end, electrons tend to move away from the hot end toward the cooler end. This is true of most metals. However, in some metals, such as iron, the opposite takes place and electrons tend to move TOWARD the hot end. These characteristics are illustrated in figure 1-21. The negative charges (electrons) are moving through the copper away from the heat and through the iron toward the heat. They cross from the iron to the copper at the hot junction, and from the copper through the current meter to the iron at the cold junction. This device is generally referred to as a thermocouple.

Thermocouples have somewhat greater power capacities than crystals, but their capacity is still very small if compared to some other sources. The thermoelectric voltage in a thermocouple depends mainly on the difference in temperature between the hot and cold junctions. Consequently, they are widely used to measure temperature, and as heat-sensing devices in automatic temperature control equipment. Thermocouples generally can be subjected to much greater temperatures than ordinary thermometers, such as the mercury or alcohol types.

VOLTAGE PRODUCED BY LIGHT

When light strikes the surface of a substance, it may dislodge electrons from their orbits around the surface atoms of the substance. This occurs because light has energy, the same as any moving force.

Some substances, mostly metallic ones, are far more sensitive to light than others. That is, more electrons will be dislodged and emitted from the surface of a highly sensitive metal, with a given amount of light, than will be emitted from a less sensitive

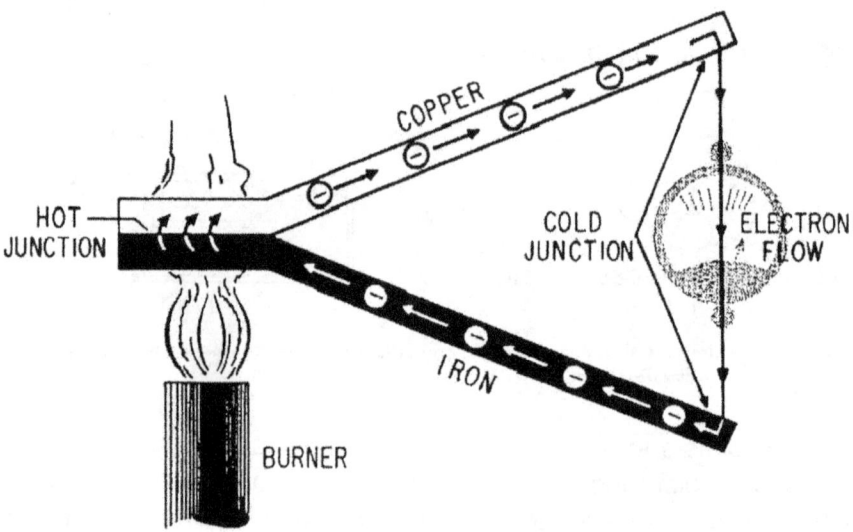

Figure 1-21.—Voltage produced by heat.

substance. Upon losing electrons, the photosensitive (light sensitive) metal becomes positively charged, and an electric force is created. Voltage produced in this manner is referred to as "a photoelectric voltage."

The photosensitive materials most commonly used to produce a photoelectric voltage are various compounds of silver oxide or copper oxide. A complete device which operates on the photoelectric principle is referred to as a "photoelectric cell." There are many sizes and types of photoelectric cells in use, each of which serves the special purpose for which it was designed. Nearly all, however, have some of the basic features of the photoelectric cells shown in figure 1-22.

The cell shown in part (A) has a curved light-sensitive surface focused on the central anode. When light from the direction shown strikes the sensitive surface, it emits electrons toward the anode. The more intense the light, the greater is the number of electrons emitted. When a wire is connected between the filament and the back, or dark side, the accumulated electrons will flow to the dark side. These electrons will eventually

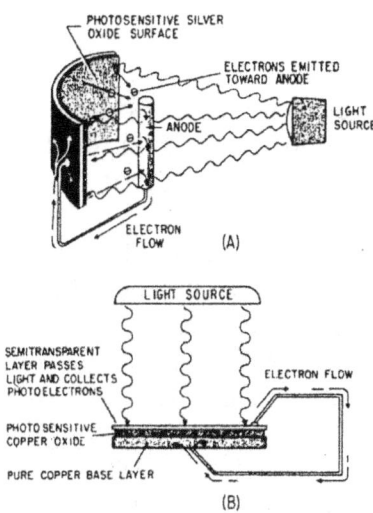

Figure 1-22.—Voltage produced by light.

pass through the metal of the reflector and replace the electrons leaving the light-sensitive surface. Thus, light energy is converted to a flow of electrons, and a usable current is developed.

The cell shown in part (B) is constructed in layers. A base plate of pure copper is coated with light-sensitive copper oxide. An additional layer of metal is put over the copper oxide. This additional layer serves two purposes:

1. It is EXTREMELY thin to permit the penetration of light to the copper oxide.

2. It also accumulates the electrons emitted by the copper oxide.

An externally connected wire completes the electron path, the same as in the reflector type cell. The photocell's voltage is utilized as needed by connecting the external wires to some other device, which amplifies (enlarges) it to a usable level.

A photocell's power capacity is very small. However, it reacts to light-intensity variations in an extremely short time. This characteristic makes the photocell very useful in detecting or accurately controlling a great number of processes or operations. For instance, the photoelectric cell, or some form of the photoelectric principle, is used in television cameras, automatic manufacturing process controls, door openers, burglar alarms, and so forth.

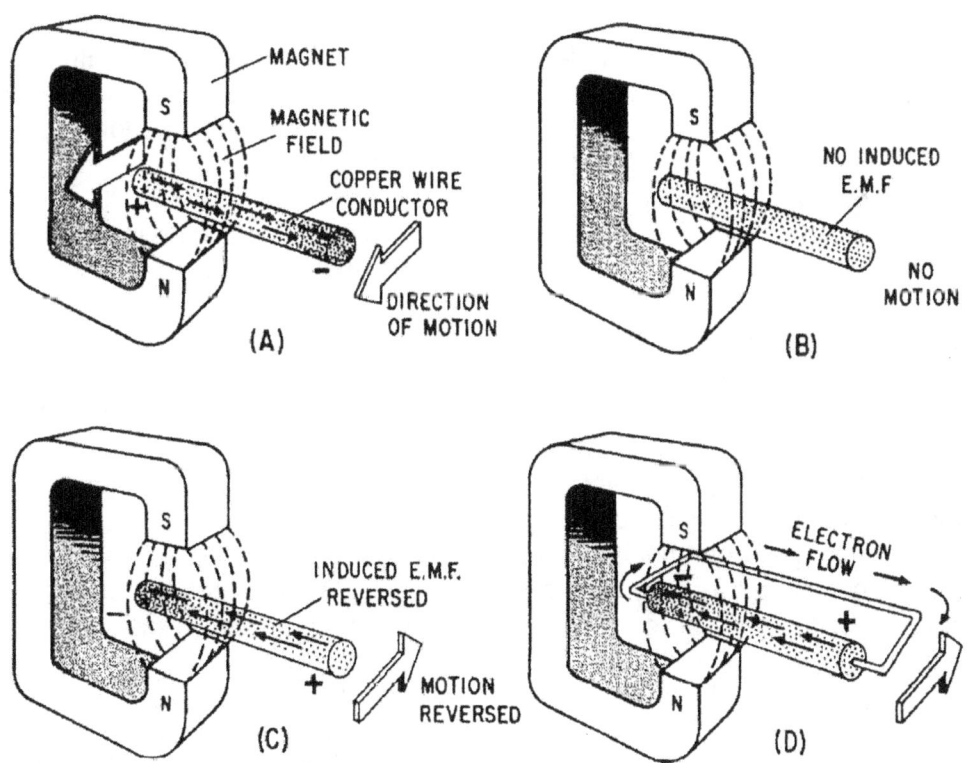

Figure 1-23.—Voltage produced by magnetism.

VOLTAGE PRODUCED BY CHEMICAL ACTION

Up to this point, it has been shown that electrons may be removed from their parent atoms and set in motion by energy derived from a source of friction, pressure, heat, or light. In general, these forms of energy do not alter the molecules of the substances being acted upon. That is, molecules are not usually added, taken away, or split-up when subjected to these four forms of energy. Only electrons are involved. When the molecules of a substance are altered, the action is referred to as CHEMICAL. For instance, if the molecules of a substance combines with atoms of another substance, or gives up atoms of its own, the action is chemical in nature. Such action always changes the chemical name and characteristics of the substance affected. For instance, when atoms of oxygen from the air come in contact with bare iron, they merge with the molecules of iron. This iron is "oxidized." It has changed chemically from iron to iron oxide, or "rust." Its molecules have been altered by chemical action.

In some cases, when atoms are added to or taken away from the molecules of a substance, the chemical change will cause the substance to take on an electric charge. The process of producing a voltage by chemical action is used in batteries and is explained in chapter 2.

VOLTAGE PRODUCED BY MAGNETISM

Magnets or magnetic devices are used for thousands of different jobs. One of the most useful and widely employed applications of magnets is in the production of vast quantities of electric power from mechanical sources. The mechanical power may be provided by a number of different sources, such as gasoline or diesel engines, and water or steam turbines. However, the final conversion of these source energies to electricity is done by generators employing the principle of electromagnetic induction. These generators, of many types and sizes, are discussed in later chapters of this course. The important subject to be discussed here is the fundamental operating principle of ALL such electromagnetic-induction generators.

To begin with, there are three fundamental conditions which must exist before a voltage can be produced by magnetism. You should learn them well, because they will be encountered again and again. They are:

1. There must be a CONDUCTOR, in which the voltage will be produced.

2. There must be a MAGNETIC FIELD in the conductor's vicinity.

3. There must be relative motion between the field and the conductor. The conductor must be moved so as to cut across the magnetic lines of force, or the field must be moved so that the lines of force are cut by the conductor.

In accordance with these conditions, when a conductor or conductors MOVE ACROSS a magnetic field so as to cut the lines of force, electrons WITHIN THE CONDUCTOR are impelled in one direction or another. Thus, an electric force, or voltage, is created.

In figure 1-23, note the presence of the three conditions needed for creating an induced voltage:

1. A magnetic field exists between the poles of the C-shaped magnet.

2. There is a conductor (copper wire).

3. There is relative motion. The wire is moved back and forth ACROSS the magnetic field.

In part (A) the conductor is moving TOWARD you. This occurs because of the magnetically induced electromotive force (e.m.f.) acting on the electrons in the copper. The right-hand end becomes negative, and the left-hand end positive. In part (B) the conductor is stopped. This eliminates motion, one of the three required conditions, and there is no longer an induced e.m.f. Consequently, there is no longer any difference in potential between the two ends of the wire. In part (C) the conductor is moving AWAY from you. An induced e.m.f. is again created. However, note carefully that the REVERSAL OF MOTION has caused a REVERSAL OF DIRECTION in the induced e.m.f.

If a path for electron flow is provided between the ends of the conductor, electrons will leave the negative end and flow to the positive end. This condition is shown in part (D). Electron flow will continue as long as the e.m.f. exists. In studying figure 1-23, it should be noted that the induced e.m.f. could also have been created by holding the conductor stationary and moving the magnetic field back and forth.

In later chapters of this course, under the heading "Generators," you will study the more complex aspects of power generation by use of mechanical motion and magnetism.

Electric Current

The drift or flow of electrons through a conductor is called ELECTRIC CURRENT. In order to determine the amount (number) of electrons flowing in a given conductor, it is necessary to adopt a unit of measurement of current flow. The term AMPERE is used to define the unit of measurement of the rate at which current flows (electron flow). The symbol for the ampere is I. One ampere may be defined as the fow of 6.28×10^{18} electrons per second past a fixed point in a conductor

A unit quantity of electricity is moved through an electric circuit when one ampere of current flows for one second of time. This unit is equivalent to 6.28×10^{18} electrons, and is called the COULOMB. The coulomb is to electricity as the gallon is to water. The symbol for the coulomb is Q. The rate of flow of current in amperes and the quantity of electricity moved through a circuit are related by the common factor of time. Thus, the quantity of electric charge, in coulombs, electricity moved through a circuit are is equal to the product of the current in amperes, I, and the duration of flow in seconds, t. Expressed as an equation, $Q = It$.

For example, if a current of 2 amperes flows through a circuit for 10 seconds the quantity of electricity moved through the circuit is 2 x 10, or 20 coulombs. Conversely, current flow may be expressed in terms of coulombs and time in seconds. Thus, if 20 coulombs are moved through a circuit in 10 seconds, the average current flow is 20/10, or 2 amperes. Note that the current flow in amperes implies the rate of flow of coulombs per second without indicating either coulombs or seconds. Thus a current flow of 2 amperes is equivalent to a rate of flow of 2 coulombs per second.

Resistance

Every material offers some resistance, or opposition, to the flow of electric current through it. Good conductors, such as copper, silver, and aluminum, offer very little resistance. Poor conductors, or insulators, such as glass, wood, and paper, offer a high resistance to current flow.

The size and type of material of the wires in an electric circuit are chosen so as to keep the electrical resistance as low as possible. In this way, current can flow easily through the conductors, just as water flows through the pipe between the tanks in figure 1-19. If the water pressure remains constant the flow of water in the pipe will depend on how far the valve is opened. The smaller the opening, the greater the opposition to the flow, and the smaller will be the rate of flow in gallons per second.

In the electric circuit, the larger the diameter of the wires, the lower will be their electrical resistance (opposition) to the flow of current through them. In the water analogy, pipe friction opposes the flow of water between the tanks. This friction is similar to electrical resistance. The resistance of the pipe to the flow of water through it depends upon (1) the length of the pipe, (2) the diameter of the pipe, and (3) the nature of the inside walls (rough or smooth). Similarly, the electrical resistance of the conductors depends upon (1) the length of the wires, (2) the diameter of the wires, and (3) the material of the wires (copper, aluminum, etc.).

Temperature also affects the resistance of electrical conductors to some extent. In most conductors (copper, aluminum, iron, etc.) the resistance increases with temperature. Carbon is an exception. In carbon the resistance decreases as temperature increases. Certain alloys of metals (manganin and constantan) have resistance that does not change appreciably with temperature.

The relative resistance of several conductors of the same length and cross section is given in the following list with silver as a standard of 1 and the remaining metals arranged in an order of ascending resistance:

Silver	1.0
Copper	1.08
Gold	1.4
Aluminum	1.8
Platinum	7.0
Lead	13.5

The resistance in an electrical circuit is expressed by the symbol R. Manufactured circuit parts containing definite amounts of resistance are called RESISTORS. Resistance (R) is measured in OHMS. One ohm is the resistance of a circuit element, or circuit, that permits a steady current of 1 ampere (1 coulomb per second) to flow when a steady e.m.f. of 1 volt is applied to the circuit.

BASIC FUNDAMENTALS OF ELECTRICAL MEASUREMENT

CONTENTS

		Page
I.	INTRODUCTION TO DC PARAMETERS	1
II.	AMMETERS, VOLTMETERS, WATTMETERS, OHMMETER, AND OSCILLOSCOPE	5
III.	AC VOLTAGE AND CURRENT	8
IV.	MEASUREMENT OF INDUCTANCE AND CAPACITANCE	10
V.	MEASUREMENT OF FREQUENCY	12
VI.	ACTIVITIES	13

BASIC FUNDAMENTALS OF ELECTRICAL MEASUREMENT

I. INTRODUCTION TO DC PARAMETERS

The use of electrical instruments and equipment to make measurements has become a major source of information and data in the complex manufacturing system as it is known today. Sophisticated techniques for electrical measurement were not introduced until the twentieth century, although the study of electrical phenomena dates back to the time of Benjamin Franklin and the American Revolution.

Measurement for electrical parameters is primarily the measurement of voltage, current, resistance, and frequency. However, most electrical measurements require only the measurement of current and voltage. The symbols for the basic electrical measurement parameters are:

I = Current   where   I =

E = Voltage   E =

R = Resistance   R =

F = Frequency

Diagrammatic symbolization of these basic parameters in direct and alternating current are:

(I) and → = Current

↕ = Voltage

〜 = Resistance

Voltage is the force that makes current move through the wires of a circuit. Current is the actual movement of electrons through a wire. Resistance is the force that controls the amount of current that can pass through a wire. Frequency in alternating current is the number of cycles occurring in each second of time.

Both voltage and current can be measured with a simple electrical meter which uses magnetism and magnetic characteristics to measure the amount of current that flows. When a meter is connected to an electrical circuit, the flow of current through the coils of the meter creates a magnetic force. This magnetic force is used to move a needle. The amount of voltage, current, and resistance is shown by the position of the needle. The greater the current or voltage, the more the needle moves. To make the measurement easier, a scale is placed behind the needle to measure its movement. This scale is marked to show the value of current on voltage or resistance. The element the meter will measure is determined by the way the meter circuit is constructed and the way the meter is connected to the electrical circuit.

Where a meter is used to measure electrical values, a different circuit is required for each type of measurement. To determine the circuits used, a definition of series and parallel circuits must be made. Resistance in a series circuit is depicted as follows:

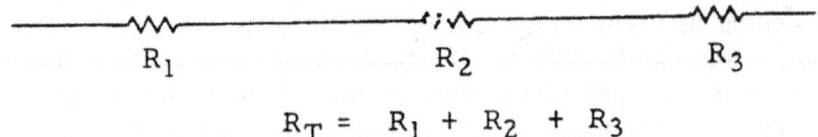

$$R_T = R_1 + R_2 + R_3$$

When two resistors are connected in parallel, they are illustrated as:

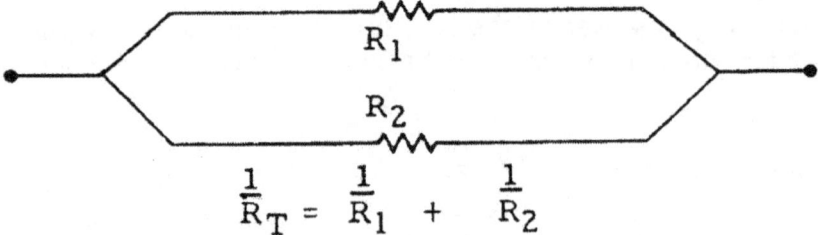

$$\frac{1}{R_T} = \frac{1}{R_1} + \frac{1}{R_2}$$

In a parallel circuit, if either resistor is disconnected, current can still flow through the other resistor. In a series circuit, if either resistor is disconnected, current flow stops because the circuit is broken.

Most circuits have both series and parallel connections and they are called series-parallel circuits. The following figure shows two resistors in series and both in parallel with a third resistor.

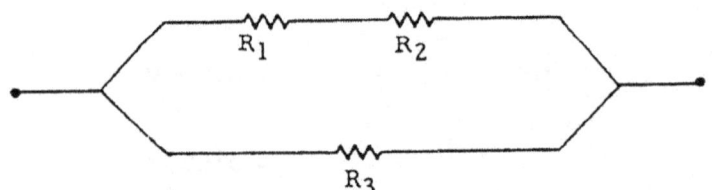

The figure below depicts two resistors in parallel and the parallel resistors in series with a third resistor.

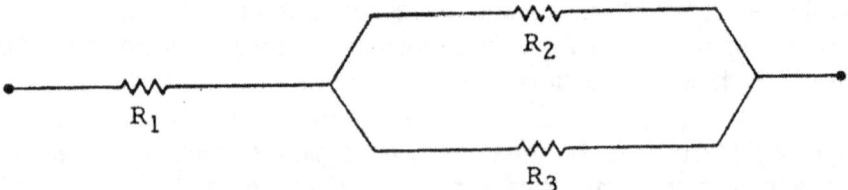

The coil in a meter has some resistance, but more resistance is usually needed. To measure voltage, a large resistance is placed in series with the meter coils as shown below:

For this circuit, the meter is called a voltmeter.

To measure current flow, a small resistance is placed in series with the meter coil and a second small resistor is placed in parallel with the meter and first resistor as shown below:

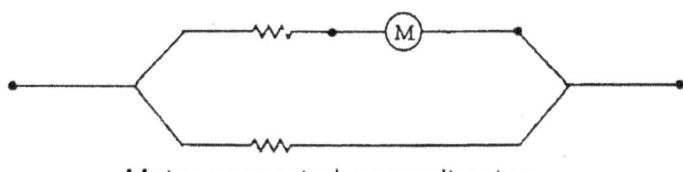

Meter connected as a voltmeter.

A simplified diagram of a D-C moving galvonometer is shown below:

D-C Moving-Coil Galvanometer.

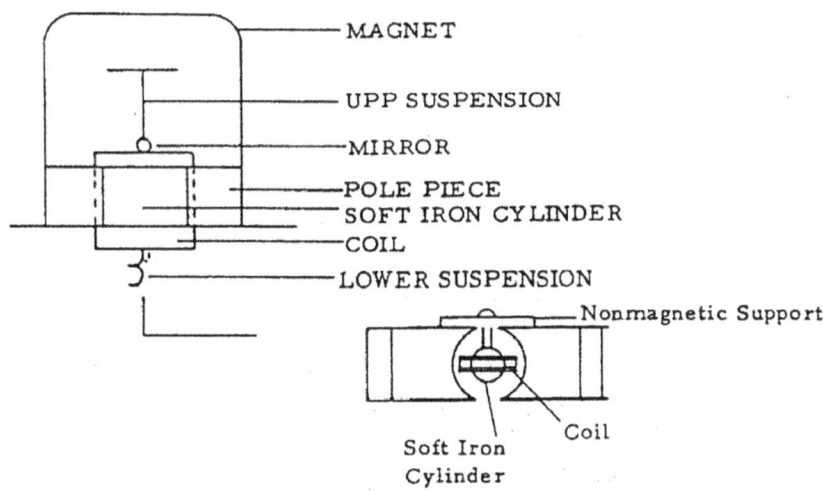

The galvonometer is a basic D'arsonval movement consisting of a stationary permanent magnet and a movable coil with attached mirror and pointer. The use of a pointer permits over-all simplicity in that the use of a light source and a system of mirrors is avoided. However, the use of a pointer introduces the problem of balance, especially if the pointer is long.

II. AMMETERS, VOLTMETERS, WATTMETERS, OHMMETER, AND OSCILLOSCOPE
Ammeter

The basic D'arsonval movement may be used to indicate or measure only very small currents. A simplified diagram of an ammeter is shown below:

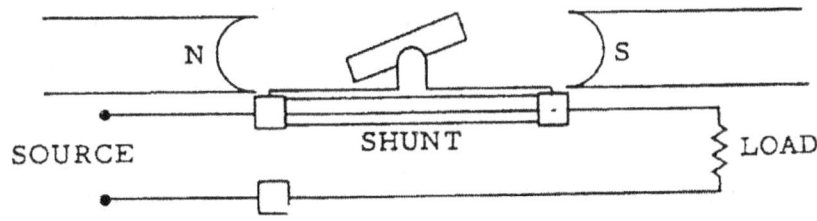

The resistance of the shunt is equal to the voltage drop for full-scale deflection divided by the rated current of the shunt.

Current measuring instruments must always be connected in series with a circuit and never in parallel.

Most ammeters indicate the magnitude of the current by being deflected from left to right. If the meter is connected with reversed polarity, it will be deflected backwards, and this action may damage the movement. The proper polarity should be observed in connecting the meter in the circuit. The meter should always be connected so that the electron flow will be into the negative terminal and out of the positive terminal. Common ammeter shunts are illustrated below:

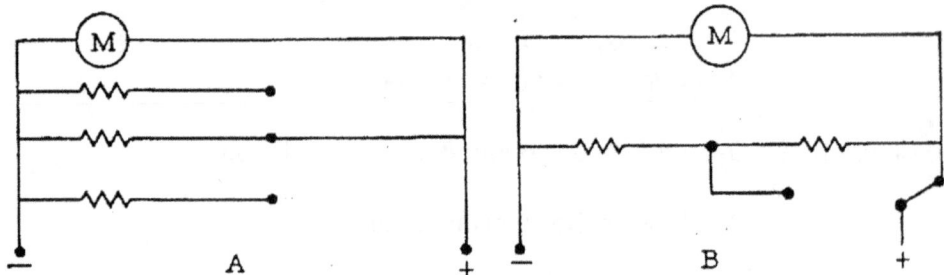

Voltmeter

The D'arsonval meter used as the basic meter for the ammeter may also be used to measure voltage if a high resistance is placed in series with the moving coil of the meter. A simplified voltmeter circuit is:

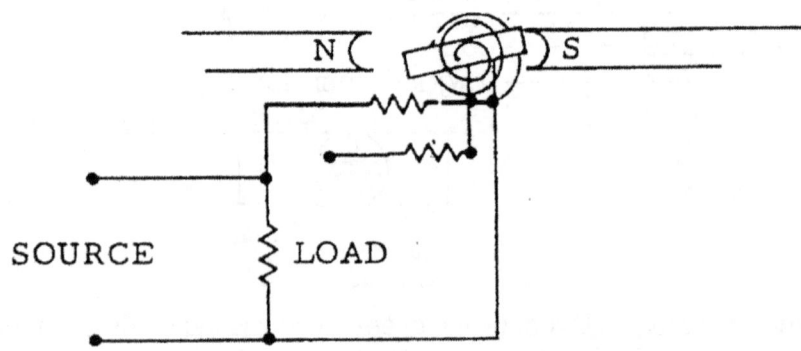

The value of the necessary series resistance is determined by the current required for full-scale deflection of the meter and by the range of voltage to be measured. As an example, assume that the basic meter is to be made into a voltmeter with a full-scale reading of 1 volt. The coil resistance of the basic meter is 100 ohms, and .0001 ampere causes full-scale deflection. The total resistance, R, of the meter coil and the series resistance is:

$$R = E/I = 1/.0001 = 10,000 \text{ Ohms}$$
and the series resistance alone is:
$$R = 10,000 - 100 = 9,900 \text{ Ohms}.$$

Voltage measuring instruments are connected across (in-parallel with) a circuit.

The function of a voltmeter is to indicate the potential difference between two points in a circuit.

Wattmeter

Electric power is measured by means of a wattmeter. Because electric power is the product of current and voltage,
$$P = IE.$$

A wattmeter must have two elements, one for current and the other for voltage. For this reason, wattmeters are usually of the electrodynamometer type which multiplies the instantaneous current through the load by the instantaneous voltage across the load.

Ohmmeter

The series-type ohmmeter consists essentially of a sensitive milliammeter, a voltage source, and a fixed and a variable resistor all connected in series between the two terminals of the instrument, as shown below:

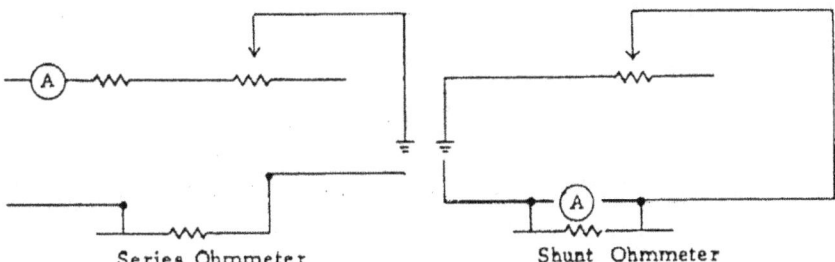

Series Ohmmeter   Shunt Ohmmeter

Before the unknown resistance is measured the test leads are shorted together and the variable resistance is adjusted for full-scale deflection. The point on the meter scale corresponding to full-scale deflection is marked "zero resistance."

The Oscilloscope

Oscilloscopes are used to obtain information about current or voltage in an electrical circuit either to supplement the information given by indicating instruments or to replace the instruments where speed is inadequate. Oscilloscopes permit determination of current and voltage variations that take place very rapidly. These devices are frequently used to obtain qualitative information about a circuit such as current and voltage waves or time relationships between events in a circuit.

This form of measurement also allows determinations of frequency in the form of a graphical illustration. Some examples of the various forms that can be illustrated on an oscilloscope are:

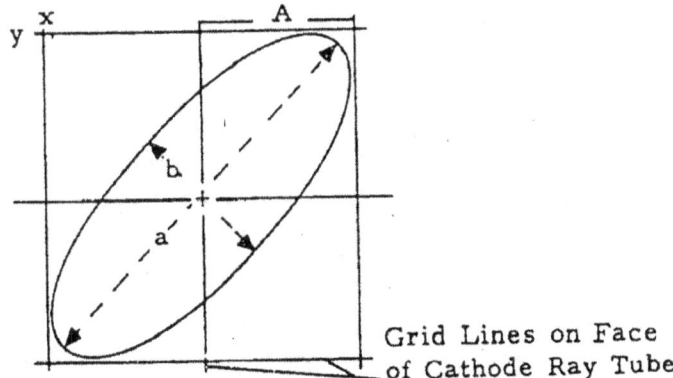

Grid Lines on Face of Cathode Ray Tube

Determination of phase difference of two sinusoidal voltages of same frequency by the pattern on the face of cathode-ray tube.

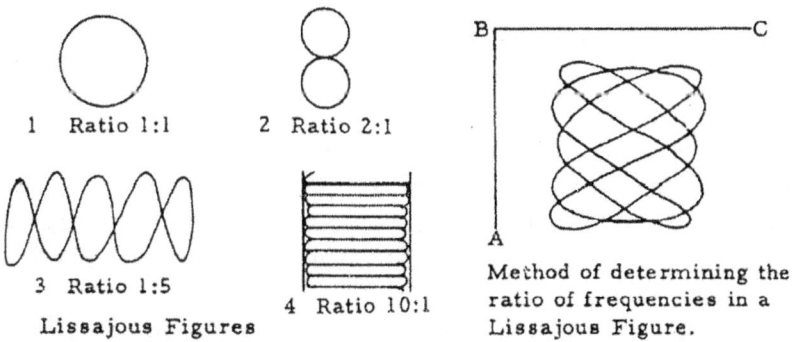

1 Ratio 1:1
2 Ratio 2:1
3 Ratio 1:5
4 Ratio 10:1
Lissajous Figures

Method of determining the ratio of frequencies in a Lissajous Figure.

Lissajous figures are patterns of voltages of different frequencies but related by a simple integral ratio as shown in the preceding figures.

III. AC VOLTAGE AND CURRENT

An alternating current (AC) consists of electrons that move first in one direction and then in another. The direction of flow changes periodically. Because most of the theory of electric power and communications deals with currents that surge back and forth in a certain manner known as sine-wave variation, the sine-wave is of considerable importance in alternating current. Symbols are:

I or → = Current   ⌇ = Resistance   ⎍⎍⎍ = Inductance
⊙ = Voltage   ꞁ = Capacitance   Ⓩ = Impedance

Important characteristics of alternating current are:
1. Cycle - As rotation of a generator continues, the two sides of the loop interchange positions and the generated voltage in each of them is the opposite direction. One complete revolution of the loop results in one cycle of induced AC voltage. This theory is illustrated as shown in the following diagram:

Points 0 to 1 represent one complete cycle of voltage in sine-wave form.
2. Frequency - The number of complete cycles occurring in each second of time. This is symbolized as "F".
3. Period - The time for one complete cycle of the generating force. This is illustrated as 1/f. (For example, the period of a 60-cycle voltage is 1/60 of a second.)
4. Phase Angle - The angle between vectors relative to the positions these vectors represent at any instant of time. This parameter is illustrated as angle 9. One complete cycle of 360 electrical degrees is indicated in the equation:

$e = E\eta \sin \theta$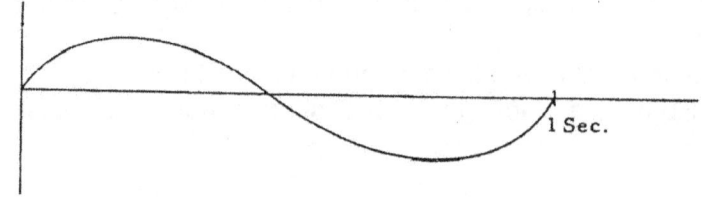

where   e = instantaneous voltage
          $E\eta$ = maximum voltage
          0 = the angle in electrical degrees representing the instantaneous position of the rotating vector. Therefore, when $6 = 60'$, $E\eta = 100$ volts, $e = 100 \sin 60° = 86.6$ volts.

    a. Inductance
Inductance is that property of a circuit that opposes any current change in the circuit. It is also the property whereby energy may be stored in a magnetic field. Therefore, a coil of wire possesses the property of inductance because a magnetic field is established around the coil when current flows in the coil. The relationship of inductance is illustrated by the symbol "L".
In a simple circuit, the relationship of inductance is shown as follows:

In a simple circuit, the relationship of capacitance is *shown* as follows:

> Where E is the applied voltage and L is the inductance.

b. Capacitance

Capacitance is that quality of a circuit that enables energy to be stored in the electric field. In simple form, it has been shown to consist of two parallel metal plates separated by an insulator, called a dielectric.

In a simple circuit, the relationship of capacitance is *shown* as follows:

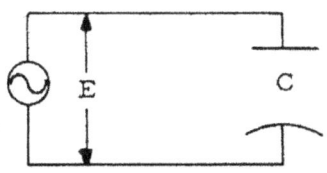

> Where E is the applied voltage and C is the capacitance.

IV. MEASUREMENT OF INDUCTANCE AND CAPACITANCE

Measurements of inductance and capacitance may be made conveniently and accurately by A-C bridge circuits. The simple form of the A-C bridge bears a strong resemblance to the wheatstone bridge. It consists of four arms, a power source furnishes alternating current of the desired frequency and suitable magnitude to the bridge. A four-arm bridge is illustrated in the following diagram:

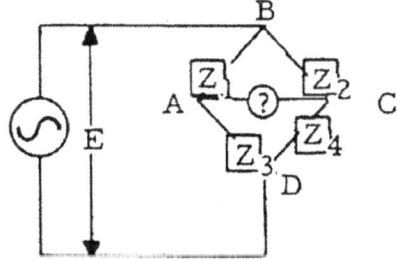

Four arm A-C bridge (using Impedances Z_x).

An inductance comparison bridge is similar to form except that the bridge is made up of resistance and inductance relationships. An illustration is as follows:

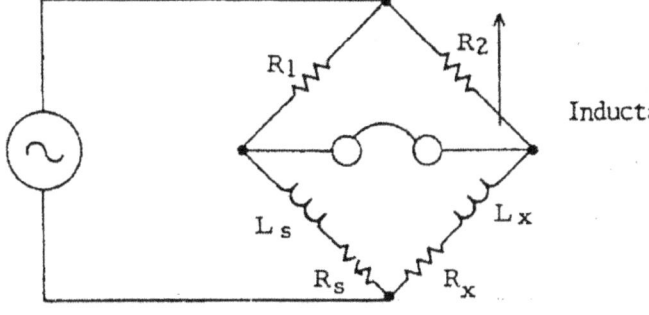

Inductance Comparison Bridge

In the inductance bridge, the relationship shows that the unknown inductance L_x is derived from the equation--

$$L_x = L_s \frac{R_2}{R_1}$$

A capacitance bridge relationship is used to determine an unknown capacitance by comparison to a known capacitance. The relationship is illustrated in the following diagram:

Capacitance Comparison Bridge

Other measurements of inductance and capacitance can be made by using the following bridges:
1. Maxwell Bridge - Permits measurement of inductance in terms of capacitance.
2. Hay Bridge - Differs from the Maxwell Bridge only in having a resistance in series with the standard capacitor, instead of in parallel with it.
3. Owen Bridge - Another circuit for measurement of inductance in terms of a standard capacitor. One arm consists of the standard capacitor only, and an adjacent arm contains a resistance and capacitance in series.
4. Schering Bridge - One of the most important A-C bridges. It is used to measure capacitance in general and in particular, is used to measure properties of insulators, condenser bushings, insulating oil, and other insulating materials. This bridge is illustrated diagrammatically since it is very important.

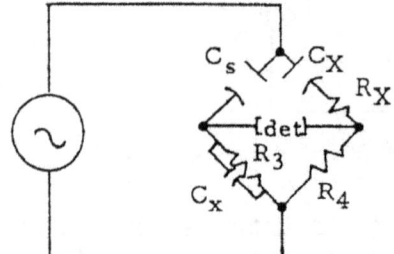

Schering bridge.

R_x = resistance in unknown Capacitor Cx
C_x = adjustable capacitor.
C_s = a high grade mica capacitor.
C_x = air capacitor
The equation is: $C_x = C_s R_3/R_4$

V. MEASUREMENT OF FREQUENCY

Several types of instruments have been devised to determine frequency. Some of them are: (refer to section on oscilloscope operation and use.)

1. Moving Iron Type - Has a moving element consisting of a soft-iron vane and two crossed stationary coils that are connected with some sort of frequency-discriminating network, so that one coil is stronger at low frequencies and the other at high frequencies.
2. Resonant Electrical Type - Two tuned circuits, one tuned to resonance slightly below the low end of the instrument scale, the other slightly above the high end. These two circuits may be combined with a crossed-coil instrument or an electro-dynamometer to make a frequency meter.
3. Mechanical Resonance Type - A series of reeds fastened to a common base that is flexibly mounted and that carries the armature of an electromagnet whose coil is energized from the A-C line whose frequency is to be measured.
4. Transducer Type - The frequency measuring function is entirely separated from the indicating instrument, which in this case is a simple D-C meter. Two parallel off-resonance circuits are used, one resonant below the instrument range and one above.

VI. ACTIVITIES

1. It is possible to make a simple meter to measure electricity. The materials needed to build a meter are as follows:
    a. One frozen concentrate juice container made of cardboard or a cardboard cylinder of about the same diameter.
    b. One 10 D (penny) nail or a piece of soft steel rod about three inches long and one eighth (1/8) inch diameter welding rod obtained from your teacher.
    c. Enameled wire approximately 28 gauge (American Wire Gauge) about 25 feet. Sources: Industrial Arts or Science teacher, the coil on the back of an old TV picture tube or a hobby store. NOTE: Get the wire from an old TV, unwrap it carefully so that it does not break, kink, or knot up.
    d. One "D" cell battery or any flashlight battery with 1.5 volts (a 9-volt transistor radio battery will not work for this meter).
    e. Two 3x5 note cards.
    f. One small elastic or rubber band.
    g. One flash light bulb.
    h. Masking tape.
    i. Tools: scissors, file, pliers, hacksaw, ruler, and permanent magnet.

    The steps for the construction of the meter are as follows:

    Once the juice container has been washed out, measure two inches along the side of the container, from the open end, and cut this part off to make a cylinder two inches long. This will open the cylinder at both ends. Cut two "V" notches as shown in Figure 4(a), page 16.

Now wrap the wire around the outside of the cylinder. To do this, begin about six inches from the end of the wire and tape the wire to the cylinder 1/8" below one of the "V" notches. Beginning at the notch, wrap the wires neatly around the cylinder each turn next to the other covering approximately one inch of the cylinder. At this point, begin another layer of wire and continue winding on top of the first. Wind this layer in the same direction as the first. Wind layer on layer until sixty-five turns have been made. When it is done, finish at the notch opposite one at which you started and tape the wire in place with a small tab of masking tape. Cut the wire leaving about six inches of lead, save the rest of the wire.

The pointer is made by cutting the head off of the nail. Then mark a point one-third the length from the end of the nail. File both sides of the nail for the two-thirds length until the nail balances at the mark [Figure 4(b), page 16[4]].

Once this is finished, the short round end of the pointer must be magnetized. To do this, rub one pole of a permanent magnet in one direction over the short round end of the pointer until it is magnetized.

Cut a two-inch piece from the end of a note card. Fold this in half, parallel to the long side to make a "V" shape three inches long and one-inch on a side.

Push the pointer through the center of the card and fasten in place with the elastic, Figure 4(c), page 16 . Position the pointer so that when the card is placed in the "V" notches of the cylinder, it balances and stands up straight.

Attach a 3 x 5 note card to the cylinder so that it is vertical and the pointer can move freely in front of the card. This is a place to mark your readings when you experiment with your meter, Figure 4(d), page 18.

Once the meter is made, you can take measurements. This meter will measure low value of DC (Direct Current) only. <u>CAUTION - DO NOT MEASURE ANY ELECTRICITY OTHER THAN BATTERIES LABELED 1. 5 V DC.</u> These batteries are marked "D", "C", "A", "AA", "AM", "AAAA".

Scrape the insulation off the ends of the wires from the meter coil. Connect each of the meter leads to one of the poles of a "D" cell battery. The meter pointer should move. The position in which it stops should indicate 1.5 volts. Note where this position is.

Clean the varnish insulation from the ends of the wire left over after you wound the meter coil. Connect one end of this to one of the meter leads. Now reconnect the battery with the long length of wire in the meter circuit. Does the meter pointer move as far this time?
Connect a flashlight bulb to the battery so that it lights. Touch the two leads of the meter to the contacts of the bulb. The movement of the pointer to a position on the scale shows the amount of voltage used to get the light to light.

Disconnect your meter and reconnect it so that one end of the battery is connected to the meter and the meter to the bulb, and then the other contact of the bulb to the battery (this is a series circuit). See Figure 5, page 17: The deflection of the meter needle is showing the current used by the light bulb.

The meter constructed is a device much the same as meters made and used in industry. Electrical properties measured are basic to the study and use of electricity. If more information is required on the subject, it is available from several sources.

Among the best sources for information is the nearest library, for both basic and advanced manuals and textbooks. Science teachers in high schools or colleges or graduate engineers, electricians, telephone repairmen, can also help. Many hobby shops and electric supply stores have a selection of basic manuals for sale which provide good background material and a number of experiments with electricity.

In order to build the circuits found in most of these books, a meter movement of greater sensitivity is needed. This can also be purchased at low cost from hobby or electrical supply houses. The meter con-structed from this instruction is only a model to demonstrate how simple electricity is to measure.

2. Visit the electrical laboratory in your school and ask the teacher to demonstrate basic electrical measurements on the meter available. Perhaps the teacher will allow you to practice making simple measurements under close supervision.

3. Arrange a plant visitation at a local electronic or electrical assembly plant. Ask the tour guide to demonstrate the different meters and how they are used in basic measurements.

4. Purchase a Heath Kit or similar meter brand name and assemble as directed. A basic ohmmeter or vacuum tube voltmeter would be a good starting point.

STEPS FOR CONSTRUCTION OF A METER

Figure 4

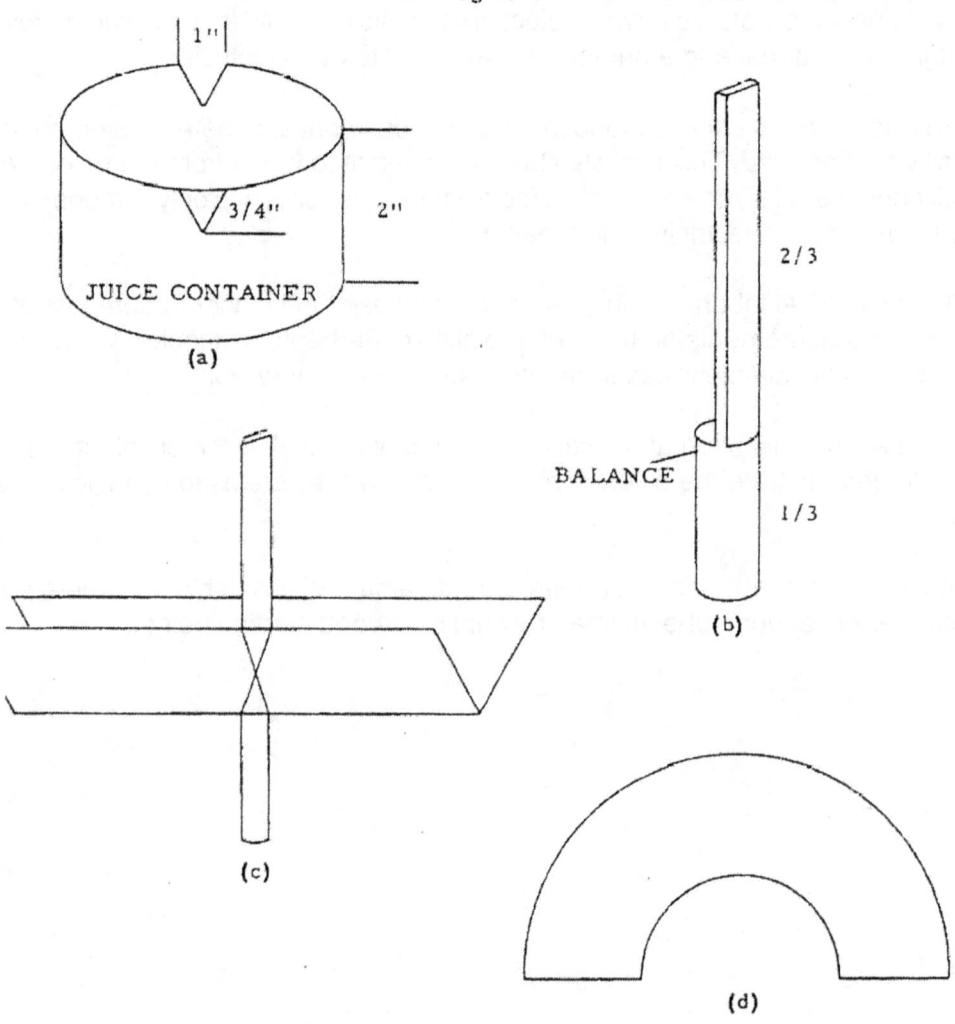

SERIES CIRCUIT
Figure 5

SERIES CIRCUIT

Figure 5

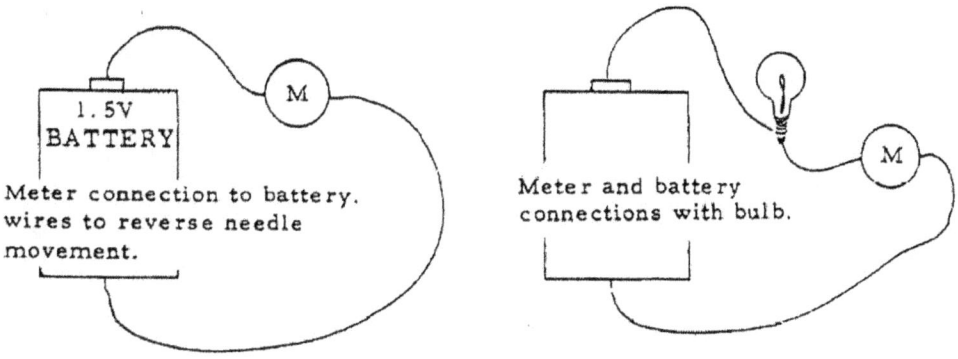

www.ingramcontent.com/pod-product-compliance
Lightning Source LLC
Chambersburg PA
CBHW081806300426
44116CB00014B/2257